The Civic Gospel

The Civic Gospel:
A Political Cartography of Christianity

William Reynolds
Georgia Southern University

Julie A. Webber
Illinois State University

SENSE PUBLISHERS
ROTTERDAM/BOSTON/TAIPEI

A C.I.P. record for this book is available from the Library of Congress.

ISBN 978-90-8790-481-4 (paperback)
ISBN 978-90-8790-482-1 (hardback)
ISBN 978-90-8790-483-8 (e-book)

Published by: Sense Publishers,
P.O. Box 21858, 3001 AW
Rotterdam, The Netherlands
http://www.sensepublishers.com

Printed on acid-free paper

Cover photo: Redux Pictures

All Rights Reserved © 2009 Sense Publishers

No part of this work may be reproduced, stored in a retrieval system, or transmitted in any form or by any means, electronic, mechanical, photocopying, microfilming, recording or otherwise, without written permission from the Publisher, with the exception of any material supplied specifically for the purpose of being entered and executed on a computer system, for exclusive use by the purchaser of the work.

For our mentors and friends,
Bill Pinar and Diane Rubenstein

CONTENTS

List of Abbreviations		ix
Preface		xi
Introduction	The Age of Ressentiment: Bodies Without Souls	1
	Free-Market Fundamentalism	2
	Microfascism and Control Societies	5
	Christian Fundamentalism	16
	Ressentiment	19
	Cartography	21
Chapter Two	Christocrats and the Civic Gospel: The Backlash of the Culture Wars	25
	The Backlash and the Resurgent Right	26
	The Social Gospel	35
	The Civic Gospel and Dominion/Reconstructionist Theology	39
	The Chistocratic Agenda	45
	Church and State	45
	Intelligent Design	48
	Homophobia	52
	A Regime of Dualistic Madness	55
Chapter Three	The Secular Strategies of the Christian Right: A Political Curriculum to Disestablish Critical Thought	59
	The Joiners	65
	Perverse Joiners	69
	The Bully Pulpit and Executive Order	73
	The Curriculum of the Christian Right	77

CONTENTS

Chapter Four	Humanism and the American Political Imaginary	83
	The Posthumanism of the Christocrats and the Neoconservatives	83
	"Because Humanity Repeatedly Fails…"	88
	Life, Or Quality of Life: Natal Fascism?	94
	Producing Modernity	99
	Pragmatism and Anti-Intellectualism	104
	Beyond Flesh	107
Chapter Five	The Significance of Place: The Civic Gospel in the South and the Midwest	109
Part I:	The Land of a Thousand Churches: The Ex-Confederacy and the Resurrection of the South	109
	The South Becomes Republican	114
	The Christocrats, the Southern Baptist Convention and the South	116
	The Southern Nation – To Jesusland and Beyond: A Faith-based War	121
Part II:	The Myth of the Common Culture, Rustbelt Religion & Right-Wing Politics	125
	A Midwestern Mega Church	131
	Common Culture	134
	Rustbelt Religion	135
	Other People's Children	136
Epilogue		139
Notes		155
References		157

LIST OF ABBREVIATIONS

ACLU	American Civil Liberties Union
ACTA	American Council of Trustees and Alumni
AOL	America On-Line
BYOI	Bring Your Own Irony
CBN	Christian Broadcasting Network
CDC	Centers for Disease Control
CIA	Central Intelligence Agency
CPA	Coalition Provisional Authority (Children Playing Adults)
C-PAC	Conservative Political Action Committee
CPD	Committee on the Present Danger
CR	Christian Right
CWA	Concerned Women for America
ESA	Evangelicals for Social Action
ERA	Equal Rights Amendment
FDA	Food & Drug Administration
FEPC	Federal Employment Practices Commission
FOF	Focus on the Family
GOP	Grand Old Party (Republican Party)
IMF	International Monetary Fund
IVF	In Vitro Fertilization
IWF	Independent Women's Forum
IWN	International Women's Network
MOAB	Massive Ordinance Air Blast (Mother of All Bombs)
NAACP	National Association for the Advancement of Colored People
NAE	National Association of Evangelicals
NAEA	National Abstinence Education Association
NCLB	No Child Left Behind
NSA	National Security Agency
PIP	Partners in Prayer
PR	Protestant Right
SBC	Southern Baptist Coalition
SUV	Sport Utility Vehicle
TBN	The Bible Network
TINA	There Is No Alternative
UN	United Nations
USA	America
USAID	United States Agency for International Development
W	George W. Bush, 43rd President of the U.S.A.
YMCA	Young Men's Christian Association

PREFACE

> Never can there be fog too thick, never can there be mud and mire too deep, to assort with the groping and floundering condition which is this High Court of Chancery. Most pestilent of these hoary sinners, holds this day in the sight of heaven and earth (Dickens, 2002, p. 1)
>
> Nobody told me there'd be days like these strange days indeed – strange days indeed (Lennon, 1988).

This book is a result of the times in which we are living. These times demand a response. When we began to write this book, it was not popular to dissent against the Bush administration. In fact, dissent was and still is equated with terrorism. In 2007, with the president's poll numbers hovering in the 30% range, the resignation of Karl Rove and Alberto Gonzales it might seem that the tide was turning and maybe since the 2008 election some of this nightmare we have been experiencing will change. At least that is the optimistic view. But there are small traces that the struggle we discuss in this book will continue well into the 21st century. On August 11, 2007 Dr. Wiley S. Drake pastor of the First Southern Baptist Church of Buena Park, California and second Vice President of the Southern Baptist Convention issued a press release on church letterhead endorsing Republican presidential candidate Mike Huckabee. He also endorsed Huckabee on a church affiliated radio show. On August 14, 2007, The Americans United for the Separation of Church and State (AUSCS) then asked the Internal Revenue Service to investigate the First Southern Baptist Church of Buena Park, California for possible violation of federal tax law barring electioneering by non-profit groups. Drake's press release was a clear endorsement. "I Announce," said the pastor:

> That I am going to personally endorse Mike Huckabee. I ask all of my Southern Baptist brothers and sisters to consider getting behind Mike and helping him all you can. First of all pray and then ask God, what should I do to put feet to my payers. Do what God tells you to do. I believe God has chosen Mike for such an hour, and I believe all those running Mike Huckabee will listen to God (Wiley, 2007, p. 1).

This language is certainly reminiscent of the early days of the Bush campaign when Bush was discussed as the anointed one (see the introduction). But, the story gets more involved. On the Christian Newswire the same day that AUSCS urged the IRS to investigate the Rev. Wiley's Church. Rev. Wiley fired back. "I am calling out to the "children of God" for action in the form of Imprecatory Prayer, particularly against American United for Separation of Church and State. "I ask the children of God to go into action with Imprecatory Prayer. Especially against Americans United for the Separation of Church and State – Specifically target Joe Conn or Jeremy Learning. They are those that lead the attack" (Wiley, 2007, p. 1). What is an imprecatory prayer? It is a prayer that is a curse. They are prayers for another's misfortune or for vengeance against God's enemies. This is just a new example of the issues and dilemmas we highlight in this text. So, the intermingling of the political and the religious was still swirling in the 2007 context. The Civic Gospel, as we discuss it, is the notion that preaching the Gospel is preaching politics and vise versa. This book is about that struggle and the issues related to it.

Many of this issues discussed in this book are a result of complicated conversations in Bill's curriculum studies classes at Georgia Southern University, particularly in courses on cultural studies and were inspired by Julie's teaching of several courses in the open curriculum available at Illinois State University's Politics and Government Department and Women and Gender Studies, where she is part of the faculty. Especially important were Julie's summer courses Gay and Lesbian Politics in 2006 and 2007. Students in those courses studied the effects of political evangelicals in mobilizing discourses of homophobia in ways that cohered with their larger mission concerning "family values." Also important were the sections in graduate seminars dedicated to understanding so-called "neo-conservative" foreign policy as it impacts on domestic social movements and institutions, especially education. Finally, in the annually offered course Julie developed to engage youth politics, where youth is understood to mean the "new" in Arendtian fashion student feedback on papers, exams and in-class presentations sharpened her thinking about the contemporary politics of education in a neoliberal framework. The title of that course "Playground to Politics" highlights the increasingly blurred boundaries between the child and the adult in spaces of development and in spaces of politics. Adults are considered unfinished while children are considered outright political agents. This aspect of contemporary politics was made abundantly clear in the spring of 2007 when conservative columnist Ann Coulter was caught at the C-PAC conference saying "I would address John Edwards but apparently you have to go into rehab for using the term 'faggot' "and later responded to remarks criticizing her comments by saying she was just "slinging sand in the sandbox." (CNN, 2007). What Coulter missed was that sandbox politics were brought to the forefront of political agendas in the U.S. by this new evangelical-inspired movement of the political right-wing. While sandbox politics may always have been the domain of powerful men in any professional context, what Coulter's comments made clear was that the conservative revolution brought them to the public debate with women as their authors. Now if women were to have an equal voice in politics, they could do so as long as their comments were only homophobic and immature: Ann Coulter had now showed the public that it wasn't just left-leaning feminists who had to mime men to get attention in political debates, conservatives did too. The key sentiment mobilizing the political agenda in the past decade has without a doubt been homophobia, which worked well with rising fears about family composition and globalization threatening what many came to believe were a stern set of maxims called family values.

Several versions of the final chapters were presented at academic conferences also known for their open formats and Julie missed presenting chapter three a "Secularism and the American Political Imaginary," for the JCT Conference, Dayton, OH, October 19-21 however, Bill did present her ideas to audiences. Later, the best insights came (as usual) from outside the formal discursive spaces of the conference where Julie benefited from discussions about megachurches from graduate students in the Georgia Southern University doctoral program. As well she presented chapter five as "The Myth of the Common Culture," at the American Association for the Advancement of Curriculum Studies, University of Illinois at Chicago, April 8, where Julie was able to return the favor and present Bill's portion of the chapter for him. Julie has also benefitted greatly from experiences on the board of the Center for Reading and Literacy at Illinois State University where annual conferences are held to study the effects of No Child Left Behind on Illinois teachers. Finally, local school problems of bullying and the community's ignorance of bullying tactics (e.g. homophobia) were especially highlighted through work in PFLAG (Parents and Friends of Lesbians and Gays) as well as with work on Safe Schools Bloomington-Normal. It is interesting to note that while the larger discourse of politics is thoroughly saturated in bullying tactics that largely rely upon an unnamed homophobia, kids on playgrounds mimicking adults openly use homophobia as a tactic and the teachers, parents and supervisors in charge of them routinely ignore this aspect of bullying, until it is brought to their attention by groups such as PFLAG and Safe Schools. Julie also thanks Ali Riaz, T.Y. Wang and Kam Shapiro for their friendship and intellectual support during this process.

Thanks to an Illinois State undergraduate assistant, Steve Reising, for merging the bibliographies of the chapters into a coherent, final version and for composing the appendix of acronyms, to C. Steven Page a doctoral student at Georgia Southern University for his helpful suggestions, to Jason Ogalsby, doctoral fellow at Georgia Southern University for his research help, and to Mark Mohr assistant professor in media studies at Georgia Southern and doctoral student for making Bill aware of interesting newspaper, journal and internet articles many of which have been cited in this book. Thanks also to William F. Pinar for his suggestions on readings concerning the South. Thanks to Diane Rubenstein, master of the American political imaginary, for sharing her knowledge with Julie and putting it in print (Rubenstein 2008). Finally, we wish to thank Shirley Steinberg a friend and colleague without whose support many great books in many fields would not exist.

CHAPTER ONE

THE AGE OF RESSENTIMENT

Bodies Without Souls

I trust God speaks through me. Without that, I couldn't do my job (Bush, 2004).

There will never be world peace until God's house and God's people are given their rightful place of leadership at the top of the world. How can there be peace when drunkards, drug dealers, communists, atheists, New Age worshipers of Satan, secular humanists, oppressive dictators, greedy money changers, revolutionary assassins, adulterers, and homosexuals are on top (Robertson, 1992, p. 227)?

We've got a lot of rebuilding to do ... The good news is — and it's hard for some to see it now — that out of this chaos is going to come a fantastic Gulf Coast, like it was before. Out of the rubbles of Trent Lott's house — he's lost his entire house — there's going to be a fantastic house. And I'm looking forward to sitting on the porch (Bush, 2005).

In our previous edited collection, *Expanding Curriculum Theory* (2004), we were concerned with the manner in which both in the larger social context and in the curriculum studies field as well there exists a movement to shut down, close off, capture and curtail lines of flight research and writing with the various authors demonstrated that it was possible to establish lines of flight to temporarily escape this closure. This work also cautions that lines of flight are not always liberating and productive.

> Deleuze and Guattari's analysis of Nazism leads them to conclude that with absolute deterritorialization along the line of flight the question of interest is no longer so certain. There is a peculiar odour of death along this line, and it may turn out that the most deterritorialized movements are indeed the Nazi line of self-immolation, which indeed escapes the moralism of Oedipus (Beasley-Murray, 2005, p. 5).

The present text we view as a necessary continuation of the earlier work. It is an attempt to broaden the scope of the discussion to the current historical conjuncture and its consequences. The current milieu is a time when the closing down of alternative discourse is gaining strength, it is a time when dissent is equated to terrorism, a time when surveillance is ubiquitous, a time when homophobia helps to win presidential elections, a time when freedom is given up in the name of security, a time when being a good citizen means being a good consumer and a time when schools have become the home of information processing and warehousing.

CHAPTER 1

> But as curriculum theorists have long appreciated, the exchange and acquisition of information is not education. Being informed is not equivalent to erudition. Information must be tempered with intellectual judgment, critical thinking, ethics, and self-reflexivity (Pinar, 2004, p. 8).

What are the various trajectories that operate in such a time? In this introduction we present a limited discussion of the major conceptualizations to be explored in-depth within the text. For Bill, the current text results from eleven years of working in the South in a university that he has mournfully and angrily witnessed rapidly sliding along the path that Readings (1996) so aptly describes.

> The contemporary University is busily transforming itself from an ideological arm of the state into a bureaucratically organized and relatively autonomous consumer-oriented institution (Readings, 1996, p. 11).

Like many of our colleagues in the field of curriculum studies, we came into academic life hoping that is was centered on scholarship and dialogue, that what we did at the university was study and develop complicated conversations about that study. After twenty years in academia, we realize, however, that universities want to develop capitalist consumers, not critical scholars. The desire in this slide is for larger classes, efficient teaching, mind-numbing meetings and hierarchical administration. All of this is under the watchful eye of surveillance cameras in the hallways. In many ways the universities are much like the public schools.

> What is at stake in the right-wing reform – which has converted the school into a business, focused on the "bottom line" (test scores) – is control of the curriculum, what teachers are permitted to teach, what children are permitted to study (Pinar, 2004, p. xii).

How has the larger socio-economic-political context operated to foster this sad development? We hope that this present study provides some insights into this phenomenon. The major thesis of this book is that when free market fundamentalism, microfascism and religious fundamentalism all conjoin, interweave and connect the ideology of Empire exists. It is not only as Giroux (2004) claims "American Supremacy," but Empire and it operates in particular ways. In order to address these issues we orient our text to a number of specific areas. In this introduction we trace and highlight the concepts that will be given attention in the body of our text. First, we discuss free-market fundamentalism and Christian fundamentalism and then we provide an exploration of the ways in which these fundamentalism(s) operate with our analysis of ressentiment, malice and envy. We think, indeed, that rather than a time of bodies without organs (Deleuze and Guattari, 1983) it is a time paradoxically of bodies without souls.

Free-Market Fundamentalism

> The sales department becomes a business' center or the "soul." We are taught that corporations have a soul, which is the most terrifying news in the world. The operation of markets is now the instrument of social control and forms

the impudent breed who are our masters. Control is short-term and of rapid rates of turnover, but also continuous and without limit, while discipline was of long duration, infinite and discontinuous (Deleuze, 1995, p. 181).

Free-market fundamentalism, a term coined by George Soros, is the first area that requires discussion. "The basic tenet of market fundamentalism is that the most efficient way to deliver services and goods, to keep an economy humming, to provide for members of society, and even, in its more advanced formulations, to maintain social order, is to conceive of virtually all human activity in commercial terms, with values negotiated between the contracting parties without outside interference, according to the laws of supply and demand. The market fundamentalist seeks to solve any imbalance by trying to reduce the role of government and expand the options of those operating in the market" (Ambrose, 2004). The compassionate conservative agenda of reducing the size of the federal government has more to do with disallowing government intervention in business than with concerns about the cost of big government. "Market fundamentalists insist that failures to provide adequately for people result not so much from imbalances in wealth or power, but in restrictions placed on the "invisible hand" of market logic – restrictions created by governments becoming economic actors who do not obey market logic, or through government's efforts to regulate private economic actions. Hence the demand is usually to "free" the markets so they can reach their own potential and so create a healthy economy: free markets, free trade, and free enterprise" (Ambrose, 2004). "Free Market Capitalism has become the dominant American ideological truth –a fundamentalism of sorts. The decline of communism opened the door for unrepentant free marketers to boldly espouse market competition as the final solution for global harmony" (Phillips, 2001, p. 1). According to the "American market scripture, if given the opportunity to freely develop, the marketplace will solve all evils. We will enjoy economic expansion, individual freedom, and unlimited bliss by fully deregulating and privatizing society's socio-economic institutions" (Phillips, 2001, p. 1). "The "reelection" of G.W. Bush as the U.S. President placed into power the party that is the strongest supporter of this American free market fundamentalism. Bush's business/government revolving-door cabinet is comprised of more corporate CEO's than any presidency in recent history" (Phillips, 2001, p. 1). The new government elite works to see that markets remain safe, globalized, and unchallenged. "A closer examination of the American market scripture reveals that "free market" essentially means constant international U.S. government intervention on behalf of American corporations. A public-private partnership that utilizes U.S. embassies, the CIA, FBI, NSA, U.S. Military, Department of Commerce, USAID, and every other U.S government institution to protect, sustain, and directly support our vital interest—U.S. business and its corporations" (Phillips, 2001, p. 1). Witness the no bid contracts for companies like Halliburton in Iraq and most recently in the wake of Katrina. According to McLaren (2005) citing Greider (1997) there exists a strong connection between free market capitalism and conservative political ideology.

> We are returning to a form of pre-welfare competitive capitalism that is driven by the motor of conservative political ideology – one that is capable of

suturing together the discourses of freedom, family values, civic authority, nationalism and patriotism. Of course, the term "freedom" is used in a decidedly and perniciously manipulative fashion. Only the market remains "free" and the people must submit to the dictates of the market (McLaren, 2005, p. 77).

This free market fundamentalism is wrapped within the larger context that liberal democracies are the last and final stage of the development of humanity. The classic statement of this proposition is made by Francis Fukuyama:

> Liberal democracy may constitute the "end point of mankind's ideological evolution" and the "final form of human government," and as such constituted the "end of history." That is, while earlier forms of government were characterized by grave defects and irrationalities that led to their eventual collapse, liberal democracy was arguably free from such fundamental internal contradictions. This was not to say that today's stable democracies, like the United States, France, or Switzerland, were not without injustice or serious social problems. But these problems were ones of incomplete implementation of the twin principles of liberty and equality on which modern democracy is founded, rather than of flaws in the principles themselves. While some present-day countries might fail to achieve stable liberal democracy, and others might lapse back into other, more primitive forms of rule like theocracy or military dictatorship, the ideal of liberal democracy could not be improved on (Fukuyama, 1992, p. 1).

One of the major consequences of this free market fundamentalism is that citizenship becomes a question of consumption. Being a good citizen no longer concerns participation, questioning and involvement in the crucial issues that we face politically and socially, but about buying things. Of course, there is little discussion concerning who has the wherewithal to buy it is just a question of buying. And, we can buy anything and that purchasing can define and construct our identities. It is possible to, as bizarre as it seems, purchase our social consciousness. Henry Giroux discussed this development in *Disturbing Pleasures: Learning Popular Culture* (1994). In essence consumers can feel socially concerned and responsible by buying products from companies that corporate marketers have constructed as socially concerned. In the wake of 9/11 for example, people could feel patriotic and socially aware by buying a new SUV as GM and Ford produced television advertisements stating that buying one of their vehicles demonstrated the consumers' patriotism and pride in America. Free market fundamentalism affects our society and the education provided in our schools and universities. It is interwoven and connected to the postmodern phenomenon of microfascism.

This consumerism is also evident in the curriculum of public schools and universities. Children in public schools are inculcated into the consumer mentality by a curriculum that emphasizes consuming information in books to pass tests or token economies that reward students with either the academic currency of good grades or currency in the form of stickers or prizes. In universities students learn that education is about consuming courses to get a degree. In neither case is education about a complicated conversation.

The complicated conversation that is curriculum requires multidisciplinary, intellectuality, erudition, and self-reflexivity. This is not the recipe for high test scores but a common faith in the possibility of self-realization and democratization, twin project of social and subjective reconstruction (Pinar, 2004, p. 8).

Microfascism and Control Societies

> It is no longer a question of freeing ourselves from repressive institutions and ideologies, but rather freeing ourselves from our own love of the very things that dominate us (Marks, 1998, p. 94).

"Fascism is the common name we accord to totalitarian power. However, we often do it irresponsibly or ahistorically, categorically identifying the concept with limited, sociological understandings of the German or Italian scenarios around the great wars, or confining it to grotesque figurations of human agency, like that of Mussolini or Hitler" (Why-War, 2004). If the concept is to have any critical credibility whatsoever in our global, neo-liberal historical moment, it needs to be unpacked and re-articulated before we begin to transpose it here and there. Deleuze and Guattari elaborate upon the fact that totalitarian regimes are not necessarily synonymous with fascism.

> The concept of totalitarian State applies at the macropoliticial level, to a rigid segmentarity and a particular mode of totalization and centralization. But, fascism is inseparable from a proliferation of molecular focuses in interaction, which skip from point to point, before beginning to resonate together in the National Socialist State. Rural fascism and city or neighborhood fascism, youth fascism and war veteran's fascism, fascism of the Left, and fascism of the Right, fascism of the couple, family, school, and office: every fascism is defined by a micro-black hole that stands on its own and communicates with others, before resonating in a great central black whole (Deleuze and Guattari, 1987, p. 214).

Deleuze in *Postscript on Control Societies* (1995) has re-articulated Walter Benjamin's argument by transposing it into sub-human, molecular-pragmatic one—control societies (see Basu, 2005).

> In control societies, on the other hand, the key thing is no longer a signature or a number but a code: codes are passwords, whereas disciplinary societies are ruled (when it comes to integration or resistance) by precepts. The digital language of control is made up of codes indicating whether access to some information should be allowed or denied (Deleuze, 1995, p. 180).

According to Deleuze, "the discourses of fascism, as dominant myths of our time, establish themselves by an imperial-linguistic takeover of a whole social body of expressive potentialities (Basu, 2004, pp. 26–27):

CHAPTER 1

We're (Deleuze and Guattari) signaling the rise of a comprehensive fascism. We can see nothing, no reason, to stop its spreading. Or rather: either a revolutionary machine that can harness desire and the phenomena of desire will take shape, or desire will go on being manipulated by the forces of oppression, of repression, and so threaten from within, any revolutionary machine (Deleuze, 1995, p. 18).

There are:
…different forms of life and expressive energies in any situation of the historical epoch which are capable of generating multiple instances of thought, imaginative actions, and wills to art. Fascism destroys such pre-signifying and pre-linguistic energies of the world, extinguishes pluralities, and replaces them with a monologue of power that saturates space with, and only with, the immanent will of the dictator. This is the moment in which the language system sponsored by the sovereign is at its most violent; it seeks to efface historical memory by denying its constitutive or legislative relation with non-linguistic social energies; it casts itself and its unilateral doctrine as absolute and natural (Basu, 2004, p. 29).

Hardt and Negri in *Empire* (2000) discuss a new face of world order – that of empire. As they write, "Empire exhausts historical time, suspends history, and summons the past and future within its own ethical order. In other words, Empire presents its order as permanent, eternal and necessary (Hardt and Negri, 2000, p. 11).

> For Deleuze, this is a psycho-mechanical production of social reality more than an organicity of community torn asunder by human alienation and the incursion of reactionary ideologies, false consciousnesses, and agents. Not that the latter do not exist, or are unimportant components in this matter, but that this technology of power cannot be simply seen as a neutral arrangement of tools misused by evil ones. The figure of the dictator is therefore not that of the aberrant individual madman, but a psychological automaton that becomes insidiously present in everything, in the technology of massification itself. The images and objects that mass hallucination, somnambulism, and trance produce are attributes of this immanent will to power. (See Deleuze's *Cinema 1&2*) The hypnotic, fascinating drive of fascism is thus seen to paradoxically operate below the radar of a moral and voluntaristic consciousness of the human subject; fascism becomes a political reality when knowledge based exchanges between entities of intelligence give way to bio-technologism of informatics or information (Basu, 2004, pp. 28–29).

When information exchange replaces knowledge we see evidences of fascism. This pervasive fascism has been called "eternal/ur-fascism" (Eco, 1995), and most recently "proto-fascism" (Giroux, 2004). We would like to refer to fascism for the purposes of our discussion as microfascism. Microfascism displays the characteristics of rhizo (rhizomatic) in the sense Deleuze and Guattari discuss in it in *Anti-Oedipus: Capitalism and Schizophrenia* (1983) and *A Thousand Plateaus* (1987) but using the notion of rhizomatic and applying it to negative consequences. That is, the microfascist order extinguishes these pre-signfying energies and impulses by co-opting them into the technological milieu of

Empire. Thus, "freedom" becomes the central password that paradoxically robs us of our will to act in self-determined ways. This happens when information becomes ubiquitous and equated with critical knowledge. As Eco rightly states this time fascism will not appear as black shirts (see McLaren, 1995):

> Ur-fascism is still around us, sometimes in plain clothes. It would be so much easier for us if there appeared on the world scene somebody saying "I want to reopen Auschwitz, I want the Black shirts to parade in the Italian squares." Life is not that simple. Ur-fascism can come back under the most innocent of disguises. Our duty is to uncover it and to point our finger at any of its new instances. (Eco, 1995, p. 58)

There are several characteristics of what we identify as microfascism. This notion of rhizome indicates that this fascism has multiple tubules that interweave throughout and at times intersect with one another and at times connect. It is also used to indicate that fascism is ever-present, as micro-fascism described by Deleuze and Guattari (1987) and not always obvious. Deleuze and Guattari see fascism as a permanent feature of social life. They are concerned with what they call "microfascism", the fascism that lurks in heart of each and every one of us.

> It's too easy to be antifascist on the molar level, and not even see the fascist inside you, the fascist you yourself sustain and nourish and cherish with molecules both personal and collective (Deleuze and Guattari, 1987, p. 215).

In this analysis we build on the conceptualizations of microfascism, Umberto Eco's (1995) eternal/ur-fascism and Henry Giroux's proto-fascism (2004). This allows us to elaborate the characteristics of microfascism. First, there is the "cult of tradition and the rejection of modernism" (Eco, 1995). According to Eco's definition of this feature of fascism, it reveals itself by believing that "Truth has already been spelled out once and for all, and we can only keep interpreting its obscure message" (Eco, 1995, p. 1). This was in evidence in many of the machinations of the compassionate conservative agenda. There was an effort to reinforce so-called traditional American values. In a speech delivered at a YMCA picnic in 2001 Bush stated:

> Now, this is a nation of character and values, and I'm so honored to being in a place that teaches values, that heralds character, that's not afraid to say there are right choices in life to make and wrong choices in life to make; a community of conscious and a community of character that aims to say to our young, this American experience is a fantastic experience (Bush, 2001).

Second, corporatization and the development of free market capitalism are part of this microfascism (Giroux, 2004; Klein, 2007). The concept of free market capitalism has been discussed in the previous section. Third, there is a rise in nationalism, fear and the just and perpetual war on terrorism (see Hardt and Negri; 2000, 2004). The revival of nationalism in the United States has risen precipitously since 9/11. It manifests itself in some interesting ways. Immediately following 9/11 the sales of American flags reached all time highs. Flag distributors reported flag sales tripled during the period between 2001 and 2003. The flag as a symbol for nationalism is reinforced by public statements to that effect. The prevailing idea was/is that the American flag represents us in the war on terrorism. This is the notion, frequently invoked since September 11, of the struggle between Good—America and those who unreservedly agree with it—and Evil. "Wherever we carry it," George W. Bush told the graduating cadets at West Point in June 2002, the American flag will stand not only for our power, but for freedom." (Urquhart, 2005). The most recent manifestation is the overabundance of yellow, or red, white and blue ribbons magnets for automobiles. It is difficult to drive down American roads today without seeing a yellow ribbon magnet on a car, pick-up truck or SUV. These magnets usually reflect the motto, "Support our Troops."

The rise in nationalism and the war on terrorism all takes place within a "culture of fear" (Glassner, 1999). Fear in microfascism enables manipulation and diversion. If the people are constantly bombarded by things to fear, they spend their time concerned about those fears and their attention is directed away from the critical issues that are most significant to the development of a democratic society and its striving for social justice. What are we afraid of? There is a long list of fears and as each fear is either moved to the background or dismissed a new fear emerges. So, if it is not the fear of terrorism, it is the fear of natural disasters or avian flu or road rage or young African-American male criminals as disproportionately portrayed in the media (*Cops*), or illegal drugs or plane crashes or wild fires or killer prescription drugs and on and on. Our youth has also become the object of fear. Rather than having youth-at-risk, we are witnessing the change to youth-as–risk. Youth are viewed as super predators. Both Henry Giroux and Barry Glassner have discussed this.

> If not represented as a symbol of fashion or hailed as a hot niche, youth are often portrayed as a problem, a danger to adult society or, even worse, irrelevant to the future (Giroux, 2003, p. xiv).

> The misbelief that every child is in imminent risk of becoming a victim has as its corollary a still darker delusion: Any kid might become a victimizer. Beneath such headlines as "Life Means Nothing," "Wild in the Streets," and "Super predators Arrive," the nation's news media have relayed tale upon blood-soaked tale of twelve- and fourteen year olds pumping bullets into toddlers, retirees, parents and one another… journalists stress that violent kids live not just in the South Bronx or South Central L.A. but in safe-seeming suburbs and small towns (Glassner, 1999, p. 68).

Fear is manifested in the popular culture as well as so-called journalistically generated fears. Movies and televisions shows make us fear the other. Particularly interesting is the relatively recent plethora of alien television shows and films. During the 2005 television season all three major networks had new alien series, which helped us fear the other. *Surface* (NBC), *Threshold* (CBS), and *Invasion* (ABC). *Threshold* was the series in which the aliens are in disguise, you never know who the aliens might be so you have to be constantly on guard. It is reminiscent of the different colored levels of terror alert. You must constantly be on guard and fearful because terrorists can be disguised and they are certainly "alien." These shows assist in maintaining fear. The remake of films such as, *War of the Worlds* starring Tom Cruise also creates the mind set to fear the other, while also trading on the national myth that vulnerable girls must (and can be) only protected by wayward muscular men from terrors within such as child predators (Faludi, 2007). We live in this culture of fear and all our energies are spent dealing with the consequences of this fear. In this way our ability to seize those pre-signifying energies is hijacked by a continual barrage of fear-based information. Because we are a Nation at Fear we lose our ability to be concerned with developing and creating a language that would assist us in moving beyond this fear, a language of critique and/or lines of flight.

There is also the phenomenon in this culture of fear, particularly the fear of terrorism, that we have finally, after years of dealing with the Vietnam syndrome, a just war. The concept of the *bellum justum* or just war is symptomatic of Empire. In their controversial book *Empire* (2000) Hardt and Negri refer the concept of just war(s).

> The traditional concept of just war involves the banalization of war and the celebration of it as an ethical instrument; both of which were ideas that modern political thought and the international community of nation-states had resolutely refused. These two traditional characteristics have reappeared in our postmodern world: on the one hand war is reduced to the status of police action and on the other; the new power that can legitimately exercise ethical functions through war is sacralized (Hardt & Negri, 2000, p. 12).

The War in Iraq demonstrates these qualities. In this war we were, according the Bush administration, bringing democracy to the barbaric and destabilizing Middle East. Acting alone, our military and corporate contractors severed a policing function: sweeping for and killing terrorists and training the Iraq military and police to serve this function. The enemy-the terrorists- were viewed as threats to the ethical world order and its stability. It is, therefore, our "democratic" if not moral responsibility to weed out the terrorists and kill them. It is broadcasted as our sacred duty.

> Evoking the role of the divine prophet who identifies with the sword arm of retribution, Bush reveals the eschatological undertow to the war on terrorism, perhaps most evident in his totalizing and Manichean pronouncements where he likens bin Laden and chthonic warriors to absolute evil, and the United States to the apogee of freedom and goodness (McLaren, 2005, p. 262).

Another quality of the war on terrorism is its duration. It has no end. In fact, Dick Cheney called it a "never-ending-war." According to the Bush administration estimates, it would take as long as it takes. So, we are faced with the reality that this war could be perpetual. The reality of a perpetual war is significant. It is connected to notions of sovereignty and exception. The Italian philosopher, Giorgio Agamben in his text, *Homo Sacer: Sovereign Power and Bare Life* (1998), explicates sovereignty and exception. Both of these concepts have direct application to the present in the United States. In simple terms, in times of war the citizens of a country are willing to grant the sovereign exceptions. Exceptions, particularly to their freedoms as citizens are granted.

CHAPTER 1

> One of the theses of the present inquiry is that in our age, the state of exception comes more and more to the foreground as the fundamental political structure and ultimately becomes the rule (Agamben, 1998, p. 20).

For example, during World War II Americans were willing to grant the exception(s) to ration gasoline, monitor their speech ("loose lips, sink ships") and various other rights in order to assist in the war effort and for their own security. It was recognized, however, that those rights would only be abrogated for the duration of the conflict. The duration was always seen as limited and as soon as the war was over, the rights would return. Fast-forward to the present. We now are engaged in a perpetual war and the exceptions have been granted. The exception was codified in the Patriot Act and the suspension of *habeus corpus*. The United States government can now because of this exception, name individuals as terrorists without offering them a hearing or even legal council. They can detain people secretly and indefinitely without access to lawyers or a jury trial. They are able to subpoena anybody's telephone, medical, bookstore, library or university records by simply certifying that the records are needed for an investigation of international terrorism. We suspect that Americans would have a hard time giving up these rights, making this exception, even for a limited time. But in this case it just might be perpetually. And it is ensconced in The USA Patriot Act. The point is that Americans have given up their rights in order to feel more secure. Fear has once again reared its ugly head. Whenever the feeling of safety or security returns the government can issue another colored terror alert. There has been some public protest against the Act. Of course, protest in the present historical moment can be equated with terrorism.

> There is strong evidence to suggest that the USA Patriot Act is being used to target certain forms of political activities, intimidate protesters, and stifle the free-speech rights of those protesting the policies of the Bush administration (Giroux, 2004, p. 9).

Fourth, the media comes under concentrated ownership. Television networks, local and cable television channels, publishing, film production studios, internet access companies all concentrated in major media corporations.

> Time Warner the largest media company in the world is the standard bearer of vertical integration in the modern digital age. The marriage between "old" media Time Warner and "new" media AOL in 2000 was heralded by many experts as a sign of a new era. The belief was that traditional media companies had to align themselves with online partners or risk the chance of finding their business model and methods obsolete. A weak ad market, subscriptions for new online users hitting a plateau, and a less than expected demand for broadband Internet service are just some of the reasons why AOL Time Warner never jumped started an overhaul of the entire media industry as first predicted. The company dropped AOL from its corporate name in 2003 in an effort to show Wall Street that it still valued its core assets. With such influential brands as CNN, Warner Brothers studio, Sports Illustrated and AOL Instant Messaging, a Time Warner property is never too far away from any consumer's

fingertips. Another of the largest global media empires, Viacom has a financial interest in broadcast and cable television, radio, Internet, book publishing, and film production and distribution. Some of this vertically integrated conglomerate's highly recognizable properties include the CBS network, MTV, Infinity broadcasting, Simon & Schuster, Blockbuster and Paramount Pictures. With such a diverse portfolio of properties, Viacom is one of the most profitable media giants as CBS is a top draw for older viewers while MTV remains the most popular teen orientated media outlet. Disney is not a media company that relies solely upon Mickey Mouse and amusement parks. From the ABC network to ESPN, Disney is an extremely well diversified corporation with so many holdings that they seemingly contradict one another. The same company that brings Peter Jennings and the ABC Family channel into living rooms is also the parent company of Miramax Films, a production unit specializing in violent and risqué features. Disney's roots date back to the early 20th century; however the company truly became the vertically integrated giant it is today after it acquired Capital Cities/ABC in 1995 (Columbia Journalism Review, 2007).

When discussing media ownership the name of Rupert Murdoch can not be ignored. In recent years, right–wing, Australian-born billionaire Rupert Murdoch has used the U.S. government's increasingly lax media regulations to consolidate his hold over the media and wider political debate in America. Consider Murdoch's empire: According to *Businessweek*, "his satellites deliver TV programs in five continents, all but dominating Britain, Italy, and wide swaths of Asia and the Middle East. He publishes 175 newspapers, including the *New York Post* and *The Times of London*. In the U.S., he owns the Twentieth Century Fox Studio, Fox Network, and 35 TV stations that reach more than 40% of the country...His cable channels include fast-growing Fox News, and 19 regional sports channels. In all, as many as one in five American homes at any given time will be tuned into a show News Corp. either produced or delivered (Center for American Progress, 2004).

The development of these major media conglomerates concentrates media ownership into progressively fewer companies or individuals. It becomes increasingly difficult for anyone who is critical of the conglomerates with their vertically integrated practices to find an outlet for their point of view.

> Concentrated corporate control does not welcome stories or investigative reports that are critical of corporate culture and its policies and practices. For example, soon after Disney bought ABC, Jim Hightower, a popular radio talk show host, was fired for making critical remarks about the Telecommunications Act of 1996 and the Disney Corporation (Giroux, 2000, p. 4).

Fifth, like George Orwell's novel *Nineteen Eighty-Four*, there are evidences of newspeak or doublespeak. The word doublespeak was coined in the early 1950s. It is often incorrectly attributed to George Orwell and his dystopian novel, Nineteen Eighty-Four. "The word actually never appears in that novel; Orwell did, however, coin newspeak, oldspeak, and doublethink. Doublespeak may be considered, in Orwell's lexicography, as the B vocabulary of Newspeak words "deliberately

CHAPTER 1

constructed for political purposes: words, that is to say, which not only had in every case a political implication, but were intended to impose a desirable mental attitude upon the person using them" (Knowledgerush, 2006). In his bestselling book *Doublespeak*, William Lutz notes that doublespeak is not an accident or a "slip of the tongue." Instead, it is a deliberate, calculated misuse of language. Lutz provides several defining attributes of doublespeak. "It misleads, distorts reality, pretends to communicate, makes the bad seem good, avoids or shifts responsibility, makes the negative appear positive, creates a false verbal map of the world limits, conceals, corrupts, and prevents thought, makes the unpleasant appear attractive or tolerable, and creates incongruity between reality and what is said or not said" (Lutz, 1989, p. 28). The Bush administration was notorious when it comes to double speak. In the areas of environmental polices and the war in Iraq, Bush doublespeak flowed freely.

First, the Healthy Forests Initiative (HFI) – leave no tree behind. Pretend to protect our forests while allowing more logging. Couple the HFI with the Bush Administration's desire to repeal the Roadless Area Conservation Rule, and the result is opening up the Ozark and Ouachita National Forests for logging in previously protected areas. It is likely that there will be healthy profits for the timber companies, at the expense of Arkansas citizens. Second, there is The "Clear Skies" Initiative. This allows our dirty old power plants to continue polluting. The Bush administration's Environmental Protection Agency proposed weakening programs that would require power plants built in the last century to meet modern pollution control standards. More pollution in our air means more public health problems, especially asthma in young children. Third, there was the Clean Water Act. The Food and Drug Administration issued warnings to pregnant women to avoid eating tuna fish because of accumulated mercury from the water, since mercury is a known toxin that causes developmental problems in young children. On the other hand, the administration's EPA proposed delaying mercury cleanup at coal-fired power plants, the major source of airborne mercury contamination of water (Sierra Club, 2004, pp. 1–2).

In the war with Iraq there are/were numerous examples of doublespeak. The administration used them from 9/11 on.

> The list of misrepresentations and rhetorical contortions includes the claims that Iraq was building nuclear weapons and was engaged in the production of biological and chemical agents, and that Saddam Hussein was working with Osama bin Laden and had direct ties to Al Qaeda. Even after the CIA reported that the charged that Saddam Hussein had brought uranium from the African nation of Niger in pursuit of developing nuclear weapons was fabricated, Bush included the assertion in his 2003 State of the Union Address (Giroux, 2004, p. 25).

So, the use of doublespeak is rampant in the current socio-political context.

Sixth, one political party radically changes its identity. The Republican Party certainly since the time of Ronald Reagan has morphed its identity. Although always conservative in the 20th century, the Republican party has become the party of the Fundamentalist Right-Wing. They oppose abortion, same-sex marriage, and embryonic stem-cell research; they also favor school prayer and the interpretation of the establishment clause of the First Amendment which prohibits only the official establishment of a state church, as opposed to the more secularist view that the clause requires a strict separation of church and state (Since the 1960s, the latter interpretation has generally been favored by the Supreme Court.) Some argue that the American colonies and the United States were founded to be Christian societies, although also they profess to be tolerant of other Abrahamic religions.

Seventh, there is a collapse of the separation of church and state. The division between church and state increasingly decreases as we proceed through the 21st century. The Bush administrations' public communications and policies contained four characteristics that are simultaneously rooted in religious fundamentalism while offering political capital and a political agenda. There were simplistic black-and-white conceptions of the political landscape, most importantly good vs. evil and security vs. peril. There were calls for immediate action on administration policies as a necessary part of the nation's calling or mission against terrorism. There were declarations about the will of God for America and for the spread of U.S. conceptions of freedom and liberty. There was the claim that dissent from the administration is unpatriotic and a threat to the nation and the globe (see Domke, 2004).

> In combination, these characteristics have transformed Bush's 'Either you are with us or against us policy to 'Either you are with us, or you are against God.' To the great misfortune of American democracy and the global public, such a view looks, sounds and feels remarkably similar to that of the terrorists it is fighting (Domke, 2004, p. 2).

All of the Christocrats we examine in this book made continual statements of support for Bush and his policies. Three issues are representative and demonstrate the disappearing division between the state and religion. First there was the faith-based initiative movement. Second, there was the stem cell research controversy. Third, there was the intelligent design movement.

The controversy over stem-cell research is another example of the collapsing of church and state. "A stem cell is a primitive type of cell that can be coaxed into developing into most of the 220 types of cells found in the human body (e.g. blood cells, heart cells, brain cells, etc). Some researchers regard them as offering the greatest potential for the alleviation of human suffering since the development of antibiotics. Over 100 million Americans suffer from diseases that may eventually be treated more effectively with stem cells or even cured (Henning, 2004, p. 2). These include heart disease, diabetes, and certain types of cancer. Stem cells can be extracted from very young human embryos – typically from surplus frozen embryos left over from in-vitro fertilization (IVF) procedures at fertility clinics (see Young-Rahn, 2003). "In a survey taken in 2001 Among Fundamental Christians, the ratio was almost 2.5 to 1 (63% to 26%) against stem cell research. Bush decided on August 9, 2001 to allow research to resume in government labs, but restricted researchers to use only 72 existing lines of stem cells. "By May 2003, most of these

CHAPTER 1

lines had become useless; some of the lines are genetically identical to others; only 11 remained available for research. By mid-2005, all were believed to be useless for research" (The Brad Blog, 2004, p. 2) In a speech given in May, 2005 at the White House, Bush reflects the fundamentalist stance on stem cell research. Tom Delay called the stem cell research – "the dismemberment of living, distinct human beings."

> But I also recognize the grave moral issues at stake. So, in August 2000 first – 2001, I set forward a policy to advance stem cell research in a responsible way by funding research on stem cell lines derived only from embryos that had already been destroyed. This policy set a clear standard: We should not use public money to support the further destruction of human life (Bush, 2005 http://www.whitehouse.gov/news/releases/2005/05/20050524-12.html).

There was/is a split in the Republican Party over stem cell research, but the Right wing clearly has dominance on this issue and it is linked by the party to the issue of abortion and the "right to life"

The faith-based initiatives were announced by President Bush in 2003. His first executive order as president created the Office of Faith-Based and Community Initiatives in the White House. This action expanded on the "Charitable Choice" provision, passed as part of President Clinton's 1996 welfare reform bill, which allowed smaller and more overtly religious groups to receive government funding for providing social services. [In 2003, faith-based social services grants totaled $1.17 billion].

When President Bush was elected, he made his faith-based initiative a priority. He said it would be a way to help out religious charities. In Philadelphia, in a speech before the heads of community and religious leaders, the president made good on that promise.

> "The days of discriminating against religious groups just because they are religious are coming to an end," Bush said. "If a charity is helping the needy, it should not matter if there is a rabbi on the board, or a cross or a crescent on the wall, or a religious commitment in the charter"
> (http://www.citizenlink.org/CLFeatures/A000000581.cfm).

In 2002, then Secretary of Education Roderick Paige delivering a speech At the White House Conference on Faith-Based and Community Initiatives expressed the connections between government and religion.

> With the stroke of a pen, the President signaled that this Administration will knock down any barrier, will do whatever it takes to get people of faith and goodwill involved in helping solve some of the problems in our society. And I also know you have to be, you have to be good in politics to become President of the United States and people can only view him from the political lenses. But, let me explain from a person who knows him up close, this is in his heart. If you could see his heart, you would understand that as well. It's not about politics or anything like that. It's about a mission that he's on as a human being. He really, seriously wants to improve the world. He's a special human

being and I'm very pleased to serve as his Secretary of Education (Paige, 2002).

There are Cabinet Centers for Faith-Based and Community Initiatives at the Department of Health and Human Services; Department of Housing and Urban Development; Department of Labor; Department of Justice; and Department of Education.

The controversy over intelligent design is a third example of the diminishing of the borders between church and state. Intelligent design is seen by many fundamentalists as a credible and scientific alternative to evolution. Of course, it is not Creationism, the full biblical doctrine of creation, which they would prefer. The book that initiated the battle over intelligent design is *Intelligent Design: The Bridge between Science and Theology* (1999) by William A. Dembski. Dembski claims that there exists specified complexity. He argues that it is impossible for specified complexity to exist in patterns displayed by configurations formed by unguided processes (Dembski, 1999). Therefore, Dembski argues, the fact that specified complex patterns can be found in living things indicates some kind of guidance in their formation, which is indicative of intelligence. It is a reliable marker of design by an intelligent agent, a central tenet to intelligent design and he argues that instances of it in nature cannot be explained by Darwinian evolution.

Although Bush said that curriculum decisions should be made by school districts rather than the federal government, He told Texas newspaper reporters in a group interview at the White House on August 1, 2005 that he believed that intelligent design should be taught alongside evolution as competing theories.

> "Both sides ought to be properly taught…so people can understand what the debate is about, he said, according to an official transcript of the session. Bush added: "Part of education is to expose people to different schools of thought…You're asking me whether or not people ought to be exposed to different ideas, and the answer is yes" (Washington Post).

But, more than presidential speeches this intelligent design movement is having direct impact on the public school curriculum. The Dover, Pennsylvania School Board implemented a policy in December 2004 requiring all ninth-grade biology teachers to read a statement on "intelligent design" before teaching evolution lessons. The disclaimer states that evolution is a "theory…not a fact," that "gaps in the theory exist for which there is no evidence," and that "intelligent design" is a valid scientific alternative. Science teachers in Dover are also required to refer to a book describing the theory of "intelligent design," Of *Pandas and People*, to students interested in the subject. The Dover school district is believed to be the first in the country to require such a disclaimer.

Utah state legislator Chris Buttars threatened to introduce legislation in 2006 in favor of teaching "divine design" in the state's public schools. "Divine design," according to Buttars, "doesn't preach religion ... The only people who will be upset about this are atheists. ... It shocks me that our schools are teaching evolution as fact" (Canham, 2005). The issues of faith-based organizations, stem cell research and intelligent design are just three examples of the attempts to collapse the space

CHAPTER 1

between church and state within microfascism. The discussion of the collapse of the separation of church and state as the final characteristic of microfascism leads us to a discussion of Christian fundamentalism.

Christian Fundamentalism

> It was once held that if one gave up their position and money for being used for the kingdom it was a spiritual sacrifice pleasing to God. Today it is the opposite, if one is not being blessed financially and receiving all they desire they are not walking by faith and are missing God's blessings. As Benny Hinn says "Poverty is from the devil and that God wants all Christians prosperous" (Benny Hinn, TBN, 11/6/90).

In *"The Battle for God: A History of Fundamentalism* (2001) Karen Armstrong discusses the history fundamentalism in the United States. It is her contention that the term fundamentalism was first used by American Protestants. This group used the term in the early part of the 20th century during its initial phase (which ran from the 1890s to the Scopes "MonkeyTrial" of 1925) to distinguish themselves from more liberal branches of Protestantism who the fundamentalists believed were at worst perverting at best misinterpreting the Christian faith" (Armstrong, 2001, p. xii). Fundamentalism was also a "back to basics" movement in American Protestantism, in which the desire was for a reemphasis of the "fundamentals" of the Christian tradition. These were a literal interpretation of scripture and the acceptance of other core doctrines. Armstrong provides a very useful historical analysis of Christian, Jewish and Muslim fundamentalism in the 20th century by dividing their development into three periods, she names, mobilization (1960–1974), the offensive (1974–1979) and Defeat (1979–1999) (Armstrong, 2001). We would add a fourth period post fundamentalism (1999-present), to which Armstrong also refers. In this text we will elaborate and discuss how fundamentalism has operated within these historical periods. Despite the apparent toppling of various leaders, particularly of Christian fundamentalism, such as the sex and financial scandals of Jimmy Swaggart and Jim and Tammy Faye Baker, Christian fundamentalism has been able to survive and even flourish in the 21st century.

In *Fundamentalism Observed* (1991), the first volume of an extensive six-volume study of fundamentalism undertaken by Martin E. Marty and R. Scott Appleby entitled *The Fundamentalist Project*; the authors suggest that all fundamentalisms follow a certain pattern. This pattern has several particular characteristics. First, fundamentalists consider that they are embattled forms of spirituality, which have emerged in response to a perceived crisis (Marty and Appleby, 1995). This explains the phase of fundamentalism that emerged with strength in the 1970s and has continued to strengthen to the present day. There is a feeling with the fundamentalists that the United States is in moral collapse since the era of the 1960s and Christianity is under attack.

> If we are going to save America and evangelize the world, we cannot accommodate secular philosophies that are diametrically opposed to Christian

truth ... We need to pull out all the stops to recruit and train 25 million Americans to become informed pro-moral activists whose voices can be heard in the halls of Congress. I am convinced that America can be turned around if we will all get serious about the Master's business. It may be late, but it is never too late to do what is right. We need an old-fashioned, God-honoring, Christ-exalting revival to turn American back to God. America can be saved (Falwell, 1984)!

Just like what Nazi Germany did to the Jews, so liberal America is now doing to the evangelical Christians. It's no different. It is the same thing. It is happening all over again. It is the Democratic Congress, the liberal-based media and the homosexuals who want to destroy the Christians. Wholesale abuse and discrimination and the worst bigotry directed toward any group in America today. More terrible than anything suffered by any minority in history (Pat Robertson, 1993 interview with Molly Ivins).

Christians as victims is a constant refrain in the fundamentalist world view.

The United States under Bush is driving toward empire, but the domestic political fuel being fed into the engine is that of a wounded and vengeful nationalism. This sentiment is for the most part entirely sincere, and all the more dangerous for that. If recent history is any guide, there is probably no more dangerous element in the nationalist mix than a sense of righteous victimhood (Lieven, 2003)

A second characteristic of fundamentalism(s) is that they feel that they are engaged with enemies whose secularist policies and beliefs seem inimical to religion itself (Marty and Appleby, 1995). In the present case of fundamentalism secularist and secular humanist policies are most evident in the public school curriculum. In 1996 Presidential candidate Pat Buchanan, was addressing an anti-gay rally in Des Moines engaged the secular humanist enemy in this way. "We're going to bring back God and the Bible and drive the gods of secular humanism right out of the public schools of America." Pat Robertson echoes Buchanan's thoughts, "the people in the United States have allowed rampant secularism and occult, etc. to be broadcast on television (2001). Third, the battle with these enemies is not regarded as a conventional battle but is experienced as a cosmic war between the forces of good and evil (Armstrong, 2000). Many of the spokespeople for fundamentalism talk of the struggle as a battle for the soul of America. Fourth, they fear annihilation and try to fortify their beleaguered identity by means of selective retrieval of certain doctrines and practices of the past (Armstrong, 2000). Fifth, to avoid contamination, fundamentalists often withdraw from mainstream society to create a counterculture yet they are not necessarily impractical dreamers (Armstong, 2000). "They have absorbed the pragmatic rationalism of modernity and under the guidance of charismatic leaders they refine these fundamentals so as to create an ideology that provides the faithful with a plan of action" (Barkat, 2006). Most recently that plan of action has become a political agenda under the Christian Coalition and Focus on the Family. Roberta Combs a native South

CHAPTER 1

Carolinian and good friend of Lee Atwater is currently Chairperson and President. Combs served as the State Chairman of the South Carolina Christian Coalition, and was later selected by Pat Robertson to become the Executive Vice-President of the Christian Coalition of America in 1999. Upon Pat Robertson's retirement from the Coalition in 2001, the national board elevated her to the role of Chairman and President, becoming the first female to hold those positions. This organization gives fundamentalist plans for action.

> Today, Christians need to play an active role in government again like never before. If we are going to be able to change policy and influence decisions – from the school boards to Washington, DC – it is imperative that people of faith become committed to doing what Ronald Reagan called "the hard work of freedom". We are driven by the belief that people of faith have a right and a responsibility to be involved in the world around them. That involvement includes community, social and political action. (http://www.cc.org/about.cfm)

More recently the nomination of a Supreme Court justice, Harriet E. Miers, revolves around the separation of church and state. Faced with issues concerning Miers' qualifications to be a Supreme Court justice, Bush attempted to shift the discussion away from qualifications such as whether the nominee has ever been a judge to questions about her faith. Bush stated:

> "People ask me why I picked Harriet Miers," Mr. Bush told reporters in the Oval Office. "They want to know Harriet Miers's background, they want to know as much as they possibly can before they form opinions. And part of Harriet Miers's life is her religion" (Bumiller, 2005).

The president spoke on the same day that James C. Dobson, the founder of the conservative evangelical group Focus on the Family, said in remarks broadcast on his organization's radio program that Karl Rove, Mr. Bush's chief political adviser, had assured him that Ms. Miers was an evangelical Christian and a member of "a very conservative church, which is almost universally pro-life." Again we have an example of the separation of church and state collapsing.

Eighth, eventually fundamentalists fight back and attempt to resacralize an increasingly skeptical world (Marty and Appleby, 1995). All of the above instances of fundamentalism previously stated are evidence of the attempt to resacralize the United States. Resacralize the United States and perhaps the world in a particular and specific way. That way would be the fundamentalist utopic version/vision of this world and the next. These eight characteristics provide a way to look at contemporary fundamentalism and they will form the basis of the section of the text devoted to the analysis of religious fundamentalisms (particularly Christian and Muslim). How do free market capitalism, microfascism and Christian fundamentalism interweave and operate in our postmodern world? That is the question we turn to next.

Ressentiment — a self defeating turn of mind; a resentment or hatred that permeates one's emotions; yet one doesn't act on it

Hatred of certain things is a family value, and a very important one. In fact if we are going to rescue our culture, we need a lot more hate. The villainous things that must be hated are loose sexual mores, Feminism, and bad behavior by certain racial and ethnic groups (Hardisty, 1999, p. 41).

What a culture this administration has spawned. What in 1995 I labeled as 'predatory culture' has transmogrified into a lurid culture of malice (McLaren, 2005, p. 267).

Another aspect of the age of fundamentalism(s) is the manner is which it is imbued with ressentiment. Deleuze interpreting Nietzsche's conceptualization of ressentiment discusses three characteristics of ressentiment. It is closely connected to the concept of malice and envy we will discuss next. First, there is the inability to admire, respect or love. Second, there is passivity. Third, there is the imputation of wrongs, the distribution of responsibilities and perpetual accusation. (Deleuze, 1983). After an initial discussion of ressentiment, these three characteristics will be discussed in relationship to the age of fundamentalism(s).

"Ressentiment is not constituted by re-action. Ressentiment designates a type in which "reactive forces prevail over active forces. It is the case in which these forces can only prevail in one way: by not acting. It is not to re-act. It is reaction. "Reaction ceases to be acted in order to become something felt" (Deleuze, 1983, p. 111). Since it is not about re-acting, reaction can be endless. Again, it is felt instead of being acted. "This reaction therefore blames its object, whatever it is, as an object on which revenge must be taken, which must be made to pay for this indefinite delay" (Deleuze, 1983, p. 115). The object in this case is the other. The other being and defined as all of those who are considered godless. There must be the distinction made and remade between the two, between godly and godless. Defining, elaborating, and critiquing the liberal and secular continuously, and endlessly, without acting permeate this free market Christian microfascism. It is an attempt at understanding how this phenomenon operates. We are suggesting it operates on one level within ressentiment. It must be emphasized that there are actions too.

One way that ressentiment operates is through the inability to admire or respect. According to those involved with these fundamentalism(s), the liberal/left/secular/ intellectuals, those denizens of the 1960s have brought nothing but godless chaos, confusion, disarray, crisis, ideology, repudiation of history, contentiousness, homosexuality, abortion and on and on to the country and to our educational system both in public schools and the universities. Of course, in ressentiment, there must be someone or something to blame. The critique "must recriminate and distribute blame: look for the inclination to play down causes, to make misfortune someone's fault" (Deleuze, 1983, p. 117). In the aftermath of 9/11 and hurricane Katrina, for example it was the godless ones who brought about both terrorism and natural devastating destruction. In a conversation between Jerry Falwell and Pat Robertson only a few days after 9/11, we can see this ressentiment.

neo/liberalism

CHAPTER 1

> Falwell: I really believe that the pagans and the abortionists and the feminists and the gays and the lesbians who are actively trying to make that an alternative lifestyle, the ACLU, People for the American Way, all of them who try to secularize America…I point the thing in their face and say you helped this happen.

> Robertson: I totally concur, and the problem is we've adopted that agenda at the highest levels of our government, and so we're responsible as a free society for what the top people do, and the top people, of course, is the court system (http://www.ihatepatrobertson.com/archives/category/jerry-falwell/).

And, also there is the ressentiment-filled reaction to Hurricane Katrina.

> You know, it's just amazing, though, that people say the litmus test for [Supreme Court nominee John G.] Roberts [Jr.] is whether or not he supports the wholesale slaughter of unborn children. We have killed over 40 million unborn babies in America. I was reading, yesterday, a book that was very interesting about what God has to say in the Old Testament about those who shed innocent blood. And he used the term that those who do this, "the land will vomit you out." That – you look at your – you look at the book of Leviticus and see what it says there. And this author of this said, "well 'vomit out' means you are not able to defend yourself." But have we found we are unable somehow to defend ourselves against some of the attacks that are coming against us, either by terrorists or now by natural disaster? Could they be connected in some way? (Robertson, 2005)

Someone must be to blame for the uncertainty and complexity in our world. Rather than admiring or respecting multiplicity and difference as a hopeful phenomenon, there is an inability to view it that way. It must be disparaged. It must be bounded. It must be clearly defined continually. It must be othered.

Passivity is another characteristic of ressentiment. This seems to be clearly indicated in the continual replay of the call for a back to basics in the society and education. Passive doesn't mean non-active, it means "non-acted" (Nietzsche, 1987). "The term "passive" stands for the triumph of reaction, the moment when, ceasing to be acted, it becomes ressentiment" (Deleuze, 1983, p. 118).

Perpetual accusation, distribution of responsibilities and imputation of wrongs is a third characteristic of ressentiment and clearly in evidence in the current free market, fundamentalist era. Here is the dangerous side of this phenomenon, "it is not content to denounce crimes and criminals, it wants sinners, people who are responsible" (Deleuze, 1983, p. 119). There must be villains (others) who can be responsible and can be perpetually accused of (blamed for) sending the country into this "so-called" perpetual crisis. This agenda needs an enemy, an evil empire, or a mad monarch. It needs an evil to combat and, by distinguishing that which is other as evil, one confirms the goodness of its opposite. It is through defining the other that we are, indeed, defined. The various and sundry list of the godless is evil therefore the opposite is good, the godly that is ressentiment. We think, however, that fundamentalism(s) operate in a manner that includes but is more complex than just ressentiment. Again, all of these characteristics of ressentiment will be discussed throughout the text in connection with various manifestations of the era of fundamentalisms.

Cartography

What distinguishes the map from the tracing is that it is entirely oriented toward experimentation in contact with the real...The map is open and connectable in all of its dimensions; it is detachable, reversible, susceptible to constant modification. It can be torn, reversed, adapted to any kind of mounting, reworked by individual, group, or social formation. It can be drawn on a wall, conceived as a work of art, constructed as a political action or as a mediation. (Deleuze & Guattari, 1987, p. 12).

In their text *A Thousand Plateaus*, Deleuze and Guattari enumerate the characteristics of the rhizome. One of the principles of the rhizome is that of cartography or mapping. Referring to earlier work, Michael J. Shapiro elucidates his use of "violent cartographies" as ways of "imagining" warring spaces that become, in Foucaultian fashion, "frames" around which policy debates from any number of areas can be rendered intelligible to citizens. "Maps of enmity" have driven domestic U.S. elections and subsequent policy decisions by their victors, the strongest one has been the 'red/blue" state divide. Here is Shapiro's explanation of the concept:

> bases of violent cartographies are the 'historically developed, socially embedded interpretations of identity and space' that constitute the frames within which enmities give rise to war-as-policy (Shapiro, 1997: ix). Violent cartographies are thus constituted as inter-articulations of geographic imaginaries and antagonisms, based on models of identity-difference. Since the Treaty of Westphalia (1648), a point at which the horizontal, geopolitical world of nation-states emerged as a more salient geographic imaginary than the theologically oriented vertical world (which was imaginatively structured as a separation between divine and secular space), maps of enmity have been framed by differences in geopolitical location, and (with notable exceptions) state leaders have supplanted religious authorities. Moreover (also with notable exceptions), geopolitical location has since been a more significant identity marker than spiritual commitment (Shapiro, 2007, 293–4).

George Bush and his advisors had, after the resolution of the 2000 election, a "milieu" in front of them onto which they mapped a violent cartography that inhered to culture war. Drawing upon old historical grievances concerning the Civil War, the old South, Texas sovereignty and Northeastern liberal hegemony, they mapped it geographically but laid over it the veneer of spiritual commitment, lest it be questioned by those with any knowledge of American history. This milieu is "the space in which a series of uncertain elements unfold," (Foucault, 2007, 20) and in it "the apparatuses of security work, fabricate organize, and plan a milieu even before the notion was formed and isolated," (ibid, 21). Finally, it has an element in which a "circular link is produced between effects and causes, since an effect from one point of view will be a cause from another," (21). We use this concept of violent cartography because it describes most accurately the oft-mentioned polarization of American politics, which does not really inhere so much to geography despite the fact that the domestic milieu has been framed in such way. Rather, the circular link between causes and effects is produced by a missionary religious discourse that is traced back to an identity we later in describe in the next chapter as the "Christocracy." This christocracy has been a grass roots movements to redraw the contours of domestic American life by conduct, specifically a newly drawn out examples of conduct exhibited by a Christian minority that stem from counter-conducts opposed to existing institutions. Ironically, by posing as a democratic movement based on promoting "freedom" this movement has produced the very "theologically oriented vertical world" also known as the middle ages, that Shapiro describes above. To those "American exceptionalists" who would claim that the U.S. is unique for never having had a feudal past, we look with horror at the one shaping into existence in the U.S. now, and note with caution that it has visited this country before.

The chapters that follow elaborate the current conditions and discuss the cultural curriculum of the religious right in America. It is unique in that although there have been several book length treatments on the subject of the religious right in America in the popular press, this is a scholarly treatment of the subject matter. This book clarifies the parameters and cartography of this phenomenon. In the chapters we make clear the nature, make-up and consequences of what we call the Christocrats and their agenda of the civic gospel and how there is much of postmodern paradox to the present historical moment.

Chapter 2 discusses the various interpretations of the notion of the gospel. The chapter delineates the social gospel and the current manifestations of the civic gospel. Mapping the civic gospel and its interconnections with dominion and reconstructionist theology is a major emphasis. The chapter concludes with the cartography of the agendas of the civic gospel.

Chapter 3 analyzes how the term "secularism" and the institutions and ideas associated with it concerning civic life have been re-scripted by Neoconservative public philosophers to provide a moral countercultural framework from which people can satisfy the associational tug that often accompanies American feelings of vulnerability in times of economic crisis as well as in response to immigration fears. "Joiners" are Americans, but "perverse joiners" are those who satisfy their associational desires by condemning others to poverty, racism and ostracism. Encouragement for this rejuvenated culture of joining has been the reconfiguration of the office of the presidency as a religious office. Beginning with countercultural charges that President Clinton had "tarnished" the sacred office with his extramarital dalliances, Neoconservatives used existing support and primacy of the office of the presidency to hand over new ministering powers to President Bush in the aftermath of 9-11. Bush has used this "presidentialism" to consolidate a new "Executive Order" where president's act as the powerful parent to a nation of scared children. Central to all of this has been the grassroots logic promulgated by the Christian Right through it's own curriculum of free market fundamentalism and an abstract notion of individual liberty that trades on libertarian platitudes ("people should pay their own way" "lift themselves up by their bootstraps" "government out of our lives", etc.) while enforcing an agenda that restricts – severely-the freedoms and liberties of women, gays and lesbians and the working poor who are overwhelmingly minorities. While Bush has used the ideology of executive power to enforce a fundamentalist agenda at home, his more powerful cronies have used his dependence on them to their personal advantage by advancing a corporatist state that feeds on government subsidies to build the terrorism industry and profit from disasters that could have been mitigated or prevented by a different kind of governmentality (Klein, 2007).

Chapter 4 discusses the other riposte of Christian fundamentalists: humanism. The concept has inflamed popular social movements, intellectual movements and rights-based movements since its birth in the 1700s in Europe. However, in the United States, humanism is equated with an ideology of the Left wing said to be born during FDRs radical Keynesian experiment in the New Deal. Humanism and the progress it promised is actually an earlier phenomenon associated with the progressive movements of the 1910s and 20s that finally made even earlier reform movements of the late nineteenth century into recognizably human projects. Such movements included those for women's rights, anti-slavery movements, labor movements for decent wages and conditions and a separate juvenile justice system and public schooling. There is a contemporary amnesia and confusion surrounding humanism. While for the right and its fundamentalist benefactors, humanism has clear meaning as an oppositional term associated with activities like abortion, public schooling and welfare, for leftists it is often mistakenly associated with human rights. Similar confusion surrounds the term postmodern which many progressives (that is, people concerned with seeing change in the future that benefits more people rather than an elite few) confuse with the time period we live in and determine it to be a critical stance on that period. Indeed, Bush believes in postmodern fashion that he is "creating modernity" but erroneously labeled French poststructuralists such as Deleuze and Guattari, are not, and never were postmodern; they recognized the symptoms of the postmodern period and diagnosed them through the moral system of ressentiment, they did not wave flags in favor of it. One reason why poststructuralism is helpful in making a critique of the microfascism of the right is that it (the right) appeals to morality rather than empirical results or scientific fact to garner its power. Poststructualism can smell a morality play in the service of incarceration; critical Marxism, humanism and democratic frameworks cannot because they are wholly wrapped up in this very same morality tale. The morality tale of these folks who hate humanism is much like the older sibling who takes one's hand, balls it up into a fist and punches you in the face, all the while exclaiming "Why do you keep hitting yourself?"

We next take the notion of geography and mapping literally to discuss notions of place and the civic gospel. The first section of the chapter is entitled: The Land of a Thousand Churches: The Ex-Confederacy and the Resurrection of the South. Drawing upon a wide range of sources (Phillips, 2006; Frank, 2005; Williamson 2002; Kincheloe & Pinar, 1991; Pinar, 2001, 2004, 2006) this section of the chapter will discuss the notions of the southernization (Shibley, 1998) of the United States

CHAPTER 1

and the place of southern christocrats in the progress of that southernization. In this way Cash's (1991) notion of the "lost cause" of the confederacy is replaced in importance by the emphasis on evangelical religion which evolved into christocratic religion and the civic gospel which is in the mind of the resurrected South. Issues of race, religion and the South will also be discussed to demonstrate the importance of the interconnections amongst religion, race and politics in the region. Like the Midwest there is not a single southern culture. There are conflicts particularly when issues of the resurrected South are discussed economically. The South may, indeed have "lost the war, but has won the peace," (Pinar, 2004, p. 235). To that end, many self-identified with the southern values that have come to dominate Midwestern regionalisms and stand for self-righteous malice against any kind of progressive reform have thought up their own way of thinking about peace and it is distinctly southern. A bumper sticker with a peace symbol on it reads: "Footprint of the American Chicken." Need we say more?

The second part of the chapter will examine the political impact of the myth of common culture that operated in the rustbelt U.S. states. Several recent books have alerted publics to the significance of the new religious and right-wing trend (*What's the Matter with Kansas*, etc.) This section of the chapter will show how another common assumption, that the Midwest is a place that wishes it could live the morals it votes for, is a little misplaced and perhaps more appropriate when applied to the rural south (Levy, 2006). Rather, this section of the chapter will examine how the assumption of common culture worked on both sides of the political aisle (left & right) to produce confusion over the substance of a so-called "common culture." Indeed, this chapter will argue that for both ideologies it was the dearth of common civic practices, public spaces and educational understandings that produced a polarized rustbelt public searching for answers to common democratic problems from unlikely sources (corporate bureaucracies, Washington politicians, preachers?). Drawing on Wendy Brown's (2006) recent theorization of Neo's (liberalism and conservatism) this section will detail the ways in which these two ideologies nourished the myth of a common culture while destroying what might be left of a modified utilitarianism.

Using Grumet's (1988) conception of "common culture" and juxtaposing it with theories that rely upon the notion of nostalgia for the "sacred canopy" (Berger 1990) and applications of it to questions of the shrinking public sphere the chapter will examine key points of conflict in rustbelt politics that are animated by the growing interest in evangelical religious belief.

The epilogue discusses how these stories that we've told ourselves in the United States have come to dominate our future prospects. It highlights many themes from the book including the gendered and religious aspects of the backlash.

CHAPTER TWO

CHRISTOCRATS AND THE CIVIC GOSPEL

The Backlash of the Culture Wars

Like America's past Great Awakenings, the Christian nationalist movement claims that the Bible is absolutely and literally true. But it goes much further, extrapolating a total political program from that truth, and yoking that program to a political party. It is a conflation of scripture and politics that sees America's triumphs as confirmation of the truth of Christian religion, and America's struggles as part of a cosmic contest between God and the devil (Goldberg, 2006, p. 6).

It is primarily a white, middle-class movement; the policies it advocates benefit the white middle and upper classes. It manipulates working-class people by providing scapegoats for their frustrations and appealing to their fears. It is much more complex than a simple conspiracy, though much of its success can be traced to the fact that the leaders of its many sectors make a point of conspiring together. It is not a populist movement, though it promotes an anti-elite message, which has the effect of masking its anti-working class agenda (Hardisty, 1999, pp. 7–8).

After his morning run on campus, Bill drives home in his Nissan X-Terra (SUV) and has his first cup of Starbucks coffee and reads the *New York Times* on-line. This identifies him as one of the blue state liberals, even though he lives in Georgia, a true red state. For the Christian Nationalist Political Backlashers, he is one of the many enemies. Howard Dean, the former chairperson of the Democratic Party was reviled for these very things – that liberal elitism. In a 2004 TV commercial aired by the conservative Club for Growth, Dean, then a presidential hopeful, was criticized and despised by "two average people" who tell him to "take his tax-hiking, government expanding, latte-drinking, sushi-eating, Volvo-driving, New York Times-reading, body piercing, Hollywood-loving, left-wing freak show back to Vermont where it belongs" (Frank, 2004, p. 17). This is set up in stark contrast to the true American. Thomas Frank (2004) characterizes these people and states that their description reads like a "turbocharged Boy Scout Law" (Frank, 2004, p. 20). This group has been identified as the Red Staters and the portrait provides five perceived characteristics of this group of people. It must be remembered that this is a perception of the group manufactured to provide divisiveness for political ends. Apparently Red Staters are "humble, reverent, courteous, kind, cheerful, loyal, and regular down-home working stiffs" (Frank, 2004, pp. 20–23). These qualities are articulated in a widely reprinted article by a Missouri farmer, Blake Hurst. The article was originally published in *The American Enterprise Magazine*.

CHAPTER 2

> Most Red Americans can't deconstruct post-modern literature, give proper orders to a nanny, pick out a cabernet with aftertones of licorice, or quote prices from the Abercrombie and Fitch catalogue. But we can raise great children, wire our own houses, make beautiful and delicious creations with our own two hands, talk casually and comfortably about God, repair a small engine, recognize a good maple sugar tree, tell you the histories of our own towns and the hopes of our neighbors, shoot a gun and run a chainsaw without fear, calculate the bearing load of a roof, grow our own asparagus, (Hurst, 1999, p. 8).

How did we get to this place? This division of either/or? How does Christian Nationalism with its civic gospel and Right-Wing politics operate? How does the debate over moral issues and family values operate within the context of politics and class interests? How are the notions of dominion theology and Christian Nationalism part of the larger backlash and resurgence of the conservative restoration with its concomitant traces of nostalgia and ressentiment? These are the questions this chapter will explore.

The Backlash and the Resurgent Right

If we follow the narrative of the backlash, then we find that somehow the United States and most of the world went to hell in the 1960s. The backlash or the conservative restoration began with the election of Richard Nixon in 1968 and has continued ever since. The contention of the backlash is that the nation was headed down the wrong path of "liberalism/leftism" and good Americans were sick of it.

> Maybe you were one of those who stood up for the American way back in 1968, sick of hearing those rich kids in beads bad-mouth the country every night on TV. Maybe you knew exactly what Richard Nixon meant when he talked about the "silent majority," the people whose hard work was rewarded with constant insults from the network news, the Hollywood movies, and the know-it-all college professors none of them interested in anything you had to say (Frank, 2004, p. 2).

But Nixon and his administration lacked the charisma and legitimacy to make the backlash a strong revival. But they did begin it. The backlash was carried through to the Reagan administration. "[Nixon's] quiet horse became the noisy 'moral majority' in Ronald Reagan's 1980 victory. By the 1980s, political issues had made a long swing towards conservatism" (Shor, 1986, p. 5). It was in the Reagan administration that big business and the ultra-conservative churches began to turn the tide away from the protest culture of the 1960s toward the establishment of a conservative restoration – the backlash. This trend continued through the George Herbert Walker Bush era, through the Clinton era (ironically Clinton was a favorite target of backlashers) and was brought to new heights in the administration of George W. Bush.

> The Great backlash was a style of conservatism that first came snarling onto the national stage in response to the partying and protests of the late sixties. While earlier forms of conservatism emphasized fiscal sobriety, the backlash

mobilizes voters with explosive social issues—summoning public outrage over everything from busing to un-Christian art – which it then marries to pro business economic policies. Cultural anger is marshaled to achieve economic ends (Franks, 2004, p. 5).

Of course, it was more than the partying and the protest of the 1960s and early 1970s that caused such consternation. It was a time of different social movements that attempted in many ways to provide liberal reforms in areas such as civil rights, women's rights, working class rights as well as the anti-war movement. But as Jean Hardisty reminds us in *Mobilizing Resentment* (1999) protest movements can also be reactionary. "Protest movements can also be a backlash against the changes that most recently occurred" (Hardisty, 1999, p. 9).

One of the conservative restoration's primary concerns is the elimination of critical or counter-hegemonic thought. There is a distinct distaste for those historical moments of the past when critique was used and flourished. In fact in much of the cultural artifacts (particularly film and music) produced during this restoration there are carefully delineated gender roles, Christocrat churches and orderly, disciplined and accountable schools. It is nostalgia for that time past when things were certain and clear-cut, a time that never was. Nostalgia flows through the post 9/11 backlash society.

Nostalgia is interlaced within the conservative restoration that motivates this backlash. It is not necessarily a cause or a result of it but there is always that trace. Nostalgia is most likely to become magnified when there are times of uncertainty, fragmentation and fear. "Nostalgia (from nostos – return home, and algia—longing) is a longing for a home that no longer exists or has ever existed" (Boym, 2001, p. xiii). It is Reagan's "shinning city on the hill." It is that urge for simpler times and a simpler society. Mary Kaldor in *New and Old Wars* (1999) discusses the notion that looking backward is the alternative when looking forward is troublesome and hopeless. Boym in *The Future of Nostalgia* (2001) contends that there are at least two types of nostalgia. The first type she describes as restorative nostalgia and the second type is reflective nostalgia (Boym, 2001). These two types of nostalgia are evident in the backlash. A typology of restorative and reflective nostalgia is helpful. Restorative nostalgia has three major characteristics. First, restorative nostalgia does not consider itself to be nostalgia. It considers itself to be truth and tradition and consequently it serves to protect the absolute truth (Boym, 2001, p. xviii). In the conservative restoration we witness this restorative nature as the basis for policy as it manifests in the notion that the truths of times past have been corrupted and the goal is to return those "real" truths to a place of prominence. The compassionate conservative agenda or binary links as causal the problems in our country with the collapse of morality and Western cultural values so there is a desire for a nostalgic re-turn to the truth. This is reflected later in ressentiment where there is perpetual accusation of the other who is/are responsible for this moral collapse. William Bennett, a spokesperson for conservatism, of the compassionate variety, stated.

I have come to the conclusion that the issues surrounding the culture and our values are the important ones…they are at the heart of the knottiest problems

CHAPTER 2

of public policy, whether the subject be education, art, race relations, drugs, crime, or raising children (Bennett, 1992, p. 36).

The conceptualizations of Ralph Reed former Christian Coalition Leader and current head of the Georgia Republican Party reinforce this. For Christocrats like him have the notion that we must return to the traditional Truth in the form of a biblically based Christian Nation with no separation between church and state.
Protecting the absolute truth is a nostalgic movement consistently addressed by compassionate conservatism and President Bush. In a speech delivered on October 10, 2002 at White House Conference on Faith-Based and Community Initiatives by Secretary of Education, Roderick Paige, he makes the connection among truth, morality and nostalgia as truth. Speaking of President Bush, Paige stated:

> He grew up in church, but like most of us, he didn't always walk the walk. Many years ago, at a particularly low point in his life, he realized that something was missing. Fortunately for him, he bumped into the Reverend Billy Graham. And they had a long, long, long conversation. And he made a decision coming out of that conversation that changed his life. And he believes that if it can change his life, that it can change the lives of others as well. And that's why he's so committed to this (Paige, 2002).

Second, nostalgia's plot is the return to origins (Boym, 2001, p. xviii). The plot of the backlash is to return to the "origins" of America before it was corrupted by the 1960s and early 1970s which the conservative restoration clearly views as something that must be overcome, forgotten and rewritten. Myron Magnet editor of the ultraconservative Manhattan Institute's City Journal and a former member of the editorial board of *Fortune* magazine argues that during that period American values deteriorated as a result of a cultural revolution led by "by an elite of opinion-makers, policymakers, and mythmakers—lawyers, judges, professors, political staffers, journalists, writers, TV and movie honchos, clergymen and it was overwhelmingly a liberal left-of-center elite" (Magnet, 2000, p. 20). Of course this led to a host of movements that were left wing including the War on Poverty, court-ordered busing, affirmative action, drug treatment programs, and the political correctness movement at colleges (see Spring, 2002, pp. 1–25). Magnet in nostalgic fashion advocates a return to the values of individualism, hard work, and a belief that success is a sign of God's favor. Notions of prosperity as a sign of God's favor manifests itself in the form of praying and preaching for prosperity. Briefly, "Name it and claim it", "The Prosperity Gospel", "Positive Confession or "Word of Faith" movement believes that Christians are promised health and wealth.

The message preached today is God desires His children to be wealthy. Pentecostal preacher Kenneth Hagin (1917–2003), of Tulsa, Oklahoma said that God not only wants to deliver believers from poverty, "He [also] wants His children to eat the best, He wants them to wear the best clothing, He wants them to drive the best cars, and He wants them to have the best of everything." (McConnell, 1995, p. 175) Another Word-Faith preacher is Kenneth Copeland. The Kenneth Copeland ministries provide the Faith Vision Network, which broadcasts on the internet Christian programming twenty-four hours a day, seven days a week. This praying for prosperity is intermixed with the Christocrat's notions that "The expulsion of God from the classroom, the rise of the drug culture, the "sexual revolution" and multiculturalism are unmistakable symptoms of cultural decadence and national decline" (Spring, 2002, p. 5) and the call for a return to our origins is clear. There is almost a crusade-like fervor to save Western culture from this detour into decadence. In fact, it has become one of the major political focuses of compassionate conservative backlash and apparently being a Christocrat can be profitable.

Third, there is always a conspiracy. Conspiracy is always used in the perjorative sense to designate a "subversive kinship of others, an imagined community based on exclusion more than affection, a union of those who are not with us but against us" (Boym, 2001, p. 43). That detour into the decadence produced by the 1960s and early 1970s is clearly the other -the conspiracy. Those who cling to those notions, which are primarily responsible for the moral and spiritual dilemma that we find ourselves in, they are the other(s) who are against the Truth. This notion of conspiracy in nostalgia is closely connected to the reaction of ressentiment, which is discussed below.

Reflective nostalgia, another characteristic, "is more concerned with historical and individual time, with the irrevocability of the past and human finitude" (Boym, 2001, p. 49). Reflective nostalgia also has three major characteristics. First, it is focused on individual stories that savor details and signs. Second, reflective nostalgia "cherishes shattered fragments of memory and temporalizes space" (Boym, 2001, p. 49). Third, while "restorative nostalgia takes itself dead seriously, reflective nostalgia can be ironic and humorous" (Boym, 2001, p. 49). One further aspect of this reflective nostalgia is about a rendezvous with oneself. Reflective nostalgia, however, is not exclusively a private affair. "Voluntary and involuntary recollections of an individual intertwine with collective memories. In many cases the mirror of reflective nostalgia is shattered by experiences of collective devastation," (Boym, 2001, p. 50). There is also a sense of awareness in reflective nostalgia.

> Nostalgics of the second type are aware of the gap between identity and resemblance; the home is in ruins or on the contrary, has been renovated and gentrified beyond recognition. This defamiliarization and sense of distance drives them to tell their story, to narrate the relationship between past, present and future (Boym, 2001, p. 50).

The past in this way is not only that which does not exist anymore but "might act and will act by inserting itself into a present sensation from which it borrows the vitality" (Bergson, 1996, p. 35). Deleuze (1991) discusses Bergson's metaphor of the cone, which represents the totality of virtual pasts that spring from a moment in the present.

> The idea of contemporaneity of the present and the past has one final consequence: Not only does the past co-exist with the present that has been, but, as it preserves itself in itself (while the present passes), it is the whole, integral past; it is all our past, which coexists with present. The famous metaphor of the cone represents this complete state of coexistence. But such a state implies

finally, that in the past itself there appear all kinds of levels of profundity, marking all the possible intervals in this coexistence (Deleuze, 1991, p. 59).

Reflective nostalgia is more about the memories and the experience of memories than it is about the actual return to a place of origin or truth. "Ulysses, for example, returns home only to look back at his journey in the alcove of his fair queen he becomes nostalgic for his nomadic self" (Boym, 2001, p. 50). Reflective nostalgia plays a role as well in the backlash of the conservative restoration. We can fill pages with memories of the way things used to be. Hence, in a larger framework, reflective nostalgia explains the popularity of stories of that greatest generation. And the ways in which there are interconnections between those moments of nostalgic reflection.

What is the problem with a little nostalgia? The major concern is that as long as we are looking backward whether restoratively or reflectively in the manner described, then the new is incapable of emerging. Nostalgia is looking backward, the past in the present, rather than looking ahead or it is looking ahead and seeing the uncertainty then looking back instead. Nostalgia, which characterizes the conservative restoration, is interconnected in many ways to notions of ressentiment.

> Ressentiment is a state of repressed feeling and desire, which becomes generative of values. The condition of ressentiment is complex both in its internal structure and in its relations to various dimensions of human existence. While it infects the heart of the individual, it is rooted in our relatedness with others. On the one hand, ressentiment is a dark, personal secret, which most of us would never reveal to others even if we could acknowledge it ourselves. On the other hand, ressentiment has an undeniably public face. It can be creative of social practices, mores, and fashions; of scholarly attitudes, academic policies, and educational initiatives; of political ideologies, institutions, and revolutions; of forms of religiosity and ascetic practices. The concept of ressentiment was first developed systematically by Nietzsche in his account of the historical emergence of what he terms 'slave morality' and in his critique of the ascetic ideal. This need to direct one's view outward instead of back to oneself—is the essence of ressentiment. While references to this condition can be found throughout his works, the chief sections in which he develops this notion are in his early work *The Genealogy of Morals* (Morelli, 1999).

> This need to direct one's view outward instead of back to oneself—is the essence of ressentiment: in order to exist, slave morality always first needs a hostile external world; it needs, psychologically speaking, external stimuli in order to act at all—its action is fundamentally reaction (Nietzsche, 1989, p. 37).

During the conservative restoration at a time when politicians, journalists, church dignitaries and media broadcasters are casting around desperately for objects on which to pin the blame for the "crisis" rather than having the courage to risk their own power by addressing the deep causes, not the manifest symptoms, of the phenomena: this is manifested in education for example through training (i.e. standardized education) obedience is secured to powerful fictions of inequality, "solid" education by means of displacement, mystification, and selective forms of gratification (good test scores).

The discussion of ressentiment turns on what Nietzsche referred to as that delayed, considered and deliberatively planned action of revenge; above all, it is what Deleuze described as the situation in which, "reaction ceases to be acted in order to become something felt (*senti*)" (Deleuze, p. 111; italics in original). Arguably, it has become routine behavior in a system designed to socialize people to believe in the reality of 'inequality' and consumption to imagine that superiors in society have some 'natural' superiority, and that society would be imperiled if the majority of people should ever come to believe that equality and superiority are conventional and hegemonic fictions.

Ressentiment is a strategy of control, a tactic developed out of fear of freedom, to foster cowardice, pride and anxiety in people who will, in turn, renounce their own (unrealized/unacknowledged) power for the compensatory pleasure and reward of asserting/affirming their neighbor's, work colleague's, or even, lover's inferiority and incapacity. Thus, through jealousy, insecurity, and competition the distributory, justificatory fiction of inequality and standardized education – repeated throughout the social structure by hierarchy and models of explication – is established and socialized ('unsociably') by the endless construction of negative others (left-wing intellectuals), potentially threatening opponents (i.e., right to life, or gay marriage) As Deleuze demonstrates the negative dialectic is the ideology of ressentiment. In conditions of structured inequality, then, instability, possible loss, disadvantage and, above all, powerlessness, are generated to such an extent that the unsettled can only be restored by an act of ressentiment – invariably enacted in a horizontally – orientated situation, i.e. on peers, not 'superiors,' (see also Webber, 2001, 2003; Reynolds, 2004).

Ressentiment and the play of forces it produces is, therefore, part of a continuously produced narrative of inequality and the nostalgia of compassionate conservatism – it is one of its principal resources: a seemingly equalizing action. It is the predicate of the duel, not the reflex punch. Nietzsche considers it a strategy of the 'weak', of the 'slave', ignoring that it is an effect of, not a cause of, enslavement. Ressentiment is an imaginary, or symbolic (even if realized) revenge on the conditions, which generated it as a value, but with a real consequence at the horizontal level. Only rarely (e.g. the Spartacus revolt) do slaves take revenge on the real objects of their unequal condition.

In Deleuze's analysis of ressentiment, the 'noble' morality creatively denies difference and otherness, its view is directed back to itself; the 'slave' morality directs its view outward, affirming difference and otherness as hostile, self threatening. It is derived from an ideological, cultural narrative. A graduated society curbs liberty by making spaces for the conditions of violence by infantilizing and, even, 'maddening, people: consuming them so that all their energies are engaged in a form of paranoia or fear, with its psychical damage. Nietzsche, to be precise, does not confine his analysis of 'noble' and 'slave' simply to social rank, but also to what he calls 'spiritual' nature where these opposed values confront each other in the trajectory of a single life. Nietzsche and Deleuze's "man" of ressentiment:

> Posits himself through a double negation (projecting a fictional image of what he is not to which he opposes himself in order to establish what he is) and is invaded by mnemonic traces just as the masculine subject posits himself in opposition to a feminine other and is entombed in body no longer able to respond to the present (Lorraine, 1999, pp. 154–155).

While interpreting Nietzsche's conceptualization of ressentiment Deleuze discusses three characteristics. First, there is the inability to admire, respect or love. Second, there is passivity. Third, there is the imputation of wrongs, the distribution of responsibilities and perpetual accusation (Deleuze, 1983). After an initial discussion of ressentiment, these three characteristics will be discussed in relationship to the current political milieu.

One way that ressentiment operates is through the inability to admire or respect. According to the conservative Christocrats our morally bereft society has brought nothing but chaos, confusion, disarray, crisis, ideology, and repudiation of history, contentiousness, and on and on. Of course, in ressentiment, there must be someone or something to blame. The critique "must recriminate and distribute blame: look for the inclination to play down causes, to make misfortune someone's fault" (Deleuze, 1983, p. 117). Someone must be to blame for the uncertainty and complexity in society.

Rather than admiring critique, creativity and invention or respecting multiplicity as a hopeful phenomenon, there is an inability to view it that way. It must be disparaged. It must be bounded. It must be clearly defined continually.

> What is most striking in the man [politics of] ressentiment is not his nastiness but his disgusting malevolence, his capacity for disparagement. Nothing can resist it. He does not respect his friends or even his enemies (Deleuze, 1983, p. 117).

Passivity is another characteristic of ressentiment.

> Moreover, ressentiment could only be imposed on the world through the triumph of the principle of gain, by making profit not only a desire and away of thinking but an economic, social and theological system, a complete system, a divine mechanism (Deleuze, 1983, p. 118).

This seems to be clearly indicated in the continual replay of the call to the Ten Commandments, moral leadership, and in education for example standards and accountability and the call for a profitable education. President George W. Bush made this clear in a speech he delivered on October 17, 2002 at the Read-Patillo Elementary School.

> One of the key components to successful schools is the willingness of people to use an accountability system to reinforce the positive and to address failure before it becomes acute, and that's essential. By all of these standards, this school we're standing in is a highly effective, successful school. It is

a school, which, innovates, it uses computer programs to stimulate the students' imagination. It teaches phonics and grammar, the basics. It starts with the basics. It gives students incentives (Bush, 2002).

It appears that other forms of education are synonymous with permissiveness, chaos and poor test scores, and unprofitability. Education can stand as an example of the larger societal concerns the entire sense of indignation on the part of the Christocrats is in a sense of this passivity. Passive doesn't mean non-active, it means "non-acted" (Nietzsche, 1987). "The term 'passive' stands for the triumph of reaction, the moment when, ceasing to be acted, it becomes ressentiment" (Deleuze, 1983, p. 118).

Perpetual accusation, distribution of responsibilities and imputation of wrongs is a third characteristic of ressentiment. Here is the dangerous side of this phenomenon, "it is not content to denounce crimes and criminals, it wants sinners, people who are responsible" (Deleuze, 1983, p. 119). Responsibility, in this case, for what? There must be villains (others) who can be responsible and can be perpetually accused of (blamed for) sending the society into this "so-called" perpetual moral collapse. The political dualism needs an enemy, an evil empire, or a mad monarch—a Saddam, or a latte drinking, sushi eating, highly educated, Volvo driving liberal. And, by distinguishing that which is other as evil, one confirms the goodness of the backlash. It is through defining the other that we are, indeed, defined that is ressentiment.

> The lamb says: I could do everything the eagle does; I'm admirable for not doing so. Let the eagle do as I do (Deleuze, 2001, p. 78).

The compassionate conservative politics of ressentiment was a way of reacting to the uncertainty of the post 9/11 global phenomena, without acting upon the concrete issues (economic and social) that trouble our society and our world. It looks nostalgically backwards to a day when the United States and Americans were in-line with Biblical roots, lived in small towns, shook hands with their neighbors, behaved themselves, lived in marriages of one man and one woman, and children did what they were told. Was that ever the case? This is a politics that views attempts to be creative and critical as threats and treats those attempts as evil, and unpatriotic. It is an anti-intellectual position. It has an agenda that promotes passivity and consumption, and it is the past heavily locked in the present with no interest in the future.

There exists in this current nostalgic backlash with ressentiment an agenda with a decidedly anti-intellectual component. In the classic work on anti-intellectualism, *Anti-Intellectualism in American Life* (1962), Hofstader reminds us elections can be swayed by the type of anti-intellectualism that we have witnessed in the beginning years of the 21st century. Hofstader, writing in the early 1960s, discussed the fact that Eisenhower's victories were examples of the force of anti-intellectualism. Eisenhower brought business back into power and of all the consequences with which it was accompanied, one of those consequences was the distrust and dismissal of the intellectual.

CHAPTER 2

> Now the intellectual dismissed as an 'egghead,' and 'oddity,' would be governed by a party which had little use for or understanding of him, and would be made the scapegoat for everything from the income tax to the attack on Pearl Harbor" (Hofstader, 1962, p. 4).

Anti-intellectualism, however, according to Hofstader did not arise in the 1950s with Eisenhower or Joseph McCarthy. It is part of our national identity. He demonstrates this by citing amongst others Puritan John Cotton, who wrote in 1642, "The more learned and witty you bee, the more fit to act for Satan will you bee" (Hofstader, 1963, p. 46). Anti-intellectualism is subject to cyclical fluctuations and the virulence of it in the 1950s and now in the 21st century does demonstrate that anti-intellectualism is cyclical or reemerges at some historical points more strongly than others. When Hofstader was writing his book the Kennedy administration of the best and brightest was beginning to function and although these were some of the same men that convinced Johnson to escalate the war in Vietnam there was not a wide-spread distain for intellectuals that is in evidence presently. Anti-intellectualism, however, is not confined historically to only conservatives or even moderate Republicans. According to Todd Gitlin in his article entitled, "The Renaissance in Anti-Intellectualism" (2000), anti-intellectualism is not the sole purview of conservatives.

> A populist strain in the 60's student movement, identifying with the oppressed sharecroppers of the Mississippi Delta and the dispossessed miners of Appalachia, bent the principle "Let the people decide" into a suspicion of all those who were ostensibly knowledgeable. Under pressure of the Vietnam War, the steel-rimmed technocrat Robert S. McNamara came to personify the steel-trap mind untethered by insight and countercultural currents came to disdain reason as a mask for imperial arrogance (Gitlin, 2000, p. B7).

Hofstadter described three pillars of anti-intellectualism – evangelical religion, practical-minded business, and the populist political style. Religion was suspicious of modern relativism, business of regulatory expertise, and populism of claims that specialized knowledge had its privileges (Hofstader, 1962). Although suspicious of definitions, Hofstader provides one.

> The common strain that binds together the attitudes and ideas which I call anti-intellectual is a resentment and suspicion of the life of the mind and of those who are considered to represent it; and a disposition constantly to minimize the value of that life (Hofstader, 1962, p. 7).

Hofstadter, when discussing evangelicals and anti-intellectualism in the first half of the twentieth century, elaborates on a type of militancy that foreshadows the Christocrats of today. He distinguishes that militancy from those for whom religion is a "serene belief, personal peace, and charity of the mind" (Hofstader, 1962, p. 118). The militant strain is more an outlet for animosities,

> My concern here is with the militants, who have thrown themselves headlong into the revolt against modernism in religion and against modernity in our

34

> culture in general. We are here dealing, then with an even smaller number but still far from miniscule portion of the whole body of the evangelical tradition – a type which has found that it can compensate with increasing zeal and enterprise for the shrinking of its numbers (Hofstader, 1962, p. 118).

It is interesting to note that in the 21st century version of this anti-intellectualism and religious zeal, there is a rejection of modernism or secularism; the new Christocrats take advantage of and use the very secularism they so vociferously rail against. We discuss this in detail in Chapter Three. The backlash operates then with nostalgia, ressentiment, and anti-intellectualism in its zealous quest to overturn what is considered the blight of previous and current periods of moral collapse and intellectual deviance. After describing the major characteristics of the backlash restoration we can turn to the specific grass-roots operations of the Christocrats.

The Social Gospel

> All those social groups that distinctly face toward the future clearly show their need and craving for a social interpretation and application of Christianity. Whoever wants to hold audiences of working people must establish some connection between religion and their social feelings and experiences (Rauschenbusch, 1917/1997, p. 3).

Bill grew up in the United Methodist Church. He was even an acolyte; that is, he wore a robe and before the service started would light the candles on the altar. There were usually two acolytes and the best part of this responsibility was he got to sit in the back of the sanctuary with his friend and they could talk during the service. During that time, mid to late 1960s, his church (Aldersgate United Methodist) in Rochester, New York was promoting a social gospel. The social gospel now in somewhat a period of decline had/has as its major aims combating injustice, suffering and poverty in society. "Individual salvation was important, but considered secondary to social reform, which would convert multitudes into God's kingdom as the government and economic institutions themselves taught men and women of brotherly love" (Potter, 2001). Salvation of the individual, then, stood as an important byproduct of working for a literal kingdom of God on earth. Working for social improvement, the Kingdom of God on earth, then, was the thrust of the Social Gospel movement (see Potter, 2001).

The social gospel was developed by Protestants in the early years of the 20th century (1900–1920) to sacralize the Godless cities and factories. This was a time of mass urbanization, mass industrialization and mass immigration and the problems that arose as a result. Both liberals and conservatives were involved in social programs of the Progressive Age.

> It was an attempt to return to what they saw as the basic teachings of the Hebrew prophets and of Christ himself, who had taught his followers to visit prisons, clothe the naked, and feed the hungry. Social Gospelers set up what they called institutional churches to provide services and recreational facilities for the poor and for new immigrants (Armstrong, 2000, p. 169).

CHAPTER 2

Walter Rauschenbusch (1861–1918) was the primary theologian of the Social Gospel movement of the first two decades of the twentieth century. There were a number of prominent ministers of the day that became involved in the mission of the Church to meet social needs through the workings and theology in institutional churches, and Rauschenbusch gave the social a theology (Potter, 2001). He attempted to legitimize it in mainstream American Protestantism.

> The social gospel calls for an expansion in the scope of salvation and for more religious dynamic to do the work of God. It requires more faith not less. It offers thorough and durable salvation. It is able to create a more searching sense of sin and to preach repentance to the respectable and mighty who have ridden humanity to the mouth of hell (Rauschenbusch, 1917, p. 11).

The social gospel arose in response to the horrendous conditions and injustices brought about by the Industrial Revolution. Interestingly enough the key villain in this theology was industrial capitalism. The industrial capitalists, according to those that advocated the social gospel, appeared unrestrained by any moral or ethical principles when it came to the treatment of the workers in the factories. Those advocates of the social gospel favored the workers' right to humane and fair treatment. Rauschenbusch wanted the social issues of the period to be foremost in the hearts and minds of Christians and all Americans. His social gospel and the conceptualizations of the progressive movement were closely aligned in this respect. Perhaps, Rauschenbush, through his writings, made the social gospel less of a marginalized segment of the Christian orientation of the time. At least that was one of his goals. He was able to connect the purposes of Christianity with social justice. Rauschenbusch published a number of well-received books outlining then systematizing social problems and the Church's responsibility. These writings have gone through several reprints. These books included *Christianity and the Social Crisis* (1907/2007), *Christianizing the Social Order* (1912), and *A Theology for the Social Gospel* (1917).

> In the early years of the century, conservative Christians were just as involved in social programs as the liberal Protestants; however, their ideology was different. They might see their social crusades as a war against Satan or as a spiritual challenge to the prevailing materialism, but they were just as concerned about low wages, child labor, and poor working conditions (Armstrong, 2000, p. 170).

The notions, theology and strategies of the Social Gospelers appalled the conservative Christians of the time and they fought this perceived liberal danger. The thinking was that the social gospel extended beyond the basic mission of the Christian Church which was the salvation of human souls through belief in the death and resurrection of Jesus Christ and the literal interpretation of the Bible. One opposing position to this liberal theology of the social gospel and its practice was scientific Protestantism. The Presbyterians of Princeton, a group associated with the New Light Presbyterian seminary at Princeton, New Jersey in 1910, issued a fundamentalist doctrine of the infallibility of scripture. There were five principles that were considered essential.

(1) inerrancy of Scripture, (2) the Virgin Birth of Christ, (3) Christ's atonement for our sins on the cross, (4) his bodily resurrection, and (5) the objective reality of his miracles (Armstrong, 2000, p. 171).

This group practiced what became known as scientific Protestantism. The American Protestant, Arthur Pierson (1837–1911), wanted the Bible explained in a scientific manner. In his text *Many Infallible Proofs* (1900) he demonstrates that he desires that religion demonstrate a type of scientific certainty. There was a scientific basis to religion and belief. The Bible would serve as the basis for general deductions that would lead to laws for Christians. Wherever possible the mythical language would be replaced by rational discourse. In a way this orientation to the Bible is much like the New Criticism in literary criticism which stated that interpreters should stick to the text and only the text to make their deductions. All other considerations such as the needs of the poor or sick were secondary theologically to scientifically explicating sacred texts. This notion of rationality and science in religion brought religion into controversy. But, it did contest social gospel notions. Interestingly enough, this orientation foreshadows the "scientific orientation" of intelligent design in our present time. For many of the supporters of either "scientific creationism" or intelligent design there can exist Biblical principles with "scientific orientation."

This is worth study since it foreshadows the battles of the early 21st century. The social gospel, of course, was not simply a white-middle class movement. The Civil Rights Movement and in particular the theological and political beliefs of Martin Luther King Jr. were also within an African-American tradition of the social gospel.

> There were these beliefs in the King family's long-standing ties to Ebenezer Baptist Church and the social gospel ministries of his father and grandfather, both of whom were civil rights leaders as well as pastors King's public, transracial ministry marked a convergence of theological scholarship and social gospel practice. "Drawing upon a variety of intellectual and religious traditions to arouse and enlighten his listeners, King was profoundly affected by his experiences both as a preacher's son at Ebenezer and as a diligent student at Crozer Seminary and Boston University" (Johnson, 1994, p. 177).

In 1973 at a workshop organized on evangelicalism and social concerns, forty-three prominent evangelicals met to discuss the need to strengthen the connections between evangelicalism and social concern. The leader of the workshop was Ron Sider a Canadian-born, American Theologian and activist. Sider has been called one of the representatives of the Christian Left although he denies any political affiliation. The meeting was organized by the Evangelicals for Social Action (ESA). ESA has become a National organization. It publishes a national journal, *Prism* and has a national network, Network 9:35. Currently the organization assists local churches in combining their evangelical interests with social action. In 1973 the group that met discussed the intersections between evangelicalism and social concerns. The result of the November 25, 1973 workshop of the ESA was the 1973 Chicago Declaration of Evangelical Social Concern in which the evangelicals

CHAPTER 2

confessed their failure to confront injustice, racism and discrimination against women, and made a pledge to do better. This was a powerful document in 1973 and demonstrates that the social gospel was still being influential in the early 1970s.

> We must attack the materialism of our culture and the maldistribution of the nation's wealth and services. We recognize that as a nation we play a crucial role in the imbalance and injustice of international trade and development. Before God and a billion hungry neighbors, we must rethink our values regarding our present standard of living and promote a more just acquisition and distribution of the world's resources. We acknowledge our Christian responsibilities of citizenship. Therefore, we must challenge the misplaced trust of the nation in economic and military might–a proud trust that promotes a national pathology of war and violence which victimizes our neighbors at home and abroad. We must resist the temptation to make the nation and its institutions objects of near-religious loyalty. (ESA, 1973, p. 6)

The minister of the church Bill attended talked about these issues from the pulpit. In 1969, he took Bill's Methodist Youth Fellowship group to Scott's Run Settlement House near Morgantown, West Virginia to help out-of-work coal miners repair their houses, and rebuild some of the Settlement house itself. Bill remembers patching mortar on the brick walls of the Settlement house. They slept at the University of West Virginia gym and would go out during the day to do the work. "This is the work of the church in America," Reverend Howe would often say. This is what Bill understood the gospel to be about. But, not every member of the church was in tune with the ramifications of the social gospel. Bill remembers distinctly the reasons for Rev. Barnard Howe's removal from the pulpit at Aldersgate. During one morning service he advocated that Kodak workers unionize, or at least consider it. He remembers his father saying to him that would be the reason for the pastor's dismissal. It was. This tradition of social gospel continued into the 1970s

The 1973 Chicago Declaration was a clear statement of the social gospel in the mid-20th century. It was a continuation and updating of the social gospel that occurred at the beginning of the 20th century. It stands in sharp contrast to the civic gospel of the early 21st century. In 1993 a second Chicago declaration was issued at a conference organized by Evangelicals for Social Action, the conference included worship services, seminars, music, and several plenary addresses for the nearly 300 participants. The new declaration still demonstrates the evidence of the social gospel.

> We weep over the growing disparity between the rich and the poor, the scandal of hunger, and the growing number of people who live in oppressive conditions, insecurity, and danger. We dream of churches that work for education, economic empowerment and justice, both at the personal and structural levels, and that address the causes and the symptoms of poverty. (http://www.cpjustice.org/stories/storyReader$928)

The social gospel still remains a viable alternative to other orientations of the mission of the church, in 2006 there was some discussion of this gospel in the Methodist and Unitarian Universalism Churches but for the most part it has declined. The Unitarian Universalist Association helps its congregations "take action on their values by providing "how-to" resources on advocacy, organizing, public policy issues and the theological motivations for our justice work" (UUAC, 2007, p. 1). The work of the social gospel also seems to be present in organizations. There is the ESA and its various publications and websites as mentioned previously. Again, in the 1970s a group, Sojourner ministries emerged. Sojourners ministries grew out of the Sojourners Community, located in Southern Columbia Heights, an inner-city neighborhood in Washington, D.C. In the early 1970s the community began at Trinity Evangelical Divinity School in Deerfield, Illinois when a group of divinity students met to discuss the relationship between faith and political issues. The publication *Post-American* was the result of these meetings. The group moved to Washington and in 1975 the magazine's name was changed to *Sojourners*. The group still publishes the magazine today and continues its interest in the intersection of faith, politics, and culture. Contrary to the declarations of 1973 and 1993 from The ESA and the work of the Sojourners are the principles, views and intent of the civic gospel – the backlash gospel. This view predominates presently.

The Civic Gospel and Dominion/Reconstructionist Theology

> Like America's Great Awakenings the Christian Nationalist movement claims that the Bible is literally true. But it goes further extrapolating a total political program from that truth, and yoking that program to a political party. It is a conflation of scripture and politics that sees America's triumphs as confirmation of the truth of the Christian religion, and the American struggles as part of a cosmic contest between God and the devil (Goldberg, 2006, p. 6).

The social gospel, which was never a majority movement in Christianity has been almost completely forgotten and replaced by what has been termed the civic gospel (see Scmidt et al., 2003), a newer more conservative and formally politicized approach to the issues of church and state. Martin Marty defines notions of the civic gospel. He summarizes the six major beliefs of evangelical political preachers based on the research from an article entitled "The Political Attitudes and Activities of Mainline Protestant Clergy in the Election of 2000: A Study of Six Denominations," which appeared in the *Journal for the Scientific Study of Religion*.

> (1) That the United States was founded as a Christian nation, (2) that free enterprise is the only economic system truly compatible with Christian beliefs, (3) that religious values are under attack in contemporary America, (4) that government needs to act to protect the nation's religious heritage, (5) that there is only one Christian view on most political issues, and (6) that it is hard for political liberals to be true Christians." On voting and opinion issues "evangelical clergy are monotonously predictable" in their Republicanism (Schmidt et al., 2003, 515–532).

CHAPTER 2

As we began to investigate the predominance of this particular brand of Christianity, it appears to be overwhelming influential and it would have been relatively easy to simply lump all Evangelical and Traditional Christians into this one monolithic Right-Wing Theology. It is not quite that simple. According to Michelle Goldberg in *Kingdom Coming* (2006), Christian Nationalism is rather a totalizing movement for those within it.

> The people who live inside this reality often call it the 'Christian worldview.' The phrase is based on the conviction that true Christianity must govern every aspect of public and private life, and that all – government, science, history, culture, and relationships – must be understood according to the dictates of scripture. There are biblically correct positions on every issue, from gay marriage to income tax rates, and only those with the right worldview can discern them. This is Christianity as a total ideology. It's an ideology adhered to by millions of Americans, some of whom are very powerful (Goldberg, 2006, p. 6)

The theologies that ground this outlook are dominionist and reconstructionist. "The most prevalent Dominionist belief is that Christians alone are Biblically mandated to occupy all secular institutions until Christ returns" (Diamond, 2002, p. 1). Christians are pledged to take over our secular society. "The idea of taking dominion over secular society gained widespread currency with the 1981 publication of evangelical philosopher Francis Schaeffer's book, *A Christian Manifesto*. The book sold 290,000 copies in its first year, and it remains one of the movement's most frequently cited texts" (Diamond, 2002, p. 1). Although Shaeffer in this book and in speeches based upon the book was clear to point out that he does not advocate a theocracy, there is a clear sense that Christians must take political action.

> Someone says that what you are after is theocracy. Absolutely not! We must make absolutely plain, we are not in favor of theocracy, in name or in fact. But, having said that, nevertheless, we must realize that we already face a hidden censorship – a hidden censorship in which it is impossible to get the other world view presented in something like public television. It's absolutely impossible (Shaeffer, 1982, p. 4).

This action Shaeffer calls 'civil disobedience'.[1] This call for Christians to engage in civil disobedience has been used as a rationale for the activism from the anti-abortion groups, like Operation Rescue, to the attempts to abolish the "teaching of evolution" in schools. Shaeffer sets up the enemy evil that Christians must battle. If they do not engage in the battle against the secularist and humanist agenda, then they have to question their own commitment to Christianity. *The Christian Manifesto* (1981) was a clear call for Christian to engage in political action.

> Every appropriate legal and political governmental means must be used. "The final bottom line" – I have invented this term in A Christian Manifesto. I hope the Christians across this country and across the world will really understand what the Bible truly teaches: The final bottom line! The early Christians, every one of the reformers (and again, I'll say in *A Christian Manifesto* I go through

country after country and show that there was not a single place with the possible exception of England, where the Reformation was successful, where there wasn't civil disobedience and disobedience to the state), the people of the Reformation, the founding fathers of this country, faced and acted in the realization that if there is no place for disobeying the government, that government has been put in the place of the living God. In such a case, the government has been made a false god. If there is no place for disobeying a human government, what government has been made God? (Shaeffer, 1982, p. 6)

The enemy Shaeffer clearly identifies as humanism (this will be discussed in chapter 3). And, Shaeffer blames complacent Christians for the turn toward a humanist country, a country that allows abortion, godless schools, and the separation of church and state. Schaeffer's conceptualizations of theology in many cases parallel those of a little known Christian Reconstructionist, Rousas John Rushdoony (1916–2001).

Rushdoony's 800 hundred page major opus was *The Institutes of Biblical Law* (1973). The title and the format of the book are based upon John Calvin's (1509–1564) magnum opus, *Institutes of Christian Religion* (1560). Rushdoony, is not well known outside Christian circles, but is still one of the driving forces behind the Reconstructionist notions of Christianity. The Reconstructionists want to reconstruct our society based on Biblical principles. He founded the Chalcedon Foundation. Its website pronounces its vision.

Chalcedon labors to articulate in the clearest possible terms a distinctly Christian and explicitly Biblical solution to the prevalent evils of the modern world. Our objective is nothing short of setting forth the vision and program for rebuilding the theological fortifications of Christian civilization. These fortifications have been eroded by the forces of humanism and secularism over the past three centuries. We are not committed, though, merely to reproducing a glorious Christian past. We work to press the claims of historic Christianity as the Biblical pattern of life everywhere. We work for godly cultural change across the entire spectrum of life (Chalcedon Foundation, 2007, p. 2)

In a study of the Rushdoony movement by Bruce Prescott, a Presbyterian minister involved with the progressive Interfaith Alliance Forum on Religious Extremism, the essentials of reconstructionism are listed by the author.

Stripped to its barest essentials, here is their blueprint for America. Their ultimate goal is to make the U.S. Constitution conform to a strict, literal interpretation of Biblical law. To do that involves a series of legal and social reforms that will move society toward their goal. 1) Make the ten commandments the law of the land, 2) Reduce the role of government to the defense of property rights, 3) Require "tithes" to ecclesiastical agencies to provide welfare services, 4) Close prisons – reinstitute slavery as a form of punishment and require capital punishment for all of ancient Israel's capital offenses – including apostasy, blasphemy, incorrigibility in children, murder, rape, Sabbath breaking, sodomy, and witchcraft, 5) Close public schools – make parents totally responsible for the education of their children, and 6) Strengthen patriarchically ordered families (Prescott, 2002, p. 2)

These basic principles of reconstructionism are reflected in the core of the civic gospel as mentioned earlier. The terms fundamentalist, evangelical, religious extremist, and Christian conservatives are all used to describe those that believe in making Christianity into a political movement to create a Christian nation. According to Rudin in *The Baptizing of America* (2006) many of these terms are not adequate and can even be misleading when trying to determine meaning for this group. Fundamentalist is inadequate and incomplete. First, there are fundamentalists in every religion and can be used to describe Muslims, Jews, Hindus and others. Second, even if we use this term Christian fundamentalist for our analysis it falls short because there are many fundamentalist Christians who do not believe in a political agenda to change society. It is quite simply an overgeneralization to use the term "fundamentalist," even though it is the shorthand in most political debates in the United States. Similarly, evangelical is another term frequently used to describe this group. Although the majority of the supporters of a Christian Nationalism are drawn from this group, many evangelicals are not interested in these political strategies or activities. The term religious extremist is also used. This term has been conflated with the activities of violence and terrorism. It has been applied to a great extent to describe the anti-American, anti-Christian, anti-Jewish Muslim terrorists, who use the Muslim religion to justify their actions. Christian conservative is yet another term used to describe this group. But these Christians do not always support the political agenda of the civic gospel (Rudin, 2006).

The terms we would borrow from Rabbi James Rudin are Christocracy and Christocrats. Rudin concedes that the term is not new in American history. It first appeared in the work of Dr. Benjamin Rush (1745–1813) one of the signers of the *Declaration of Independence*. He used the term in a positive way to differentiate himself from both aristocrat and democrat. According to Rudin (2006), Christocrats have several basic attitudes. First, that the United States has a Christian "manifest destiny" and that it is off the path of that destiny. It is a necessary to bring the country back to that religious path if it is to be "saved" (p. 10). Second, there is a fear of people from urban areas (those latte drinking folks are the foil in their rhetoric for the poor minorities and immigrants they truly disdain) Thus, they are threatened by demographic diversity and the "liberals" are the people who defend it (p. 10). They long for the comfort, safety and purity of exurban areas of traditional rural space, a mainly white existence. (see Chapter 3 for an extended analysis). Third, a commitment to Jesus as a personal savior is a necessary but not sufficient action for Christocrats. A national repentance and acceptance of Jesus is necessary. Fourth, there will be a national atonement before the Christocracy can be instituted over every aspect of American life. Fifth, this control is divinely ordained and Biblically inspired. "America requires a system of moral safeguards that will move the nation from its decadent, wanton, secular humanist ways," (pp. 10–11).

A study released in September 2006 by the Baylor Institute for Studies in Religion was helpful in clarifying some of the issues surrounding this Christian Nationalism and the Christocrats. The Baylor study helped to clarify the demographics of this movement. This study allows us to be a bit more specific about the nature and size of the Christocratic, civic gospel movement. The Baylor study provides "some key initial findings related to the measurement of religion, the nature of religious belief, the relationship between religious, moral and political attitudes, and religious spending habits" (Baylor et al., 2006, p. 6). The study demonstrates that Christocrats are comprised of evangelicals, but also conservative Roman Catholics, traditional Protestants or Eastern Orthodox Christians. The majority of the movement is Caucasian, but an increasing number of African Americans and Hispanics are also Christocrats.The Baylor study indicates that the United States population is largely affiliated with some religious preference.

> Barely one in ten Americans (10.8%) is NOT affiliated with a congregation, denomination, or other religious group. Less than five percent of the U.S. population claims a faith outside the Judeo-Christian mainstream. Fully a third of Americans (33.65), roughly 100 million people areEvangelical Protestant by affiliation (Baylor et al., 2006, p. 8).

Unsurprisingly, the study concludes that the heaviest concentrations of evangelicals, the group from which most of the Christocrats come, are in the South and Midwest. In the South 50.3% of those participating in the study consider their selves evangelicals and in the Midwest it is 33.7%. This is in contrast to the East with a 13.1% and the West with a concentration of only 1.3% (the geographic phenomenon will be discussed in depth in Chapter 5), The demographics of the evangelical are as follows. They are more likely to be female 36.7% as compared to male 30.0%. White 35.4% as compared to Black 9.5%, evenly distributed across age groups (18–30, 31–44, 45–64, and 65+)., and 40% having an income of $35,000.00 or less and 26.9 % having an income of more that $100,000.00 (Baylor et al., 2006). According to the Baylor study this group emphasizes the "authority of the Bible, salvation through a personal relationship with Jesus Christ, personal piety, and the need to share the "Good News" of Jesus Christ with others" (Baylor et al., 2006, p. 9). This is not the agenda of the Christocrats, but is fertile ground for recruitment to their causes. An attempt to determine the exact percentage of those evangelicals that are Christocrats will have to wait for another survey. It is probable that Christocrats with their civic gospel agenda of Christian Nationalism do not represent the majority of Americans or even a majority of evangelicals, "but it does represent a significant and highly mobilized minority (Goldberg, 2006, p. 8). There is a website devoted to Christocrats (www.christocrat.com). At this site one can obtain civic lessons for Christocrats during elections; that is, how to tailor their personal religious convictions to their political cause. There are available are a number of downloadable versions of ad copy for the print media. One example of that free ad copy is Had Enough Yet? It is a clarion call for Christocrats to unite for elections:

HAD ENOUGH YET?

In 1947 liberal judges changed the first amendment and invented the phrase "Separation of Church and State," which restricts religious activity in public.

In 1962 liberal judges prohibited school prayer.

CHAPTER 2

In 1973 liberal judges legalized abortion resulting in the death of over 40 million babies, mostly for birth control purposes. And your child can have an abortion without your knowledge or consent.

In 2003 the liberal judges have challenged the traditional family, promoting same sex marriage.

At this time liberals are challenging – "One Nation Under God" in our Pledge of Allegiance – the display of the Ten Commandments in public places – the mention of God in public places – removal or God from money.

CALLING CHRISTIANS TO UNITE!

[Non denomination – No doctrine]

No single group or denomination possesses enough strength alone to return America back to its Biblical roots. Yet it CAN be put back on track by Christians of all dominations committed to the moral law of God (Christocrat.com, 2007). A visitor to the site can also find plans to win elections, comments on evils of the separation of church and state, information on how we lost God, and a host of other political advice. And, not surprisingly merchandise. Christocrats can obtain license plates proudly proclaiming Christocrat status and even a mouse pad that has the American Flag as its background with various Christocrat quotations and in large block letters God Bless America. One final and important connection is made between the Christocrats and their political agenda on this site. There is a section entitled "Guidelines for Voting"

– Don't let candidates, the news media, or friends and relatives confuse you with rhetoric. All you need to know is," does the candidate promote a moral agenda?" How does he vote on abortion issues? How does he feel about homosexual behavior? What's his perspective on the relationship between God and government?
– If there is more than one candidate running that has a moral agenda, then you can choose the one that best suits your special interest.
– If none of the candidates are pro-moral, vote the one that is the closest to a moral agenda. Get involved. If there is time, run someone against him. If not, get started on the next election.
– Don't be afraid to vote your morals. Trust God. Matthew 6:33 says "But seek ye first the kingdom of God, and his righteousness; and all these things shall be added unto you (everything else will fall into place) (http://www.christocrat.com/voteguide.htm).

Despite the inability to determine the percentage of Christocrats, it is clear that it is a highly organized and well- funded militant minority. It harkens back to Hofstadter's comments concerning evangelicals in the 20th century. Regardless of the size of this group, they have a clear agenda and the requisite Christian soldiers to fight for it (www.christocrats.com).

The Christocratic Agenda

> Vote to stop abortion; receive a rollback in capital gains taxes. Vote to make our country strong again; receive deindustrialization. Vote to screw those politically correct college professors; receive electricity deregulation; Vote to get government off our backs; receive conglomeration and monopoly everywhere from media to meat-packing; Vote to stand tall against terrorists; receive Social Security privatization. Vote to strike a blow against elitism; receive a social order in which wealth is more concentrated than ever before in our lifetimes, in which workers have been stripped of power and CEOs are rewarded in a manner beyond imagining (Frank, 2004, p. 7).

When we discuss the agenda of the Christocrats there is a long list of their causes that are relevant. Overshadowing those causes, however, is the resentment discussed in the introduction. For the Christocrats, there must be a public enemy. The enemy must be demonized and continually mobilized in media discourse to provide objects for followers to rally against. The main goal is to articulate an "us against them strategy." As we shall see in Chapters Three and Four, this rhetoric works for domestic and foreign policy concerns simultaneously (Williams, 2005). As George W. Bush would have it; you are either for us or against us. It is a dualism of ressentiment that perpetuates itself through Christian rhetoric and a decisive opposition to secular humanism and its supposed institutions and ideals. Jean Hardisty in *Mobilizing Resentment* (1999) discusses the use of resentment as a political strategy for the Right:

> The right has captured the citizen anger and mobilized it to express intolerance against individuals and groups. Such organizing provides a release for feelings of anger and frustration. The Right uses three specific forms of intolerance – stereotyping, scapegoating, and demonizing – to mobilize and organize recruits (p. 51).

This intolerance materializes in the political agenda of the Christocrats. This group uses intolerance to frame a number of issues in their agenda. It might seem to some to be paradoxical that a religion that emphasizes love and care would be the same religion that exploits intolerance for political and financial gain. Three issues that are preeminent in the Christocrat demonization and intolerance that are used to mobilize the faithful are the case against separation of church and state, the teaching of intelligent design, and the demonization of gays and lesbians. There are other issues such as abortion, AIDS, faith-based organizations, abstinence, environmentalism and a host of others. We will confine our comments to the former three in this chapter. Some of the latter issues are subsumed in them.

Church and State

The division between church and state increasingly decreases as we proceed through the 21st century. G. W. Bush clearly saw himself as the born again, sword-bearing leader of the United States. Prior to becoming president and as an official act as governor of Texas, Bush on April 17, 2000 proclaimed that June 10, 2000 would be declared Jesus Day. Bush did not simply decide to create an arbitrary 'Jesus Day' for the State of Texas. His proclamation was issued in support of a national celebration of Jesus Day, an annual event supported by proclamations from other governors and mayors throughout America as well. In *The Faith of George W. Bush* (2003) a sympathetic author, Stephan Mansfield writes that, "in the election year 2000, Bush told Texas preacher James Robinson, one of his spiritual mentors:

> I feel like God wants me to run for president. I can't explain it, but I get the sense my country is going to need me…I know it won't be easy on me or my family, but God wants me to do it," (Mansfield, 2003, p. 109).

His administrations' public communications and policies contained four characteristics that are simultaneously rooted in religious fundamentalism while offering political capital and effective political dualisms. There were simplistic black-and-white conceptions of the political landscape, most importantly good vs. evil and security vs. peril – the major binary. There were calls for immediate action on administration policies as a necessary part of the nation's calling or mission against terrorism. There were declarations about the will of God for America and for the spread of U.S. conceptions of freedom and liberty. There was the claim that dissent from the administration is unpatriotic and a threat to the nation and the globe (see Domke, 2004).

> In combination, these characteristics have transformed Bush's 'Either you are with us or against us policy to 'Either you are with us, or you are against God.' To the great misfortune of American democracy and the global public, such a view looks, sounds and feels remarkably similar to that of the terrorists it is fighting (Domke, 2004, p. 2).

Bush's Republican Party was supported by the Christocrats and by its well-known political organizations and leaders. The Moral Majority once led by the late Jerry Falwell. This organization which emerged in 1979, changed its name in 2004 to the Moral Majority Coalition reflecting its move to directly influence politics. Jerry Falwell died in May 2007 and his successor was his son Jonathan Falwell. He assumed leadership roles as Senior Pastor of the Thomas Road Baptist Church, leader of the Moral Majority Coalition and Executive Vice-President of *Spiritual* Affairs at Liberty University (the university Jerry Falwell founded). The Moral Majority Coalition was and continues to be very helpful with its get out the vote campaigns. The Christian Coalition founded by Pat Robertson and Ralph Reed the first executive director of the Christian Coalition, and former Chair of the Georgia Republican party who also headed Bush's southeastern presidential campaign. Reed lost his 2006 primary bid to become the Republican candidate for Lieutenant Governor of Georgia. Reed currently kept a low profile because of his Jack Abramoff baggage. But, he was involved in the 2008 elections. James Dobson is leader of Focus on the Family and currently the most powerful of the Christocratic leaders. Rick Santorum, the anti-gay, anti-abortion, former senator from Pennsylvania is also enmeshed with the Bush elections. Currently Santorum is a Senior Fellow of the Ethics and Public Policy Center, established and directs EPPC's Program to Protect America's Freedom. All of these Christocratic leaders have made continual statements of support for Bush, his policies and the general Christocratic political agenda.

This diminishing line separating church and state is viewed by the Christocrats as re-establishing the rightful relationship between them, and that is no separation at all. One famous case begins to illustrate this fusion of them. It is the case of Roy Moore the former Alabama Supreme Court justice. In 2003, Moore had a 5,300 lb., Ten Commandments monument installed in the Montgomery judicial building. He was ordered by a judge to remove the monument from the building and he defied the order. He was subsequently removed from his position. Although to many his case is an example of the "latest in the line of grotesque Southern anachronisms" (Goldberg, 2006, p. 25), he became a martyr and a hero for the Christocrats. He is viewed as a defender of the faith for his stand. It even propelled him to run in the Republican primary for Governor of Alabama in 2004. He did not win that primary; however, his hero status lives on. He has his own website entitled Foundation for Moral Law, a book, entitled, *So Help me God*, and Ten Commandments lapel pins. He advocates a Christian Nation founded on and committed to strong Biblical principles like, well, the Ten Commandments.

One of the strongest and most political of the proponents of a Christocracy (read a Christian Nation) is David Barton a graduate of Oral Roberts University, and president of Wallbuilders, a Texas based organization devoted to remaking America as a Christian Nation. In 1997 he was also the vice president of the Texas Republican Party. His most famous work is *The Myth of Separation* (1992). In this book Barton attempts to prove that the constitutional support for a separation of church and state is a myth. When asked in 2002 by Pat Robertson if he had proof that American was a Christian nation Barton replied that he did, indeed.

> There is a lot of proof. Not the least of which is a great Fourth of July speech that was given in 1837 by one of the guys who fought in the revolution, who became a president, John Quincy Adams. His question was why is it in America that the Fourth of July and Christmas are the most celebrated holidays? His answer was that at Christmas we celebrate what Jesus Christ did for the world [with] his birth, and on the Fourth of July we celebrate what Jesus Christ did for America, since we founded it as a Christian nation. (http://www.beliefnet.com/story/154/story_15469.html)

In his book Barton has twelve quotes concerning the myth of separation of church and state that have been found to be false. He even has admitted to the spuriousness of the quotes. But, it has not stopped the influence of his Wallbuilders organization. His Wallbuilders website has for sale numerous books and pamphlets proclaiming the Christian nation, the evils of activist judges, the responsibility for Christians to vote, the sanctity of marriage (there are Christmas cards devoted to this), Bibles in

CHAPTER 2

schools, defending liberty mouse pads, and a newsletter. Why the name Wallbuilders? The website explains:

> In the Old Testament book of Nehemiah, the nation of Israel rallied together in a grassroots movement to help rebuild the walls of Jerusalem and thus restore stability, safety, and a promising future to that great city. We have chosen this historical concept of "rebuilding the walls" to represent allegorically the call for citizen involvement in rebuilding our nation's foundations. As Psalm 11:3 reminds us, "If the foundations be destroyed, what shall the righteous do? (http://www.wallbuilders.com/aboutus/)

The Wallbuilder's organization also actively recruits ministers to become politically involved with the Christocratic agenda. A passage from the website describes this activity.

> For the past 6 years, Wallbuilders has brought ministers from across the nation to Washington, DC, for exclusive briefing sessions with some of the top Christian Senators and Representatives now serving in the Congress. The members brief pastors on a variety of issues related to Biblical values and share their hearts regarding their personal faith and its application in public office. Additionally the members impart practical information for pastors to carry home and implement in their communities and congregations. (http://www.wallbuilders.com/events/PastorsBriefing/briefing.htm).

The message is clear that there is no dividing line between church and state in a Christocrat's view. Christocrats should have a political agenda and that agenda should be preached in the pulpits of the nation's churches, reinforcing the message that we are a Christian Nation and those that even partially agree or support the religiously correct issues should be politically supported. If there is no separation between church and state then, the curriculum in schools should be part of the agenda to take back the United States with Biblically correct ideas.

Intelligent Design

The controversy over intelligent design is another example of the diminishing borders between church and state and the Christian activist's intrusion into public education. Intelligent design is seen by many Christocrats as a credible and scientific alternative to evolution. Of course, it is not Creationism, the full biblical doctrine of creation, which they would prefer. The book that initiated the battle over intelligent design is *Intelligent Design: The Bridge between Science and Theology* (1999) by William A. Dembski. Dembski claims that there exists specified complexity. He argues that it is impossible for specified complexity to exist in patterns displayed by configurations formed by unguided processes, ignoring the fact that natural selection is a process guided by the rationality of nature, the logic of which supports their favored economic system, free market capitalism. Therefore, Dembski argues, the fact that specified complex patterns can be found in living things indicates some kind of guidance in their formation, which is indicative of intelligence. It is a reliable marker of design by an intelligent agent, a central tenet to intelligent design and he argues that instances of it in nature cannot be explained by Darwinian evolution, but instead are consistent with the notion of intelligent design (Dembski, 1999).

Although Bush said that curriculum decisions should be made by school districts rather than the federal government, he told Texas newspaper reporters in a group interview at the White House on August 1, 2005 that he believes that intelligent design should be taught alongside evolution as a competing theory.

> Both sides ought to be properly taught . . . so people can understand what the debate is about," he said, according to an official transcript of the session. Bush added: "Part of education is to expose people to different schools of thought. . . . You're asking me whether or not people ought to be exposed to different ideas, and the answer is yes." (*Washington Post*).

But, more than through presidential speeches this intelligent design movement is having direct impact on the public school curriculum.

One of the first instances of this battle against evolution in the late 20th century and early 21st century was in Kansas. In 1999 the Kansas State Board of Education deleted references to macroevolution and the age of earth from the state science standards. The mandate caused a political debate which split the Republican Party between moderates and conservatives (Christocrats). The major political supporter of the anti-evolution position for candidates on the Kansas Sate School Board election in 2000 was Kansas Senator Sam Brownback. Brownback, who converted to Catholicism in 2002, is linked to various extreme right Christian organizations such as Opus Dei, "the ultraconservative prelature renowned for its role in the Franco regime in Spain" (Frank, 2004, p. 71) and The Family or fellowship.

> When in Washington, he lives in a town house operated by a Christian group know as the Family or the Fellowship, who mission seems o be bringing together American lawmakers with capitalists and dictators from around the world (Frank, 2004, p. 72).

In the election the conservative candidates for the board were defeated. The newly elected board reversed its position on evolution by a 7 to 3 vote. There were, however, statements in the Kansas science standards that were included to lessen the impact for conservatives. There was a warning placed in the Kansas science standards.

> Teachers should not ridicule, belittle or embarrass a student for expressing an alternative view or belief. If a student should raise a question in a natural science class that the teacher determines to be outside the domain of science, the teacher should treat the question with respect. The teacher should explain why the question is outside the domain of natural science and encourage the student to discuss the question further with his or her family and other appropriate sources (Fountain, 2001)

The Dover, Pennsylvania School Board implemented a policy in December 2004 requiring all ninth-grade biology teachers to read a statement on "intelligent design" before teaching evolution lessons. The disclaimer states that evolution is a "theory...not a fact," that "gaps in the theory exist for which there is no evidence," and that "intelligent design" is a valid scientific alternative. Science teachers in Dover were also required to refer to a book describing the theory of "intelligent design," *Of Pandas and People*, to students interested in the subject. The Dover school district is believed to be the first in the country to require such a disclaimer. In November of 2005 a school board election was held and all eight of the school board members who had supported the introduction of intelligent design into the science curriculum were swept out of office. Reporting on the case *New York Times* reporter Laurie Goodstein wrote, " In the end voters here [Dover, PA] said they were tired of being portrayed as a northern version of Dayton, Tennessee, a Bible Belt hamlet where 80 years ago a biology teacher named John Scopes was tried for illegally teaching evolution" (Goodstein, 2005, A-15). The controversy became a federal case, *Kitzmiller verses Dover Area School District*. In December 20, 2005, Judge John E. Jones III, in The United States District Court ForThe Middle District Of Pennsylvania, ruled that the Dover District School Board violated the US Constitution when they changed the 9th grade Biology curriculum to include Intelligent Design. The ruling is 139 pages and Jones goes into great detail to demonstrate how he came to his conclusion. Judge Jones found: The Board's actions violated the establishment clause and failed the "purpose" and "effect" prongs of the Lemon Test (*Kitzmiller v. Dover Area School District 2005*). That Intelligent Design is not science and that is in fact "creation science" with a different label. The Board members at the heart of the case, the ones' who led the effort to put Intelligent Design in the curriculum, "lied under oath and that the Board attempted to hide their real intentions about the change after they found out it might cause a legal case" (Doug, 2005). While Intelligent Design is not appropriate for the science classroom, the court wasn't saying it couldn't be studied in a more appropriate context. The ruling centers on intelligent design not being taught in *science* classrooms but leaves open the possibilities for it to be placed in other subjects within the curriculum. The Cobb County Board of Education in Georgia ordered in 2002 that more than 34,000 of the school district's biology textbooks contain a disclaimer referring to evolution as a disputed fact. The sticker reads:

> This textbook contains material on evolution. Evolution is a theory, not a fact, regarding the origin of living things. This material should be approached with an open mind, studied carefully and critically considered. Five parents of students and the American Civil Liberties Union had challenged the stickers in court, arguing they violated the constitutional separation of church and state. The case was heard in federal court in November of 2004. The school system defended the warning stickers as a show of tolerance, not religious activism as some parents claimed. In January of 2005, U.S. District Judge Clarence Cooper in Atlanta, Georgia, ruled that Cobb county school district's textbook stickers referring to evolution as "a theory not a fact" were unconstitutional.It is not that the school board should not have called evolution a theory or that the school board should have called evolution a fact. Rather, the distinction of evolution as a theory rather than a fact is the

distinction that religiously motivated individuals have specifically asked school boards to make in the most recent anti-evolution movement, and that was exactly what parents in Cobb County did in this case. By adopting this specific language, even if at the direction of counsel, the Cobb County School Board appears to have sided with these religiously motivated individuals. The sticker sends a message that the school board agrees with the beliefs of Christian fundamentalists and creationists. The school board has effectively improperly entangled itself with religion by appearing to take a position, therefore, the sticker must be removed from all of the textbooks into which it has been placed (CNN, 2005)

Utah state legislator Chris Buttars threatened to introduce legislation in 2006 in favor of teaching "divine design" in the state's public schools. "Divine design," according to Buttars, "doesn't preach religion. The only people who will be upset about this are atheists. It shocks me that our schools are teaching evolution as fact." (National Center for Science Education, p. 1). In this controversy the binary is maintained by posing the so-called atheistic evolutionists against the God-fearing believers of intelligent design (read creationism). It presents the controversy as if there are no religious-minded or agnostic people who also support evolution, only atheists.

The battle over the teaching of evolution is a small example of the Christocrats and their political allies on the right to battle science. In a book entitled, *The Republican War on Science* (2005) by Chris Mooney the larger question concerning science and issues such as global warming, stem cell research and intelligent design is examined. The war pits the Christocrats, the God-fearing against the atheistic scientific community. The binary is portrayed as the intellectual snobs continuing to push the atheistic agenda of science on the "common" people. The binary is maintained on a larger scale.

In an interesting analysis of the case against evolution Frank (2004) elaborates on the manner in which the Christocrats or Neocons (neo-conservatives) are able to turn their own offenses into the offenses of the scientific community of intellectuals. It is the scientific community that is evil and promoting an agenda. He states that anti-evolution crusaders in Kansas (and we can project in other areas as well) are saying that it is the scientific community not the fundamentalists (read Christocrats) that are:

> Trying to impose its religious views on everyone else; that is the scientific community not the fundamentalists—that it engages in 'censorship of contrary evidence'; that it is the science experts who are 'dogmatic' and 'narrow-minded'; that it is these same experts who are irrational and emotional, unable to face reality; and that the reason no articles refuting evolution are ever published in professional, peer-reviewed journals is that the journals are biased (p. 211).

The blurring of the lines between church, state, and the scientific community is maintained as well as the binary in the controversies and conundrums over evolution and intelligent design. The court defeats of the intelligent design movement are viewed as proof that the scientific community is waging war on the Godly. And, proof of the need to battle against judges who defeat their gains. "Teach the controversy" now becomes the likely ground on which the seemingly never-ending

CHAPTER 2

evolution battle will be fought (Mooney, 2005, p. 193). The only thing that seems certain, according to Mooney, is that much more litigation lies ahead.

In a recently released documentary *Jesus Camp* created by Hedi Ewing and Rachel Gray, we are taken to the American Heartland for an examination of the lives of Christocrats and the education of their children. This film demonstrates that the education of children is not overlooked in the perpetuation of a Christocratic political agenda. The site of the "Kids on Fire" summer camp is ironically Devil's Lake, North Dakota. The leader of the camp is Pastor Becky Fischer. Most of the children in the camp are young children. The film focuses on three children ranging in age from ten to thirteen.

> Outfitted in war paint and army fatigues, the kids are first shown taking part in a choreographed dance number that evokes both Jesus Christ and combat. The images imply—and more explicitly so as the movie goes on—that these youngsters are "warriors" for God, engaged in a Christian jihad to change the face of the nation. Islamic radicals may garner the newspaper headlines, but as Jesus Camp makes clear, America's own homegrown radical fundamentalists may prove just as dangerous. Pastor Fischer puts it this way, "I want to see young people as committed to the cause of Jesus Christ as the young people are to Islam … laying down their lives for the Gospel." (Ewing & Grady, 2006)

Although we could easily dismiss this as a fringe element, the kids at "Kids on Fire" summer camp demonstrate the power and influence of the Christocratic agenda. It also demonstrates that the Christocrats have their own particular version of an educational agenda that far exceeds the battles over evolution. These children will grow up to be adult Christocratic warriors. Children and education become part of the backlash of the culture wars. As one spokesman says in the documentary; "We are engaged in a culture war. We didn't start it, but by His Grace, we're going to finish it" (Ewing & Grady, 2006).

Homophobia

> The enmity of the Christian Right toward gay people is potentially the most dangerous element of its ideology and political game plan. It is safe to say that the leadership of the Christian Right will not be satisfied until homosexuality is banned in the United States. Toward that end Christian Right leaders conduct their anti-gay activities against a backdrop of widespread and historically entrenched homophobia: homosexuals can now be blamed for the modern-day Plague, fulfilling the time-honored role of scapegoats (Diamond, 1989, p. 101).

The Christocrats most galvanizing issue is their stand against gays and lesbians. This issue emerged in the 2004 election as the debate over gay marriage, but the issue is much more complex than the obvious political tactic of polarizing the American public over the issue of marriage.

But the greatest demonization is reserved for "homosexuals." For conservative Christians especially those who read the Bible literally homosexuality is a practice condemned by God. Both the Eagle Forum and Concerned Women for America have ongoing campaigns against "militant lesbians" and "the gay agenda" (Hardisty, 1999, p. 86).

Homosexuality has become the enemy. The ressentiment the Christocrats feel for this enemy has surpassed the demonization of the old enemies of Catholics and African-Americans. Gay people have become the new demons. The rhetoric against gays and lesbians is especially ruthless. Again, in displaying the qualities of ressentiment the Christocrats see gays and lesbians as part of a conspiracy to corrupt the nation. One of the texts that articulates this point of view is entitled, *The Homosexual Agenda* (2003) written by Craig Osten and Alan Sears. These authors present the notion that the Gay agenda is a national conspiracy to silence the faithful and steal the souls of the nation's children. There message is full of ressentiment continually attributing various evils and plots to homosexuals.

> We will outline how the homosexual agenda touches every area of our lives, from the media to education to families to corporate America and to government. We will document how the religious freedoms of all Americans are under attack from radical homosexual activists (Sears and Osten, 2003, p. 14).

This notion of a homosexual conspiracy would be preposterous if it was not widely supported by the Christocrats and preached in mega churches across the country.

Another major text in the anti-gay Christocratic agenda is *The Pink Swastika* (2002) by Scott Lively and Kevin Abrams. In this book the authors make the shocking pronouncement that "Nazism was primarily a homosexual movement and that today's gay rights movement is its direct descendent and that claims to the contrary are simply part of the homosexual conspiracy" (Goldberg, 2006, p. 55). This astonishing charge is not just a couple of crazies lashing out in their homophobia but is a common belief among Christocrats.

> When Kevin Abrams and I published the first edition of this book in 1995, we knew it would cause controversy, contradicting as it does the common portrayal of homosexuals as exclusively victims of the Nazi regime. For this reason we were scrupulous in our documentation of homosexuals as the true inventors of Nazism and the guiding force behind many Nazi atrocities (Lively & Abrams, 2002, p. 1).

The authors attack on homosexuals is relentless. They feel that since homosexuals are ruthless, they must be treated in kind.

> Like their Nazi predecessors, today's homosexuals lack any scruples. Homosexuality is primarily a predatory addiction striving to take the weak and unsuspecting down with it. The 'gay' agenda is a colossal fraud; a gigantic robbery of the mind. Homosexuals of the type described in this book have no

true idea of how to act in the best interests of their country and fellow man. Their intention is to serve none but themselves (Lively and Abrams, 2002, p. 13).

It would be easy to simply dismiss Lively and Abrams as homophobic crazies, but their views are common among Christocrats. According to Goldberg (2006), their work is cited in many books on the "homosexual agenda" and is "repeated endlessly at churches, on right-wing TV and radio, at rallies, and by politicians" (pp. 55–56). It helps to explain the reasons that in 2004 millions of Americans decided to vote against gay people from getting married. The dualism continues. The evil Nazi-generating, ruthless and predatory homosexuals are pitted against God-fearing, heterosexual Americans. Alongside this talk of ruthless gays and the consequent sermons filled with the rhetoric of perversion and abomination preached at various mega churches across the country, there is also a constant refrain from Christocrats about hating the sin, but not the sinners.

> Crucial to this belief system is the conviction that homosexuality can be cured. To that end a massive network of counseling centers, inpatient programs, self-help books and seminars devoted to turning gay people straight through so-called reparative therapy. They've even invented a holiday, National Coming Out of Homosexuality Day, to mirror the pro-gay National Coming Out Day. (Goldberg, 2006, p. 76).

How does this notion operate in the interest of Christocrats? Their anti-gay agenda is based on the supposition that homosexuality is a choice. It is the key argument against gay rights. Both Exodus International (founded by Michael Bussee and Garry Cooper two ex-gay movement dropouts) and Courage (A British ex-ex-gay organization) renounce the entire notion that homosexuality is a choice and believes that it can be cured. They also announce the consequences for ex-gays such as depression, hopelessness, and even suicide. The American Psychological Association findings agree. The APA's 1998 statement stated that, "psychiatric literature strongly demonstrates that the treatment attempts to change sexual preference orientation are ineffective. However the potential risks are great including depression, anxiety, and self-destructive behavior"

The Christocrats turn this information around to debunk findings like these as proof that their opposition is biased toward gays. And, this apparently gives them strength to continue their quest or mission to prevent and treat homosexuality as James Dobson's Focus on the Family does.

> Focus on the Family is promoting the truth that change is possible for those who experience same-sex attractions — a message routinely silenced today. We want people to know that individuals don't have to be gay and that a homosexual identity is something that can be overcome. That's why we've developed a one-day conference for those seeking answers on this often confusing and divisive issue. Whether you have a gay friend or family member, are an educator, pastor or concerned citizen — or even self-identify as gay — Love Won Out will inform, inspire and offer you hope. (http://www.lovewonout.com/).

The way that Christocrats operate is to take an issue such as gay rights and make it part of the larger "us versus them" dualism that they have so carefully constructed. It is brought to national attention by making an issue that Christocrats can unite around and vote to demonstrate their feeling of righteousness. In the case of gay rights it is to form the opposition to gay marriage. In the 2004 election this opposition resulted in eleven state constitutional amendments banning gay marriage and other legal recognition for gay couples.

President Bush, again the favorite son of the Christocrats, supported the idea of a constitutional amendment banning gay marriage. No amendment proposed previously had used the constitution to negate a freedom. Bush stated that it was the corruption of marriage he was trying to prevent with the constitutional amendment.

> The union of a man and a woman is the most enduring human institution, honored and encouraged in all cultures and by every religious faith, Marriage cannot be severed from its cultural, religious and natural roots without weakening the good influence of society. After more than two centuries of American jurisprudence and millennia of human experience, a few judges and local authorities are presuming to change the most fundamental institution of civilization. Their actions have created confusion on an issue that requires clarity. On a matter of such importance, the voice of the people must be heard. Activist courts have left the people with one recourse. If we're to prevent the meaning of marriage from being changed forever, our nation must enact a constitutional amendment to protect marriage in America. Decisive and democratic action is needed because attempts to redefine marriage in a single state or city could have serious consequences throughout the country. (Bush, 2004).

The amendment failed in June 2006 in the Senate in a 49 to 48 vote. The close vote demonstrates the power of the Christocrats and their agenda. But the battle against gays continues.

A Regime of Dualistic Madness

To reemphasize, we are not asking about the meaning of the Christocratic phenomena. We are exploring how as Deleuze discussed in *Two Regimes of Madness* (2006) [1975] the question of how this phenomena, like power, "exerts itself, where it takes shape, and why it is everywhere" (Deleuze, 2006, p. 11). The manner in which the Christocrats have set up a binary relationships between good and evil, between the believer and the non-believer, and moral righteousness and deviance to name a few is one of the key ways that the power of the Christocrats operates. If we take a stand against the Christocrats then we are easily put into the category of evil, non-believers who lack moral righteousness.

We are easily swept into the debates that the Christocrats construct. We can argue and write about our "side" in the debates over abortion, evolution, stem cell research, gay marriage, and church and state and we should. The moment we enter into those debates, however, we are labeled as the liberal leftist latte drinking crowd

CHAPTER 2

(blue staters). We are defined and can easily become the object of ressentiment. We continue to allow the Christocrats to construct the arguments and vote against their own self-interest.

> And, still worse, people keep on being sunk in black holes, pinioned on a white wall. This is what being identified, labeled, recognized is: A central computer functioning as a black hole and sweeping across a white wall without contours (Deleuze, 1987, p. 18).

The Christocratic agenda filled with nostalgia and ressentiment operates with power to construct the black holes with which we so genuinely and feverishly debate. But, of course, they are black holes that we can fall into and never emerge. In many ways those black holes shift the debate from issues such as the unequal distribution of wealth to issues that make very good political sound bites. In some cases these issues operate to disguise the issues that are crucial to people's lives particularly their economic lives and well-being. In everyday political terms the Christocrats vote their morality which is stolen by the neo-conservatives for their larger agenda of free market capitalism, corporatization and privatization.

What if we didn't get trapped in the debate? Not that these issues don't deserve our attention. Of course they do. Perhaps, one way to move the questions that preoccupy us is to engage the issues in a different way. Michelle Goldberg (2006) advocates that we refute the distortions of the Christocrats.

> Liberals need to create their own echo chamber to refute these kinds of distortions while loudly supporting everyone's freedom of speech. Committed Christian nationalists [Christocrats] won't be won over, but some of their would-be-sympathizers might be inoculated against the claim that the progressives want to extirpate their faith, making it harder for the right to frame every political dispute as part of a war against Jesus. The challenge is to make reality matter again (Goldberg, 2006, p. 206).

There is, indeed, a place for direct confrontation on the issues like freedom of speech that Goldberg discusses. But there may just be another way as well.

Can we deconstruct the dualistic debate? If the Christocrats operate with power in defining the terms of the debate into a dualistic either/or, then the possibility exists to challenge the entire set up of this dualism. Of course challenging the dualisms set up by the Christocrats necessitates setting up another dualism. It is very difficult to emerge from this frame.

> We invoke one dualism only in order to challenge another. We employ a dualism of models only in order to arrive at a process that challenges all models. Each time, mental correctives are necessary to undo the dualisms we had no wish to construct but through which we pass. Arrive at the magic formula we all seek – PLURALISM=MONISM – via all the dualisms that are the enemy, an entirely necessary enemy, the furniture we are forever rearranging (Deleuze and Guattari, 1987, pp. 20–21).

We can therefore be ever constructing to deconstruct the dualisms that have been constructed by the Christocrats. Certainly even the most committed Christocrat or latte drinker can understand that the cultural bifurcations that are created in these debates simplify extremely complex issues and simply put are too multifaceted for a simple either/or.

This is the current symbolic order or "regime of signs or semiotic regime" (Deleuze, 2006, p. 13). The analysis of this order is yet another way to approach this construct of the dualistic thinking implicit in the Christocratic agenda. How do the symbols and signs that the Christocratics construct operate within our society? How are issues like secularism and humanism interwoven into this dualist symbolic order? These are questions that we address in the following chapters.

CHAPTER THREE

THE SECULAR STRATEGIES OF THE CHRISTIAN RIGHT

A Political Curriculum to Disestablish Critical Thought

"Authority untaught is the condition in which a culture commits suicide,"

-Philip Rieff, *Fellow Teachers*

Three years ago Julie published her thesis as a book, *Failure to Hold: The Politics of School Violence* with a chapter in it that never fails to shock committed Christians at around Chapter Five. This chapter "Witnessing and Salvation at School" explored the role of religion during and in the aftermath of school shootings in the United States. It presented these disastrous events as political opportunity structures for the Christian right to bolster its arguments for bringing God, the Ten Commandments and prayer into the nation's approximately 85,000 public schools. It examines "Prayer at the Pole" a student-led movement in favor of prayer in school that symbolically organizes itself around one of America's most potent national symbols: the flag pole. One way that the Christian right has been effective is at capturing imagery tied to the nation and presenting its message as inherently "American." Indeed, love and ownership of the nation is one of the major indices of desire in the U.S. political imaginary. Yet these forms of desire are linked to other very tangible political issues related to regulating private life and sexuality. But the strategies for capturing the imaginary have not been wholly separate in form from secular culture, institutions and ideas. In fact, they mime them to give the public a sense of national continuity with New Deal liberalism; mega churches look like public schools or malls, some even look like local community buildings, music is in the style of alternative or rock with lyrics about Christ, and baptismal chambers look like modern Jacuzzis oddly presented in the middle of a vestibule resembling an upscale hotel lobby. In this chapter, we explore the strategies deployed by the Christian right to mimic secular structures, arguing that while this growing political force explicitly argues that secularism is an affront to living the "good" (Christian) life, it knowingly uses these very secular forms to earn loyalty from citizens for religious and political purposes. But first, we follow other scholars in defining the Christian Right as a political movement aimed at shaping public and foreign policies for religious and conservative purposes. The Christian Right as described in this chapter and the subsequent one is a public social movement with key figures holding prominent political positions in government that models its claims for rights and agenda-setting on an ethnic-like minority status. As we shall see, while it promotes these politics of by arguing it is a persecuted minority, its political agenda has come to dominate the center of

CHAPTER 3

political ideology, an unprecedented political victory in modern times. It is not all Christians and it is not conservatives who refrain from public or political life, such as libertarians. In the sections that follow, it will become clear who encompasses the Christian Right, but first we will describe the effects of this political organizing on contemporary public life in the U.S.

Normal, Illinois is the stereotypical example of a community that Michelle Goldberg has called "exurban" to distinguish it from the urban coasts of the country as well as give more specific meaning the areas where the Christian right has been effective at gaining support for republican political candidates. Rather than refer to these as "red states" (a very misleading label as Normal is very republican but located in a blue state) or rural or Midwestern Goldberg's term refers to the rejection of urbanity implied in *choosing* to live in an exurban community. These places are defined by a rejection of all aspects of living associated with urban life: cosmopolitanism, diversity, rationality, public forums and spaces, public transportation, art galleries, sidewalks (indeed any structure that may encourage walking or riding a bicycle). There is a common sense developed in these communities that life in cities is difficult, expensive, full of traffic and inimical to raising a family. As everyone in Normal says "It's a great place to raise a family." Taxes to fund public forms of recreation and education are sacrilege. In fact, the Catholic Church provides the sex education curriculum for the Bloomington public school district with nary a public outcry. A typical mega church looks exactly like a newer public high school found anywhere in the United States. One such mega church in Normal has the exact same architectural style as Columbine High School; the same cafeteria housed on the bottom floor at the back of the building one finds scattered tables with a large terrace wrapped around the top of the cafeteria giving the person perched on it a global view of the people munching on breakfast below. As one drives into the parking lot it feels more like a mall parking lot with hundreds of spaces painted onto the flat blacktop peppered with large street lamps. Surrounding the colossal building (which is barely distinguishable from the three schools nearby) are thousands of yards of sod with yearling trees poking out of it. There are no benches or paths or flowers so the grass is completely pointless and only there as a nod to suburban aesthetics. As you walk into the building it looks exactly like a mall with an information center that displays all the activities and events, as well as information on the church and its causes (crisis pregnancy centers, for example). A map can show you how to navigate the building and where to find the "battle of the churches" softball diamond. No one speaks to you; in fact, they don't even make eye contact or smile at people that they do not already know. One wonders how anyone accidentally gets pregnant in this town! Inside the theatre (where the service is held) thousands of concert stadium seats surround a large stage with musical instruments for the band. The band is the center piece of the service playing upbeat Christian rock with lyrics that subtly damn anyone not dependent on the "rock of Christ" to walking on shallow ground. Three large flat screens adorn the walls surrounding the stage and feature the pastor freed from a pulpit dancing around with a mike in front of the band explaining why there is no "sacred feminine" and *The Da Vinci Code* is a farce. There are no hymnals or bibles. Important passages are presented on the screens detached from their narrative context. This is a third order simulacrum of religion. It is the perfect counterpart to globalized life in an exurban town. Its form resembles secular public life in every way while its content, its message is consistent with the Christian right: what is wrong with America is feminism, gay rights, abortion and cinema, and apparently, reading. What is right is absolving you of personal responsibility and giving yourself over to Christ. It is a form of the posthuman ideology as outlined in the next chapter. As Goldberg describes it,

> These churches are usually located on the sprawling edges of cities, in the new exurban developments that almost totally lack for public space-squares, parks, promenades, or even, in some places, sidewalks. With their endless procession warehouse-like chain stores and garish profusion of primary-colored logos, the exurbs are the purest of ecosystems for consumer capitalism. Yet the brutal, impersonal utilitarianism of the strip mall and office park structure- its perversely ascetic refusal to make a single concession to aesthetics- recalls the Stalinist monstrosities imposed on communist countries. The banality is aggressive and disorienting, (Goldberg, 2006, p. 58).

This church replaces every aspect of secular public culture featuring softball teams, ministries, and power lunches for men and adventure weekends for them too. There are three day care centers that are patterned on developmental stages; everything missing and under funded from the state is found here on the compound. What is striking is that most things that are provided could be provided by the state without the religious and political messages and the religion doesn't seem to the primary reason for attending a mega church. In this "joiner" culture, amenities for living the good life are only provided on a membership basis. People join churches to meet other people through activities because they can't meet them in public spaces. Women join for the children to attend a play group. Men join for the golf league and softball. The very idea of a public is tied to membership in private organization not to civic avenues. As Michael Warner writes,

> Imagine how powerless people would feel if their commonality and participation were simply defined by pre-given frameworks, by institutions and laws, as in other social contexts they are through kinship. What would the world look like if all ways of being public were more like applying for a driver's license or subscribing to a professional group – if, that is, formally organized mediations replaced the self-organized public as the image of belonging and common activity? Such is the image of totalitarianism: non-kin society organized by bureaucracy and law. Everyone's position, function, and capacity for action are specified for her by administration (Warner, 2002, p. 69).

This is how social life is engineered in contemporary U.S. society. Yet, we don't think these folks feel disempowered. We think they feel vindicated to judge others unlike themselves (and we wonder where this comes from?). We think they *enjoy* what critical scholars call totalitarianism. Yet, they do not realize the basic rights

CHAPTER 3

(of expression, of assembly, of public service, public education, etc.) that are compromised in order to gain this pathetic right to judge deviance against the current national script. In giving up the right to self-govern at the federal and local level publics have allowed politicians to gut the state of social services and fund private, mostly Christian -based private services. While some would point out that secularism (and the public services provided by welfare and public education) were themselves ideological, we would argue that those ideologies while imperfect and often discriminatory, were a better option than those presented by faith-based services, not because they were secular but because they were *public*. Since the state has retreated from public forms of servicing to "faith-based" servicing, it has also begun to destroy what public forms are left (using No Child Left Behind to excuse discontinuation of funding) and corporations have not been regulated when they decrease health benefits and lose the pensions of their employees. Faith-based servicing is *exclusive* in that groups that apply for this funding can withhold employment from members of other faiths. This points to the break down of the social contract between the sovereign and the people where the people must fend for themselves or join a faith-based organization. It is surprisingly similar to the way in which madrassahs (demonized by the corporate media outlined in the introduction of this writing) are seen as providing education for children in Islamic cultures where public schooling has never existed (Riaz, 2008).

Indeed, Goldberg's appraisal of Christian nationalism consistently describes it as a totalitarian movement as it is a totalizing ideology explaining and providing every answer and service to the public. Warner's distinction between "pre-given frameworks" and "self-organized publics" is instructive for our examination of the Christian right's imaginary. A self-organized public may have spaces provided and maintained by the state but what takes place in them should not be regulated by any particular state sanctioned religion or cultural mandate. All were governed by the state and groups that did not fit the dominant ethnic culture formed subcultures and self-fashioned neighborhoods and community services using the resources of the state to capacitate them in their endeavors. Indeed, that is why citizens pay taxes. In the midst of this ideological sandstorm, it is (mostly Anglo) protestant Christian evangelical culture that has emerged as the only culture worthy of dispensing social services. Only 66 grants out of 1600 were conferred on non-Christian faith-based organizations by five federal departments in the year 2003, and the Bush Administration had no means to evaluate the effectiveness of such federally funded programs because there's no data gathering mandated by this initiative (Goldberg, 2006, p. 121). In the past, under New Deal-inspired social services there may have been hegemonic publics dominated by one ethnic group, and indeed all publics were regulated by a heteronormative and liberal imperative, but they did not require that an individual *join* them in a formal way and subscribe to their beliefs or convert to Christianity in exchange for relief from the failure of capitalism to provide for all. If anything happened, members of a differently structured Christian right retreated from public participation following what has been described as their "intellectual humiliation" at the Scopes Trial in 1925, where evolution was defended as a valid curriculum component (Coleman, 2005, p. 656). Most sociologists and anthropologists agree that although a "Christian right" neither existed at that time, nor for several decades after, many evangelicals and Pentecostals withdrew from American politics until the election campaign of Jimmy Carter, a candidate whom they mistakenly identified as an ally in their search to bring god "back" into the schools. Not realizing that as a Baptist Carter had sustained the lifelong commitment to the separation of church and state upon which his faith was created (Richardson cited in Flint & Porter, 2005, p. 33). Also, as other close observers of the emergence of the Christian right as a political influence have documented, the evangelicals were too busy "growing their churches" during the 1950s to come out as a force (Dionne, 1992, p. 172). Finally, the evangelical movement (defined here as a movement to proselytize or "witness" to others about conversion to Christ) was not fully able to emerge on the domestic political scene until the election of Ronald Reagan in 1980, after Carter's defeat, one in which evangelicals soured on the Democrat who they felt betrayed their values. Indeed, two protestant variants known for the apolitical nature of their faiths, fundamentalist Independent Baptists and the Pentecostal Assemblies of God, were drawn out of seclusion by Carter's appointment of two pro-choice women as presidential assistants (Costanza and the lawyer for Jane Roe, Weddington); so, first Carter had alienated the evangelicals by failing to act as a pro-life Christian while conducting official duties as president (which he, in fact, is) while in office (Flint & Porter, 2005, p. 41). Then he further outraged them by appointing two feminist pro-choice advisors to the White House.

At about this time, the Moral Majority began to form riding to the forefront of American consciousness through the support of an enormously popular Ronald Reagan. Not only did he court the Christian Right, Reagan affirmed many of the issues on their narrow agenda by agreeing that homosexuality was a neurotic disorder (twelve years after the APA declared it was not). The main *wedge* issue for this coalition of elites was, of course, public schooling and children. The Briggs Amendment was proposed in California to ban teachers from mentioning homosexuality in a positive light in public schools. Christian right supporters worried that the children would be negatively affected and perhaps converted to this abnormal lifestyle if they were taught about it in public schools. However, at this phase in the movement, the Christian right became aware that it was severely disadvantaged by its extreme rhetoric. Calling pro-choice advocates "baby killers" and advocating death to gays and lesbians did not play well with a moderate American electorate more concerned about taxes and government spending. Some studies of the Christian right movement organizing have pointed out that two main strategies followed from the failures of the Christian right at the end of the 1980s that would encourage them to begin "mainstreaming" their message to the larger public. The first was to gut the rhetoric of Biblical references because they found the public did not understand them. As the leader of Virginia's Family Foundation argued,

> Now I'm proud to be a Christian and known as a Christian activist, but, right now you will not see the word 'Christian' in any of the Family Foundation literature because, in the current climate, that kind of appeal is not received (Kincaid quoted in Rozell & Wilcox, 1996, p. 280).

CHAPTER 3

Movement organizers stressed that they had to communicate more effectively with voters who were in many ways Bible-challenged, even if it meant conceding certain basic points to liberals in order to capture their attention. The second part of the mainstreaming strategy was to endorse or mimic moderate GOP issues *as if they were central* (when they were not) such as taxes and crime. All the while they diluted their message for mainstream appeal they increased their grassroots organizing by forming successful direct mail and phone campaigning. They informed their constituents about "family friendly" candidates and, framing tax policy as having a direct influence on family stability issued report cards on candidates that included such statements as "Excessive taxes are the major reason why most moms who would like to stay home and raise their young children cannot afford to do so. Clearly any bills and votes which increase the tax burden on families are not family-friendly," (Virginia Family Council quoted in Rozell & Wilcox, 1996, p. 281). These statements are of course unsupported by objective social science research. Instead the Christian right has formed its own policy centers that, like crisis pregnancy centers, mimic the features of established policy centers while promoting their own narrow political agenda as objective fact. Only 12 percent of women in the U.S. identify as "stay at home moms" and, any tax cuts passed by the Bush administration have been restricted to the wealthy. Virginia, the state where this report card was issued has had one of the worst records in funding public education in recent years. The two states whose governorships were decided by the Christian right vote during the 1980s were none other than Texas and Florida. It seems that catering to this base is what determined elections throughout the 1990s at the state level, and led to the presidency in 2001. In many ways the Christian right learned that mainstreaming its agenda by:

- Taking over the platform of the party most closely aligned to its agenda on a few non-religious issues (taxes, crime and muscular foreign policy),
- Refraining from backing candidates from religious professions (e.g. the defeat of Robertson). Other commentators who assess the campaigns of preachers turned politicians have argued that both Reagan and Bush ("W")'s success was precisely because they were "politicians turned preachers" and not the other way around (Jelen, 2005).
- Speaking in secular language about "national values" rather than in scriptural speak, this language could help them effectively overcome even the most inflammatory past mistakes as well as distance themselves from the apparent "irrationality" of the party's fringe.
- Colonizing and re-signifying words to make the objects, persons or ideas to which they refer in reality seem politically incorrect (examples include feminism and more recently, "radical feminism").
- Creating oversimplified and threatening caricatures of diverse social movements and people to rally against (from the "welfare queen" to the "gay agenda")
- Establishing itself as a persecuted minority with an ethnic-like status despite the fact that Christians are the overwhelming majority in the U.S. Its only equivalent movement would be the men's movement claiming persecution in a patriarchal country without a critique of patriarchy.[2]

All these strategies would make them into viable candidates to take control over the national agenda. Finally, the Christian right has effectively hidden its more fundamentalist leanings in order to capture the Republican Party and use it as a platform to force its more radical agenda in through grassroots organizing. As the parties become more and more polarized the Christian right can afford to take political hits, even humiliations from their fringe members. For example, what may have been observed by traditional political scientists as setbacks to the first wave of the Christian right movement such as the failure of certain premillennial prophecies to come to fruition (e.g. the Soviet Union, or Libya invading Israel in the 70s and 80s, or the First Gulf War in 1991) actually provided enemies and events around which the premillenialists or "Second Coming" believers could organize their imagery seeing in all these events "the signs" of the Antichrist (Buss & Herman, 2003, pp. 12–13). It did not matter that these prophecies did not become reality as all are signs of a future foreclosed and determined by their shared apocalyptic hues. The form of this movement is mutable; its content is not. One basic feature is its emphasis on conformity and religious identity. In order to be acceptable to the Christian right one must have converted to Christ (see Chapter Two). But one must also be fearful of being "left behind" in the present by the economy and society. This corresponds easily with being Left Behind by not converting to Christ as the popular fiction series by Tim LaHaye has threatened. "Conversion" is a profound signifier in American public rhetoric that can slither between a number of different institutional and ideological sites from capitalism to Christianity to democracy. As the Bush administration forcefully hollowed out the state (while increasing its power as a military force projecting outward to Iraq and Afghanistan) of its domestic responsibilities, citizens are left to the private sphere as the only possible hope for assistance to many social problems.[3] In addition, attempting a fringe existence as an individual is severely punished through the mechanisms of a bellicose surveillance culture. The only refuge from the disciplinary society is to join a private organization that can provide cover for one's person and supplies the social services withheld by the state. As a core value of neoliberalism is choice, citizens are of course invited to choose to join a religious organization but the state will no longer protect the exercise of independent will or thought. The choices they have are also limited. In an era when the Christian Right complains that environmentalism is a threat to privacy because it regulates patterns of consumption they, at the same time, have no problem with increasing the powers of the federal government to regulate private sex acts and the consequences that may flow from them. All of these policy contradictions matter little in a media culture that drops an issue after a day or two and relies on sound byte information as news.

The Joiners

Free thought is one of the first casualties in the war against the Enlightenment. While you still don't have to believe in a particular interpretation of Scripture to send a child to school (or at least not object to it) if you desire affordable day care or even friends in an exurban area, you must join a church. We will call this an ideology of joinerism. It has been officially endorsed by sociologist Katherine Newman in her study of school violence and the boys who perpetrate it in the exurban communities. The few singular examples of rampage school shooters showcased by the media at the end of the 1990s, in our estimation, signaled what was to come in the form of conformism and law in schools and public spaces of the U.S. following 9-11. What drove these reactions to school shootings was fear that was ratcheted up by every media presentation of "The Killer at Thurston High" or "Teenage Nazis." There were two main reactions: one was religious, the other a form of governmentality and surveillance. In law, the ideal was containment: students should be policed by school officials for deviant dress and behaviors, and fellow students were rewarded for turning in students with these behaviors. Schools increased means of surveillance that weren't effective at Columbine, such as video cameras and entry restriction. The City of Chicago alone spent $53 million on surveillance equipment in its public school system by 2001. The increased surveillance powers of the state brought on by school shootings would morph into the Homeland Security apparatus after 9-11. There is continuity between these two movements of governmentality in the way that they emotionally prepared the American public for accepting infringements on civil liberties in the name of security from school shooters and terrorists, neither of which are predictable nor especially sophisticated in their means of attack. After 9-11, federal money earmarked for schools and other social services was diverted to Homeland Security block grants. Most schools are falling apart but they have elaborate security systems and police departments have unused riot gear, new SUVs and other unnecessary equipment.

The other reaction was religious. The rhizomatic strains of the evangelical Christian right were newly empowered: had the Ten Commandments been posted on school walls, they argued, these shootings would not have happened, Satan is in the public schools and he is winning the battle because "they" (meaning secularists) took God out of them, etc. I recall attending a meeting with the parents of two victims of the Columbine attack at a First Assembly of God in West Lafayette, Indiana and seeing how in one statement the evangelical movement was merging with the militarist movement when a mother exclaimed she was so relieved to see uniformed police in attendance at the event. While this may have been a genuine reaction and reassurance for an individual who had experienced the trauma of losing a child, its *mass reception and applause* was disconcerting. Many of the survivors and parents of victims of school attacks have developed their own ministries and lecture series parlaying trauma and tragedy into political influence and grassroots penetration. Conversion experiences are political capital in these publics, as is witnessing to others about the presence of Christ in one's life. Partners in Prayer is a group that seeks to increase support for praying in public schools, at any time, and witnessing and praying for others who are alienated. It is a subtle way of prying at the separation of church and state because they add "at any time" when praying is not allowed during class periods if it disrupts others' in learning the curriculum.

Newman's conclusion (contrary to Julie's, which was precisely the public itself as the problem) is that school shooters are "failed joiners" without assessing the larger culture of joinerism. Despite the fact that she is critical of adolescent hierarchies of prestige in schools, Newman's prolific interviews capture the text proselytizing one major theme: that school shooters are failed joiners. Certainly one could read her book and find numerous examples of her sympathy for the culture that these failed joiners were immersed in before they took revenge at the school space. However, media presentations have Newman excoriating shooters for failing to fit in. Previously, Julie referred to it as "compliance" following Winnicott's psycho-analytic formulation (Webber, 2003, pp. 143–166). One was forced to be compliant without criticism or suffer social ostracism at school and home and in the American psychiatric community. Now that many areas have evacuated public spaces that are relatively autonomous and self-regulating, we have an even more intense form of compliance de-linked from independent accountable forms. What this means is that while no one tells you have to join there is no longer a public space to visit and experiment with being your individual self in the presence of others, or to engage in dialogue with people who think differently). At this end of cosmopolitanism there is only your "choice" to join a faith-based community. What is so dystopian about it is that there are no alternatives. When the options for joining or creating new forms of association are limited there is not much room for the exercise of free will and conformity becomes the ideal social and political goal. This is exactly what Julie had argued about school shooters who are alienated from the jock culture in public schools that mimics the larger adult culture in the U.S. The public that was only beginning to abandon secularism and public schooling at the end of the 1990s has now completely moved on to joinerism, aided by the Bush Administration's support for faith-based social services, as well as the fear and arrogance that inspired an intense nationalism and insularity following 9-11. We call these citizens joiners in that they do not do so out of critical knowledge of the churches they attend but out of benign acquiescence to the idea that public and governmental forms of community and social service either no longer exist or are politically incorrect. One reason public forms of assistance are deemed politically incorrect is because they feed into and nurture another ideology of social change promoted by the Christian Right: self-help. Known by social scientists for a long time as the critical tactic of semi-progressive groups concerned with the image of racial minorities in American culture, such as the Urban League or NAACP, self-help meant that groups would remain passive about institutional discrimination and attempt to blend in with the mainstream and gain more citizenship rights by presenting themselves as groups that do not rely on the government for financial assistance or formal representation. An ideology of acquiescence, self-help corresponds to one of the basic beliefs of market fundamentalism: that anyone can move up the socio-economic ladder if they work hard enough despite institutional barriers imposed by racism, national identity, sexism or heteronormativity. The federal government's non-response to Hurricane Katrina translated into an overwhelming endorsement for the ideal of self-help: mainstream American media celebrated the fact that citizens would volunteer to help those left behind in New Orleans and elsewhere. Rather than focusing on the government's inadequacies, it was politically correct to volunteer and unpatriotic to expect the government to carry out its duties when natural disaster strikes the republic. There is an effective slippage here too between assistance and association where assistance requires a specific kind of religious association followed by conversion to the belief system of that group: whether in favor of the market or religion. Without a separation between assistance and association, individuals who do not share dominant religious beliefs have no right to public assistance.

A recent study demonstrates the effect of this joinerism on American culture. In the study researchers confirmed what political scientist Robert Putnam has been arguing for a long time, that Americans are losing their sense of civic purpose and ability to form communities. The researchers also found that people are forming less intimate friendships with persons other than a spouse or partner and that this leads them to place enormous importance on that one intimate relationship. How wonderful is this for the Christian Right? What historical institution is most in need of a makeover to capture the style of the economy and polity at the present time? Marriage. James Dobson, head of Focus on the Family and a leading critic of gay and lesbian marriage was pleased to hear of this new societal development and more than happy to weigh in as an expert to counter Putnam's evaluation that this was bad for American democracy. On the contrary, for those on the Christian Right any social change that reinforces the dependency of people in marriage reinforces the centrality of the nuclear family and this family arrangement is considered by them to be the basic foundation of a strong America. This is where the idea that the family has been under attack by secularism comes from because secularism (in their logic) encourages people to go out in public and make new associations, join civic groups and exercise democratic thought. Rather than seeking out social and emotional support outside the family people will now seek it within. As Theweleit argued, under Nazi rule family was held to be the supreme value in German culture even though in practice the family (especially the father) had little real control over the socialization of his children. He further elaborated that family was designated as the place where the "promise of psychic satisfaction" would take place when in reality the family was

> "stripped of the only function that might have lent it human substance as a site of relationships, of communication, of protection; it became an organization for the terror of formal domination. But public denouncements of the family remained prohibited; this was the source of the fascist double-bind. While the state defended the dictum of 'honoring they father and mother' with increasing vehemence, it simultaneously deprived parents utterly of the qualities on which a child's respect might have been founded," (Theweleit, 1989, pp. 252–253).

In many of the Christian Right's political strategies and rhetoric we see this fascist double-bind. For example, parents have the right to home school their children or send them to charter schools and these developments away from compulsory public education delivered by the state's elected boards and officials might at first seem to

THE SECULAR STRATEGIES OF THE CHRISTIAN RIGHT

be organized around increasing parental rights. In fact that is the exact language that proponents of these educational developments have used when they alleged that the public school system's "secularism" undermined their children's religious belief as well as the parent's desired moral and sexual pedagogy. It is the same argument they use as delegates appointed by President Bush to United Nations conferences devoted to children's human rights when they oppose educating children in developing countries about their social and political rights and presume that an empowered child will challenge parental authority (Buss & Herman, 2003). In reality, the child will be challenging sex traffickers, terrorists, militias, union busters, managers and street predators because their parents can't protect them. The bind operates on two levels when the same message is delivered: on an international level, delegates presume that the children in developing countries to which these rights pedagogies are administered have living or empowered parents (a faulty and profoundly arrogant and narcissistic assumption). On a domestic level, (where this strategy is really aimed) it is aimed at making people fearful of public institutions and encourages them to prostrate themselves before the free market because "choice" is a consumer right valued highly by the Christian and political right. However, this free market undermines parental authority by advertising products and popular culture that overturn the child's religious belief and sexual innocence that they value so highly and use as justification for retreat from public education. In sum, it undermines their parental authority and any respect the children might have for their parents and their "values" are undercut by the seductions of the market. Recently at a Jehovah's Witness convention in Bloomington, Illinois audience members listen intently then applauded when school-aged children described the strategies they had used to avoid participating in extra-curricular activities at school.

Rather than resistance to surveillance culture, the diverse religions forming the Christian Right social movement coalesce over the idea that it is forms of publicity that threaten their belief systems rather than the increased policing powers of the state. Where the free market fundamentalism most obviously undercuts the family ideology of the Christian Right by undercutting parental authority is through its effects in the form of declining wages and benefits. If families cannot afford basic services like health care and groceries or are subject to the vagaries of employment fluctuations and inflated consumer prices, they cannot present themselves to their children as independent wage earners (and fathers cannot and do not earn family wages any longer). This makes it obvious to children that real authority lays elsewhere in the market and the corporate board. In this way, authority is really "untaught" as the Rieff quote at the start of this chapter contends. We will return to this notion at the end, but first an analysis of where the Christian Right's emphasis on conformity and identity clashes with its own acquiescence to micro fascism.

Perverse Joiners

The Christian Right ignores the performativity of identity and the contradictions in its totalizing ideology remain on the level of the superstructure. Unknowingly the Christian Right ideology can anticipate a moment of conjuncture when/if the

CHAPTER 3

American political imaginary is forced to confront these contradictions without mediation (i.e. the media does not frame them). The vanguard strategists will have to reconcile the antimonies of choice with the conformist ideology of market fundamentalism and the ways in which their reliance upon stable Christian or moral identities rest upon the state regulation of private behaviors. Furthermore, their own very bourgeois affinities will eventually no longer be worshipped as possibilities for the foot soldiers of the Christian Right. These contradictions are not geographically contained to red or blue states and have the potential to disrupt political certainties across the nation. For example, while Goldberg's analysis of exurban communities relies on the urban space remaining a cosmopolitan bulwark against which these banal spaces are compared, we feel compelled to note that Warner's description of pre-given frameworks and the decline of a self-regulated public is given in the context of his criticism of Mayor Rudy Giuliani's clean up program for New York City, the apotheosis of urbanity in the U.S. Warner describes how in clearing out the sex industry, he also eliminated the safe spaces (and self-regulating) for gay and lesbian community. Similar campaigns have won favor with increasingly heteronymous publics in Las Vegas, Chicago and Detroit. It is only *after* Las Vegas is turned into a safe space for middle-class family vacations that it is simultaneously marketed as the place where "What Happens in Vegas Stays in Vegas." So, the joinerism is not contained to exurban spaces (although it is more stark and unapologetic) it is also infiltrating cities who want to cater to the exurbans who might vacation there. This is the Disneyland-ization of the adult cosmopolitan public space. Or, as Lauren Berlant terms it "infantile citizenship," where adults concede political autonomy and abandon the difficult struggle of real politics for an imagined life free of decision-making and contradiction. What they gain in return is a menu of choices in leisure that will not disrupt their social and moral certainties or dare them to imagine life outside of the family.

To add an even deeper twist to our understanding of the geographic confusion over faith based influence, Judith Halberstam has argued that it is precisely the challenge of subverting or foiling the exurban community that encourages transgender people to live there, "While gender codes may be somewhat more flexible in urban settings, this also means that people become more and more astute in urban contexts at reading gender. In the context of a small town where there are strict codes of normativity, there is also greater potential for subverting the codes surreptitiously," (Halberstam, 2005, p. 44). In an analysis of *Boys Don't Cry*, Halberstam takes issue with most critics who point to the movie's seemingly correct condemnation of rural life for transgender people and instead asserts that Brandon Teena liked having the comfort of the small town and was able to assume a particular rural male role there; that was precisely what he desired, not to move to Chicago and be "out" as a lesbian. Indeed, Teena was transgender in that he did not make the "bourgeois investment in the economy of authenticity," (Halberstam, 2005, p. 70). More specifically, Teena rejected the "protocols and strictures of transsexuality," (Ibid, 54). An important distinction emerges here and demonstrates a contradiction that, while not specific to Christian right ideology, threatens to disrupt the assurances it has over who remains a part of "us" "them," "friend," and "enemy." While they are clear who their enemies are: feminists, gays and lesbians and pro-choice policy and law, how can they tolerate the passing transgender person who actually *likes* the codes of their community? One who is a transgender person but is enacting this performance to be more like them? One who refuses to make a public confession of their sexual identity? Perhaps this person even plays in the band at the mega church every Sunday or is the star of the softball team. In other words, the identity politics of the Christian right depends upon stable identities for their targeted enemies, and as long as urbanites provide them with a *stable set of representations* (and Democrats too) their stereotypes will continue to have enormous influence over the electorate. Brandon Teena is a perverse joiner, not the kind that the fundamentalist movement in the U.S. or the Christian right political ideology is able to imagine as part of their community. Brandon Teena's example, in Halberstam's view, is a positive example of a line of flight that ends tragically. However one may feel about this example, Teena did have the courage to "Live Free or Die" as the New Hampshire license plate reads. Other films have presented such passing in more dogmatic religio-political environments such as the presentation of the Taliban in the film *Osama*. In both films, the directors end with the dire consequences of failing to pass as an alternative identity but what about those ordinary people who successfully pass in small towns all over the United States and elsewhere? They present a challenge to the reproductive logic of cloning and conformity, presenting publics with the idea that identity is malleable, even rhizomatic, for non-fascist purposes.

As S. Sayyid has argued, fundamentalism cannot be defined through identity politics. Fundamentalism cannot be (and should not be) mistaken for having a definite object against which it fights, such as women or a particular vision for women's subjugation or liberation. Indeed, in his study he notes that Islamic fundamentalism has become an allegory for all forms of fundamentalism and that perhaps the practice of veiling women represents the most obvious example of female subjugation, whereas other forms are overlooked or seen as good when represented by the secular state. For example, when the French government bans wearing of the head scarf in public spaces, it becomes easy for liberals or secularists to overlook the fact that the French government is engaged in its primary mode vis-à-vis the population: governmentality. It imposes its own restriction on women's freedom in the name of secularism against this supposed "Islamic fundamentalism" that blindly drove these young women to wear headscarves. There is evidence that they chose to wear it as a sign of resistance against French governmentality, and not necessarily as a sign of submission to a particular form of Islamic patriarchy. It is here in the critical choice, in the space between resisting and submitting that political analysis has failed to capture and represent the autonomy of individuals. Again, resistance to one form of domination does not imply submission to another: this is the game that identity politics wants citizens to play and lose. Kind of like Brandon Teena posing as a stereotypical rural white man: posing as the object that would have her destroyed for being a blight on its own identity, one shown to be very fragile in the last analysis. It is a stable set of identity representations that fundamentalism needs to create its totalitarian system of meaning, where every task is performed efficiently and every person performs their "pre-given" role assigned to them by the perverse combination of capitalist economics and fundamentalist beliefs noted in the introduction: "free market capitalism has become the dominant American ideological truth – a fundamentalism of sorts," (4). But this fundamentalism cannot have its way without a market system that privileges, as argued in the beginning, the role of efficient information delivery over knowledge, the role of stereotype manipulation and its efficacy at distancing and distracting publics from questioning forms of governmentality. It obscures the existence and message of these perverse joiners in an era of joinerism: that identity is malleable and shifting, and it can be transformed into anything but essentialism.

Christian and market fundamentalism in the U.S. may be seen as the new form of "dogmatism" and often obscures the relationship between religion and politics (Sayyid, 2003, p. 15). Unlike the contemporary use of the term fundamentalism, which tends to imply that religion or interpretations of religious texts inform politics, one may see other secular or political groups as dogmatists as well. The famous example of Lincoln is often given in this context, and the best analysis of the sovereign who declares the 'state of exception" to law (Agamben, 1999). Sayyid gives numerous examples of these leaders in the West, in the very countries that preach freedom and democracy to those that might resist their capitalist and militarist impositions, such as Thatcher enjoying the phrase (TINA: There is no alternative) or Agamben's erudite point that when Bush decided to refer to himself as the "Supreme Commander of the U.S. Military" after 9-11, he was revealing to the citizens that executive power would disregard the law (Constitution). Agamben sees this as a trend in the West related to the breakdown in sovereignty and the absorption of legislative power into executive power in "states of emergency":

> This means that the democratic principle of separation of powers has today collapsed, that the executive power has in fact, at least partially, absorbed the legislative power. Parliament is no longer the sovereign legislative body that holds the exclusive power to bind the citizens by means of the law: it is limited to ratifying the decrees issued by the executive power. And it is significant that though this transformation of the constitutional order (which is today underway in varying degrees in Western democracies) is perfectly well know by jurists and politicians; it has *remained unknown by citizens*. At the very moment when it would like to give lessons in democracy to different traditions and cultures, the political culture of the *West does not realize that it has entirely lost its canon* (Agamben, 2005, p. 18, emphasis ours).

As Sayyid points out, "The concept of fundamentalism relies not on its internal coherence but, rather, on a 'shared' assumption regarding the role of politics, truth and religion," (Sayyid, 2000, p. 15). In the U.S., this translates into support for political candidates who share the values of faith-based communities and fundamentalists. They argue that they care less about a political position on a certain issue than whether or not that candidate shares their "faith" and "values," (Egan, 2006, A-1). So, those who privilege religion over politics and values over issues tend to care less about Agamben's mourning for a Western canon; to them the canon was fodder for a culture war against which they lodged a successful campaign during the 1980s and 1990s. The very assumption of a western canon is equal to secularism; political solutions to problems are themselves the result of sovereignty or secular authority that they reject. Rather, this shared assumption about religion is provided by the leader himself. His leadership consists not in overseeing the formation of public policy to address problems but of portraying the kind of moral character they see as valuable to reaffirming their faith. Indeed, for the more millennial-inclined (that is, those who believe that Jesus will return to the earth to save believers and damn the rest) they are "semiotically aroused" by events in the world that demonstrate to them the proof of his return. Hurricane Katrina for them is an example of this, as is the interpretation of the war given by a Kansas group traveling to soldiers' funerals arguing that their deaths are God's punishment for the U.S. population tolerating homosexuality. Any semiotic support that political leaders can offer to them for these apocalyptic events is seen as evidence of the moral character of the nation and that leader is lauded for his ability to embody national "values." Historically, this was the main space for a leader to inhabit while exemplifying the "shared assumption" that is not internally or textually coherent was the Oval Office or the press room; a space from which all Americans could hear a centralized message. Now, however, the role of communications technologies to implode the space of signification allows political leaders to transmit many messages to different groups that demonstrate little integrity on the part of the leader when analyzed together. The bully pulpit has imploded and national humiliation and political theology are effectively communicated with little criticism.

The Bully Pulpit and Executive Order

> "Why do we hear so often in media and academia these fears of religion? I suspect that we're seeing rampant Christophobia, which is far more prevalent than homophobia, although you wouldn't know that from press coverage." (Marvin Olasky, 2003, p. 50).

> All the theories which put conversion "of the eye of the soul' in the place of a conversion of natural and social objects that modifies goods actually experienced, is a retreat and escape from existence- and this retraction into self is, once more, the heart of subjective egoisms. The typical example is perhaps the other-worldliness found in religions whose chief concern is with the salvation of the personal soul. But other-worldliness is found as well in estheticism and in all seclusion within ivory towers," (John Dewey, *The Quest for Certainty*, p. 275).

Olasky, a convert to Christianity is a very important figure in the Christian right movement, and his endorsement of President Bush for his willingness to speak from his "heart" about faith and freedom is telling. Capitalizing on another of the Christian Right's rhetorical successes against forms of public reason, the shift to the heart as the locus of political agency from the head as the logical center where rational thought is formed then acted out by the body in political resistance obliterates all modern understandings of praxis. The heart is irrational but that is its strength and it does not compel the body into action on the material world to challenge or change it, but rather encourages the mind to become flatulent, and release whatever immediate justifications or theories for present problems without editing. Olasky praised Bush for recognizing American diversity and ending the oppression against faith-based groups through his establishment of the Faith-based initiatives, and for using the office of the presidency to do so. He is critical of congress because there are too many moderate republicans and not enough conservative democrats. Finally, Bush did for religious people what Reagan did for conservatives: made them more attractive to the political center. Olasky compares this victory for religious citizens to the potentiality of the Red Socks winning the World Series. This was not all that Bush did to cheer up the flock. Bush abandoned diplomacy and asserted a unilateral and militaristic foreign policy against both Afghanistan and Iraq. But this policy by itself is not what arouses the Christian Right; it is the way it reinscribes American national identity as "righteous."[4] It spares Israel for the end of days and converts American territory and people into a sacred political community. As Bill Callahan has argued, in countries with predominately Anglo-Saxon cultures, such as the U.S. and Britain, asserting temporal sovereignty was often an important part of building nationalism, even if it used shame as a tactic. Callahan finds that special days of memorial are chosen by leaders to form a political community out of theology. As he writes, "National humiliation days, on the other hand, were recurrent events that expressed identity in terms of a political theology that combined the spiritual and the temporal to assert the nation as a sacred political community," (Callahan, 2006, p. 397). Callahan further explains that these holidays were used to shame the identity of the "national self" and that rather than serving to excuse or absolve the domestic population of guilt over possible abuses of the Other/enemy, they cited elements *within* the domestic space as guilty. Certainly, it is clear that the Bush administration avoided courting open hostility toward the Iraqi people by using the Wilsonian rhetoric of making a clear distinction between the "leaders as dictators" and the "people" that U.S. soldiers are rescuing. Thus, for the Christian right the "other" comes from within in the form of anti-gay sentiment and marriage amendments. Other scholars focusing on the Christian Right have noted that there is confusion over where the threats to American identity might emanate from,

> "It is the PR's very inability to 'know' where the danger comes from, inside or outside, that marks an important transition in PR approaches to governmental and international institutions. In the earlier decades of the twentieth century the PR could easily identify trends and individuals in civil society of which it disapproved. 'Bad apples' within state institutions could be rooted out; leading state figures, such as J. Edgar Hoover, wrote regularly in mainstream publications explaining how they were advancing God's plan in government," (Buss & Herman, 2003, p. 33)

Now, however, the idea of the sacred community and its temporal sovereignty is challenged from any number of places. The level of analysis appropriate to understanding Christian Right thinking about foreign policy does not contain itself to one mode rather its effectiveness resides in its ability to find threats everywhere. One possible explanation for the expansion in threat perception is the role of technology in making every conceivable explanation for state or terrorist action available instantaneously and obscuring materialist explanations based on balance of power principles (as happened with interpretations for motives for school shooters who were gay, Goth, nerdy, Nazi, Godless, psychopathic, woman-hating, video game-playing, tearless, drug dealing, gun fanatic porn aficionados who refused to join school cliques all at the same time). Rather than asserting that the inside or national identity of a state is irrelevant for understanding its foreign policy, the Bush administration gave the U.S. a theological and righteous political identity that marks it for increasing hatred by those unfavorably endowed with material resources and occupied by aggressive allies of the U.S., if not the U.S. itself.

Another political use of the executive office focuses on nostalgia and national salvation. Although any number of past mistakes in U.S. foreign policy could be erased by national salvation such as Hiroshima, Vietnam, the Bay of Pigs disaster, etc., the use of the Bully Pulpit by Bush encouraged the population to focus on contemporary "blights" and future "threats" to the core of U.S. national identity, imagined as the "family." In contemporary uses of these shamings, the focus is on specific elements of the U.S. population that are exceptions to this constructed moral image and national salvation, such as gays and lesbians, unionists, activists judges and feminists. Moreover, this kind of power is *not only* a secular form of power, using the law to coerce populations from certain acts or policies but a "political theology" that after 9-11 "produces modernity more generally in the sense that security is an issue that joins the sacred and the secular in the pursuit of national salvation," (Ibid.) It is not a retro-active movement and although the function of national humiliation days is to inscribe the dominant national narrative with the sacredness of the political community, it does not do so in a way that mimics or restores any previous community. This is because, as Halberstam argues quoting Nancy, "the idea of community emerges out of the Christian ritual of communion and expresses the sense that something we once had is now lost – a connection that was once organic and lifegiving that is now moribund and redundant," (Halberstam, 2005, p. 154). Thus, Bush's bully pulpit rhetoric was nostalgic for something that Christianity already marks as dead and mourns through ritual.

This political theology focuses on reforming the identity of the nation by policing those that make up its image through the people and their practices, virtues and sins. Callahan cites Bush's "National Day of Prayer and Reconciliation" on May 1st, 2003 where he encouraged the nation to pray for the Iraq War and soldiers. However, we would argue that one finds examples of shaming and encouragement for those outsiders to the "community" that is contained to the national space in several other forums where the president reaffirmed to his Christian base that he is on their side. One particular example is the State of the Union address in 2006 where Bush's speech read "people who have lost their way, and love" however, Bush read the phrase so it came out as "people who have lost their way in love."

Another example is when Bush bellowed out support for Right to Life activists protesting at the Supreme Court on the anniversary of *Roe v. Wade*. Instead of showing up in person, his voice came out of speakers at the protest site, kind of like the Wizard of Oz. Bush sent video taped speeches of himself to the Southern Baptist Convention where Secretary of State Condoleezza Rice was a keynote speaker. At this event, the Baptist leaders discussed plans to pass a rule to encourage congregants to abandon public schooling (a place of sin) for home schooling.

As Bush and administration officials courted this base, they did so with pusillanimity; unable to step out with a party platform that directly confronts a middle class that is largely undecided about most major issues the Christian right valorizes (federal ban on abortion, school prayer, gay marriage, evolution, the Iraq war, etc.) they promoted this agenda by going to their base in public speeches and through information exchanges (recall the introduction and the insights of Eco and Deleuze and Guattari that these fascist claims are never made openly but are discreetly issued under the noses of silent majorities). The bully pulpit is not the Oval Office or the White House Press briefing room. Those are spaces where the administration attempted to say little or nothing about politics and hold democratic discussion of controversial issues to a minimum. As Sheldon Wolin has argued, most Americans do not mind this scenario as they are as afraid of democracy as they are the state (this is why discussion of limiting "Big Government" plays well to both sides of the political spectrum to woo the middle). Here the "state" is confused with representative government that is separated in powers. The trend has been to move to exclude the Supreme Court and Congress from checking the Executive unwittingly reinforcing the power of the state and undermining democracy (Wolin, 1981). As a youth minister for *See You at the Pole* told me in 2000, "Righteousness exalts a nation," and he further argued that the central place for this righteousness is the bully pulpit (code for presidency). While it was noted earlier that many analysts see the success of the conservative leaders in their ability to mime religious figures in their political strategy, others have teased out the specific form that it takes, that of the "jeremiad," as a "a call to collective repentance, generally accompanied by a warning of divine retribution if the call is not heeded," (Jelen, 2005, p. 308). Seen as a 'rhetorical strategy" used by the Christian right to foster national humiliation and condemnation of certain behaviors (such as feminist organizing or gay sex) this uses biblical scripture to bring down punishment on an entire nation. As was mentioned in the introduction, Jerry Falwell issued a jeremiad against the American people for their tolerance of these errant behaviors targeted by the Christian right, however, this political sin, as well as those committed by the organizers at soldiers' funerals were condemned by Bush as inappropriate (Jelen, 2005, p. 309). Bush admonished his base to court the middle as his ratings continued to slip and one argument for why these jeremiads don't go over well with the public is that the U.S. is so tied to individualism that people refuse collective responsibility for the sins of others, and prefer the protestant idea of an "unmediated individual relationship between Christ and each believer," (Ibid, p. 308). Jelen further argues that American liberalism, with its emphasis on individualism and the free market undermines any attempt for the Christian right to achieve many of its more radical reforms. It remains to be seen whether the biblical literalists or the more individualistic moderate Christianity will hold the center. Another scholar of secularism saw the Christian right's future message as diluted by entry into politics,

> The more that Christian belief comes into play in the political center, the more they are secularized. This is most obvious in the progression of conservative Christianity to the political center in the United States. The closer even every conservative get to congress or the White House, the more they have to substitute the language of compromise and problem solving for the rhetoric of obedience and faith, (Fenn, 2001, p. 162).

This was written before 9/11, but we must remember that Bush was elected before 9-11. And while it looked to be a one-term desperate presidency in the first few months, the events of 9-11 brought many in the middle to rally around the cause of the intervention in Afghanistan, as well as the later argument for the invasion of Iraq to depose Saddam Hussein. The reluctant "indifferent" middle voters came out in support of one of the Christian right's main agendas: a belligerent foreign policy dressed up as missionary work. The missionary aspect is important to national identity because it shores up the "righteousness factor" and dovetails nicely with the shift from thinking with one's head to feeling with the heart. Bush effectively used the bully pulpit of the presidency to bolster support for Christian charity, to enact educational legislation that discriminates against the very form and purpose of public schooling (in the name of the children), limits the teaching of sex education and bans federally funded abortion or contraception and stem cell research. This pulpit was effective because it was not located at a church but in public office, at speeches to private religious groups and in concert with highly calculated media events. Bush's strategy has been to please a minor base of support while not offending an indifferent middle by presenting conservative Christian values as mainstream ones. As we argued in our last book, *Expanding Curriculum Theory*, the main weapon against the average teacher forming a judgment about school politics was and is time; that is, time that is eaten up by work as we move into a piece rate system for compensation throughout the fundamentalist marketplace where solutions to workers with families are really attempts to increase the productivity of workers without formally challenging their rights to rest and leisure time, health care and work compensation. This very same principle animates the market fundamentalism espoused by the Christian Right. In fact, we might even argue that it is a staple of their curriculum for learning how to be an American in the 21st century. We now turn to this curriculum to understand what it avoids teaching in the name of "life" that produces a culture obsessed with apocalypse.

The Curriculum of the Christian Right

> A prerequisite for political work with potential fascists would, I believe, be the acknowledgment of they actually perceive in things they so avidly detest. To say 'yes' it is possible to see us in this way,' rather than 'no, we are quite

different,' is the minimum requirement for rapprochement," (Theweleit, 1989, p. 268).

So far we have outlined several key strategies used by the Christian Right to mimic secular policy and the ways in which they have exploited key features of American national identity – such as individualism and righteousness, even self-help—and replaced their former secular meanings with religious values and ideas about national character mirrored in appropriate behaviors. In this last section our aim is to outline what we are calling the curriculum of the Christian right which is a kind of course for *unlearning* democratic conduct. The first object of criticism for the Christian right is secularism (we discuss their willing jettison of humanism in the next chapter). They may, as William Connolly has argued, have good reason to abandon this concept as it fails to capture the emotional register of politics and life. Indeed, Enlightenment philosophy included an emphasis on the rational and a commitment to curb emotion because it was thought to impair impartial judgment. Public philosophers like John Rawls and Jurgen Habermas argue for the centrality of reasoned discourse or of political arrangements that limit the "bias" of emotion. The Christian right unleashes this unthinking emotion and celebrates it as a new incarnation of diversity. Citing their authority as a conformity to family values or national character, those on the Christian right do not need to reason or think through their ideas. In fact, it is the very *shared assumption* of self-righteousness that validates their claims and this is why secularists do not understand them; they cannot believe that they would refuse to submit their ideas to critical reflection: "For most critics of secularism who recognize the visceral register invoke it to deepen the quest for unity or community in public life, while most secularists who eschew it act as if diversity can be fostered only by leaving the guttural register of being out of public life," (Connolly, 1999, p. 24). Connolly's point is that secularism makes its own self-righteous mistakes as an ideology that believes itself to be without metaphysical support: as objective. He correctly exposes how the deployment of secularism has provided a justified enemy for the Christian right and he believes (I think) that by dispelling the illusion that secularism has no bias or under girding belief system that is totalizing, he will undermine the claims of the Christian right making space for pluralism (Connolly, 2004).

Much like Theweleit's conclusion foregrounding this last section where he argues that conceding certain political points to potential fascists opens a space for a kind of rapprochement where diplomacy or civility is renewed after conflict or war, we can remain skeptical. While we agree with the metaphysical argument; the idea that objectivity is always compromised by the vital lie that it is without metaphysical support, it seems clear that the Christian Right is not waging this political battle at the level of metaphysics but of epistemology. It is 'shock and awe' at the level of critical thought. Willing to manipulate data mined by the Bush administration's Homeland Security authorizations, the Christian Right and the Neocons show no remorse in playing fast and loose with objective facts. How do we know what we know? Also, the Christian right has, as was shown in earlier sections, diluted its message to capture mainstream support. So, in many ways the Christian Right has already taken Theweleit's advice and engaged in rapprochement

78

with secular or non-religious political elements. While the idea that one should concede ideas to potential fascists (which is what Goldberg claims about the Christian Right, and we are calling micro fascist) can buy time for those on the academic Left and independent categorys, what does this accomplish with respect to the middle voter (what Curtis White has described as the "middle mind") for whom the secular strategies of the Christian Right have found support. Religious affiliation or church attendance does not necessarily signify strict identification with fundamentalist interpretations of the Bible but may be thought of as a spirituality that helps people deal with the uncertainty created by globalization and its effects but also the lack of political leadership exhibited by the Bush administration and Congress over the past twelve years. As one social scientist explains: "Much data gathering on religion in the United States fails to account for this key demographic. Sociologists herd Americans into religions and then denominations, but they do not inquire into how our spiritual lives measure out certainty and confusion," (Prothero, 2006). This would be the affective register that Connelly mentioned. It is confusing to live in a culture where the state is the enemy even as evidence of its strength is everywhere in the form of policy to combat "crime" and the ethical delivery of public assistance and association are now left to the individual personalities of privatized firms and services—to the "market that has spoken," as Steven Colbert says.

Democracy is a method for living in common, as is fascism and totalitarianism. The difference between them is that democracy makes a pretense to being open to the future whereas fascism and totalitarianism close down meaning and issue centralized messages so comforting to their fearful citizens that they do not notice the temporal foreclosure of the future. Existing only in an imaginary past (and historically unverified) as informative of how to live each and every detail of the present, totalitarianism and fascism (with its tendency to expel those who do not fit its definitions of life in the past) are political holding patterns in that they cannot function in perpetuity the way their leaders claim. Eventually, the shared assumptions are questioned and the total meaning system breaks down because the repetitive distinctions between "good" and "bad" become boring and people crave spontaneity (Winnicott, 1986, p. 225). Here is an example of the distinctions, what Connolly calls the "ascriptive liabilities" attributed to those deserving of being left behind in apocalyptic times:

> As a crucial corollary, any individual initially marked by one or more of these ascriptive liabilities can become a full-fledged member simply by asserting aggressively the conventional code of the nation: individual responsibility for your own fate, unfettered faith in the capitalist market, belief in a moral god, the readiness to try to obey those who embody the spirit of the nation, commitment to the opportunity society, opposition to the welfare state, support for family values, identification with the military as the ultimate guarantor of the nation, commitment to normal sexuality, and the collection of all these dispositions under the general heading of common sense, (Connolly, 1999, p. 108).

They can become a full-fledged member of this "sacred community" constructed by the Christian Right and the GOP over the last thirty years. However, we might recall that faith, whether it is liberal or secular faith or religious or conservative faith, measures the political effectivity of leadership and democracy at a given time in history. At times when there has been less faith and certainty there has been the overzealous action of the state in the name of protection. There is such a thing as liberal fascism (Kroker & Weinstein, 1993). Public schoolteachers have, in the past, misunderstood the separation of church and state, as well as democratic method. For years we have witnessed critical intellectuals criticizing teaching training programs for reproducing Taylorism, an efficient means of delivering uncritical knowledge and producing fixed identities for students to inhabit as they learn to become future workers. They have punished students for praying in school. This is not the legacy we mean to defend in this text. At its core, the assumption that one has the answer (whether liberal or conservative, Christian or not) to life summed up in a discrete data set of responses is micro fascist. We are tired of reading political and educational texts whose language seemingly promises that "radical democracy" will be the answer to all our prayers (e.g. Giroux; McLaren). As a political theorist, reading these sermons made Julie want to cringe in embarrassment for them; democracy is not easy, fun or the road to salvation. Part of the problem with the Left's political strategizing is that it promised something it could not deliver: freedom from political struggle. The will to mastery is exposed in a basic contradiction at the heart of our educational systems, themselves modeled largely after the Enlightenment (at least in aspiration). Michael Warner's depiction of totalitarianism as "non-kin society organized by bureaucracy and law" could easily describe the public schools so readily defended by Leftists throughout the 80s and 90s. The Christian Right has also attempted (and at times, successfully) to rescript the purpose and meaning of democracy. They argue that feminist activism at the United Nations bypasses democratic consensus (Buss & Herman, 2003). They have also argued that the institution of the presidency does similar undemocratic things when it uses executive orders to lift the ban on federally funded abortion (as Clinton did) but was remarkably silent when Bush used it to reimpose the ban originally conceived and implemented by Reagan known as the "Mexico City Policy," in respond to population control strategies discusses at the UN Convention in 1980.

It is one thing to discuss protestant fundamentalism as a "total meaning system" stressing the role that it plays in citizens' lives by providing an "intratextuality" that conveys the authority of sacred texts to inform individual's lives, but we would argue (with other scholars cited in this text) that the Christian right mimics other national narratives in terms of political form and that the texts themselves have been imploded as much as liberalism or secularism or the Western canon.

The important question is: but what exactly do fundamentalists "get" out of this belief system? As Connolly has argued, secularism's mistakes include among them abandoning a respect for the "visceral register" that informs many political opinions and thoughts about how life should be organized and lived. Righteousness is another "shared attitude" toward politics and religion and following 9-11 the widespread sentiment that Americans were persecuted victims because of the terrorist attacks could merge successfully with the righteousness of the Christian Right to, in the words of Tocqueville "exalt a nation." And, as we have seen previously, the resacralization of the national imaginary was easy to achieve following the model that Christian groups used in local and state politics following school shootings. Another such visceral register that Julie has observed in her research is the way that fundamentalist organizing appeals to many women, even though it leaves progressive feminists and liberals baffled. In ironic ways, many to all of the items on the Christian Rights' domestic policy agenda curb the rights of and overtake not only feminist agendas but women's agendas in their main areas of concern: education, health care and employment policy. These have always been more important to women as they were inordinately affected by them whereas men's agendas (taxes and foreign policy) have remained just that (Burrell, 1994; Lawless, 2003). The policies currently in place undermine women's role in these domestic policy areas and replace them with the importance of the nuclear family. One thing that secularism has been silent about is securing women's enjoyment and one major aspect of this enjoyment has historically been romantic and the presumption that monogamy is expected of relationships. While liberal feminists argue for the protection of women from men, as well as their equality with them as noble pursuits for women that they can enjoy a sense of personal fulfillment through work outside the home, fundamentalists and conservatives on the politically active Christian right seduce women with promises of faithful husbands, monogamy and family values. They argue further that "equality feminism" cannot guarantee the "dignity" of women and that it does not ensure that they are designated a specific "role" in the sexual division of labor. In many ways, parts of this conservative movement imagine restoring the heteronormative imperative that restores for men a *status* and women a *function* in what they view as a culture of death. Secularism is equated with this culture of death and the "culture war" that Ralph Reed and others insist we are in the midst of fighting. Indeed, if we are all the "same" as indicated by formal political rights, they argue, then there is no way to maintain the difference between men and women, therefore, (in a weird twist of logic) same sex relationships become acceptable. As Buss and Herman have argued, the Christian right sees the feminist agenda as the slippery slope toward the "homosexual" one (The curious silence about these desires by secularists and feminists (even ones who argue that an ethic of care should be pursued in American life such as Noddings and Fraser) is a major problem for progressive political organizers. There is no reason why pluralists should not concede that it is perfectly worthwhile to pursue a stable romantic relationship if one desires it. Similarly, there is no reason to suggest that one cannot pursue polyamory and delight in the practice of compersion, which is the enjoyment rather than jealous response to a significant other's sexual pleasure, e.g. to disestablish monogamy (Emens, 2004, p. 79). Clearly, it is time for the progressive left to defend a kind of romantic partnership that is not tied to sexuality because it gives them free reign to promise monogamy as a national value even if it's not required of party leaders on the Right.

CHAPTER 3

As you can see, the next terrain of "secular" culture that the Christian Right is apt to mimic and then attack is the terrain of "rights" itself. If the culture of the U.S. accedes to the vision of the sacred community promoted in national humiliation days, or continues to find public assistance at the local mega church, we will witness more indifference to the increasing number of defensive marriage proposals at state level elections. These referenda are not a test of heterosexual tolerance of gay and lesbian citizens, they are a test of tolerance for the extension of rights to any person that does not fit the definition of "common sense" outlined by William Connolly above. They are a test of democratic knowledge and the willingness to pledge allegiance to authoritarianism relatively unlearned or detected by most of the public. They are also a test of the importance of humanism in American culture and politics in the fundamentalist era and the effect of it on American democracy. To that, we now turn.

CHAPTER FOUR

HUMANISM AND THE AMERICAN POLITICAL IMAGINARY

"Man will learn to face the crises of life in terms of his knowledge of their naturalness and probability. Reasonable and manly attitudes will be fostered by education and supported by custom. We assume that humanism will take the path of social and mental hygiene and discourage sentimental and unreal hopes and wishful thinking.

Eleventh affirmation of the *Humanist Manifesto*, 1933.

To put it in somewhat grandiose terms: Neoconservatism aims to infuse American bourgeois orthodoxy with a new self-conscious intellectual vigor, while dispelling the feverish mélange of gnostic humors that, for more than a century now, has suffused our political beliefs and tended to convert them into political religions. Our intellectuals may feel 'alienated' from the orthodoxy represented by the 'American way of life'; they may feel homeless and hopeless in the world this way of life has created. The American people, in their overwhelming majority, do not feel so alienated, homeless, or hopeless. It is the self-imposed assignment of neoconservatism to explain to the American people why they are right, and to the intellectuals why they are wrong. (Erving Kristol quoted in Williams, 2007, p. 108).

The Posthumanism of the Christocrats and the Neoconservatives

This chapter examines how the Christocrats have been mobilized by a political movement of elites in American politics to consolidate their hold over the American political imaginary; that is, how Americans identify themselves as a nation. Neoconservatism holds up a mirror and tells the American public what it wants to see. Neoconservatism presents itself as the ally of a confused Christian Right in that it does not disagree that there are problems with humanism and secularism but it also does not admit that it does not share the Christian right's backward-looking nostalgic mode of thinking and rejection of modernism. As we have and shall see some more in this chapter, Neoconservatism uses the domestic support of the Christocrats to make war and nationalism a popular rallying cry for its own causes through the rehabilitation of the "bourgeois populism" that Kristol describes above. As we have seen throughout this book, the hostility for "intellectuals" is shared by Christocrats and Neoconservatives; in fact, that and the heroic American nationalism we've witnessed since 9-11, are about the only two things these groups do share. Intellectuals stand for anyone who made or makes rational arguments in favor of humanism or its institutions: education, welfare, progressive penal reform, and juvenile justice—all those "gnostic humors." For both, the market, not the state, will be the arbiter of problems that are not social (which is to say, human) but are the result of character defects. And the market is directed by God for Christocrats and by responses to disaster for the Neoconservatives (Klein, 2007). They are both post-humanist in the sense that they believe that human effort and rationality do not direct the course of events, and are united in their faith in the market. This is a successful marriage where one partner takes while the other looks the other way in faith (and takes too). The Neoconservatives have used their power as elites to end the culture wars by writing the last chapter on terms that are favorable to them *as elites*, detrimental to the entire populace (this is the feudalization of America) and virtually genocidal to anyone who represents or uses critical thought. Kristol is correct that the progressive movement that promotes critical thought and rationality began over 100 years ago and is guilty of its own wishful thinking, and it is these arrogances that the Neoconservative movement has used to manipulate a downtrodden American public into following their retrograde way of thinking.

Thirty men signed the *Manifesto* to demonstrate that the fundamentalist attempt to "appeal to the state to enforce their beliefs by legislation" had "no sympathy." (Wilson, Chapter 13). It was criticized for being too "Unitarian" but the affirmations in it largely represent what has come to be known as "humanism" in the U.S. and these affirmations are rejected by the Christian Right and the Neoconservatives for different reasons. For the CR, it is a humiliating curriculum that makes their belief in Christianity seem small, for the Neoconservative, who pats the CR on the shoulder in a "there, there" fashion it represents the triumph of "self interest" without the unique American egotism attached to it that makes war and corporate profiteering possible without interference. Education looms large in the manifesto as a cause for the wrong thinking of the religious literalist, as well as the *salvation* of humankind. As the reader can see, in form, humanism does not dispense with religion; salvation is retained for education. Transcendence takes place "laterally" as it were, within the space of human existence on earth, not before or after death. Naturally, the debate over humanism has religious overtones. Yet as we move out of modern ideologies into post human ones, the debate over humanism has resurfaced around the political movement of the Christian right and the reactive response of mainstream liberals who are caught in their language traps. Powerless to respond to biblical literalism with anything but slack- jawed wonder, liberals have resorted to normative appeals about the irrationality of the Christian Right. However, were they to examine the religious overtones in their own rhetoric, they may come to see the Christian Right more clearly as a social movement aimed at transforming the organizing metaphors of American existence according to a very narrow civic agenda where to be American means to support war, abhor taxes, abolish abortion and contraception, luxuriate in facile definitions of masculinity and femininity, enforce the death penalty and fear homosexuality. Indeed, the very same categories of issues the fundamentalists have accused liberals of promoting that hinge on a basic concept of self-interest as motivation to act as a citizen or human. We believe the above statement is unfortunate for the cause of progressivism, by which we mean any ideology devoted to producing and welcoming social change and political formulations that encourage it. "Man will learn" sounds reasonable, but what is it exactly that he will learn? This statement has probably done equally enough to cripple curricular and academic freedom as any religious doctrine and it comes to blows more readily with American conceptions of "happiness" to which we all have a universal right, and "freedom" to which we devote all our labors and energies. As John Dewey once said, "Man takes his enjoyment neat, and at as short a distance as possible," (Dewey, 1952, p. 78). As a statement about the human nature of Americans, which some have described as "ludic" or "nihilistic" in its simplicity and indifference to communal or social forms of political life (i.e. its selfishness). It is apparent this arrogance of humanism goes so far as to impugn religious thinking as "dirty"; why else the reference to "social and mental hygiene?" Indeed, humanism, like all *isms* suffers from problems related to ideological modes that no longer cohere to the social realities that shaped them into being (Kishwar, 1990). Unlike Michael Barnett's neo-conservative apology for U.S. belligerency that shines through an argument for mapping danger and finding danger in geographical regions while simultaneously rejecting ideological notions of security that stem from the identities of potentially threatening people, (Elden & Bialasiewicz, 2006, p. 634) humanism can (and has also) been rejected by poststructuralist theories that do not define ideologies as necessarily ontological assumptions, but also about ways of life or the means of constructing a proper "human," "dignified" or "rational" life. What poststructuralists rejected about humanism was not its tendency to reduce conflicts to "us" versus "them" scenarios but something much more substantial about the logic of progressivism that undergirded it, about the unreflective western theories that informed it (all the while claiming a monopoly on reflection), and the contradictions it glossed over. Some of these important contradictions had to do with "rights" and "citizens" — a problem detected by Marx in early criticisms of the state (e.g. Marx *On the Jewish Question*).

Here's the rub: all progressive forms of law and order, education and tolerance have been built around this shaky and arrogant edifice of humanism. From humanitarian international law to basic rights to education, the taint of humanism's attack on religion is evident. Had humanism based itself not on a rejection of religion but on an affirmation of humans with the caveat to freedom of belief, we might not find ourselves trapped in the neoconservative moment. Yet, we do not have a time machine and cannot go back and warn progressives not to enjoy their political victories too much; *ressentiment* is a great force in American politics. And yet it would be hasty to view this as simple regression; there are differences between the religious ideas that humanists responded to in the *Manifesto* and the Christian religiosity that has become so central to many Americans during the era of globalization. The ideology of the Christocracy has been formed by globalization and the Neoconservative rhetoric that shapes the public's responses to policy issues associated with it, such as immigration and the war on terror.

In the last chapter we dealt with secularism, and in this chapter we turn to humanism's role in fundamentalist thought in the United States. We have separated them even though they are usually tied together as objects of ridicule and hatred by the Christian Right, and the principles they uphold even evoke fear in more mainstream evangelicals. Usually, the venom attached to them flows from the hatred for secular values which are seen as a sham and a disgrace because they displace the conversion to Christ and religion with the idea that government and policy should be without religious content. However, we will argue that the more threatening part of this binary is not secularism but humanism because it places human beings in a decision-making capacity that usurps God's role in determining life in the present, and in doing so, interferes with the Christian fundamentalist need to live according to judgment in the afterlife, among other ideas. Humanism, as an ideology that makes man and nature central to understanding the evolution of history and life on earth also displaces or questions God's role in its creation. Hence, our debates about the teaching of evolution in public schools and as were mentioned in the Chapter Two, the final *intellectual*[5] humiliation of the evangelical and fundamentalist churches in the U.S. during the Scopes Trial of 1925. However, given the vast changes in American life since that time it can be argued that the Christian Right does not seek to move backward to a space of the polity that no longer exists, although it does use this assumption to its own political advantage. Instead the CR is a force that is beyond humanism, just as most neoliberals are beyond humanism and into technology viz. social efficiency, so the Christian right is happy to displace the human as the central organizing principle of all social and policy oriented plans and replace it with technology and what Heidegger identified as *techne*, the logic of technical rationality as overshadowing the poetic and accidental nature of events — the unfolding of events according to a natural – if even – accidental forces. Whether this logic is fated or determined as an outcome of probability, the CR shares with its Neoconservative political elites, a profound disillusionment with humanism and the liberalism that provided it with policy sanctuary in modern U.S. institutions. We need to remind our readers that free market fundamentalism is nurtured by its own institutionalized liberalism: the freedom of capital. That 40% of the U.S. population believes in dispensationalism, the notion that events are predetermined by God, and in many cases are evidenced directly in policy outcomes in the Middle East, serves the purposes of these former "vital center liberals" whether successful or not, in many cases, the bad news is good for its synchrony with Biblical rapture. As one scholar of fundamentalism puts it, "postmillennial optimism about the progressive march of history toward a more just and humane society, linked to positive beliefs about modernity, lost ground to premillennial pessimism," (Schaefer, 2004, p. 84). What this means is that even among religious Christianity, progressive future-oriented tones have been eclipsed by nihilistic thinking as well; the very existential mode of nihilism that the Neoconservatives claim that war, character culture and nationalism will eradicate. Unable to reconcile a hopeful Christianity with American political and social realities, many have opted for the endisms associated with pre-determined patterns of thought that cross a wide range of contemporary ideologies about technology, God's grace and vital life.

The Christian right is a posthumanist force in American politics, just as *alienated* from reality and its principles in Enlightenment thought as are the poststructuralist intellectuals or the neoliberal corporate managers. The CR has always been against humanism in its opposition to the arrogance of humanism, but now it has a political environment that agrees with it, at least on this point, if not for the same reasons. The recent revelations of the administrator for faith-based programs bears on this point; charging that President Bush the person is a good Christian who believes in helping the poor, the author nonetheless charges that even the president cannot escape the cynical and hypocritical policies and fundraising tactics of the Neocons within the GOP. Another reason for the abandonment of humanism as an ideology is its inability to produce stability when applied to political and social life. As Nietzsche argued, humans are 'human, all too human" and do not remain the same or carry consistent thought or apply consistent principles in their lives. Why base a political system on such uncertain ground as man or human nature? There is in this the need for an enduring promise that social life remains unchangeable, predictable and knowable. Not that different from the secular need to produce laws that prevent the aleatory events of crime or tragedy through criminology or the scientific study of deviant and violent behavior, this perspective longs for certainty amid the natural condition of change (Dewey, 1929). However, if naturalism and humanism are rejected then there is no longer the problem of inconsistent beliefs and norms. Taking the text (the *Bible, Koran, The Republic*, etc.) as the literal guide to conduct ensures that people and polities will not change dramatically, it is assumed. Also, since the interpretation remains the same, it doesn't matter what changes are wrought in the material world since the response to them never changes. It is, in fact, in one's response to change that we find the eternal return of the same—another citizen who blinks and reads his Bible.

Furthermore, these religious interpretations begin with the presumption that "Christian communities are exempt from the moral and political failures of wider society," (Schweiker, 2003, f.n. 42). Placing the responsibility for norm endurance on moral structures and conduct makes the individual believer responsible for all accidents that may befall him or her (witness the neoconservative Christian response of the president's advisors and appointees to Hurricane Katrina). Several political outcomes result from this rejection of humanism as an epistemological guide for constructing any range of policies from breastfeeding in public to tax breaks for the wealthy and the rejection of federal minimum wage standards. The predominance of this way of thinking (as a political synecdoche, where the minority CR value system comes to stand in for the whole American public's psychic response to news events, and recall from the last chapter how they've learned to present themselves as a persecuted minority with an ethnic-like status) leads to the intended GOP platform goal of *small government*.[5] If government cannot legislate behaviors and morals and only the text can, then they do not need to have a policy agenda for the domestic scene other than dismantling the one built by previous administrations. This is "freedom from" as Maxine Greene pointed out, a freedom from governmental influence and a negative freedom at that. It all makes perfect sense, and is not irrational (as most critics would have it) as it has been made out to be. The fundamentalist rejection of humanism as "lateral transcendence" – human freedom here on earth in the present – is perfectly logical when measured according to its own goals and

CHAPTER 4

objectives, its principles and epistemological concerns, but only where that transcendence parts ways with the politics of this social movement's very specific goals and objectives. Among them, the right to life narrowly understood as the right to personhood and extension of constitutional protection to fetuses. This is an exception to the above "exemption" from the so-called failures of wider society. Here the Christocrats believe their fate is tied to the wider society's tolerance for abortion. The victory against abortion and contraception is not tied to improving the quality of life in the present, nor is it connected to ensuring that fetuses live a good life in the future. It is a precondition for Christian entry into the Kingdom of Heaven; their fate is *linked to common America's moral rectitude* with regard to the right to life. Similarly, the core of American citizenship is linked to birth, an idea borrowed by the Neoconservatives from Hannah Arendt and applied in an entirely different context. Taking Arendt's reverence for American foundation as revolutionary, and her linkage of this foundation to an abstract notion of natality (literally the "new"). This policy only fails to make sense to those who adopt a completely different view. This is why again we must disagree with Connolly (Connolly, 2004) that we can make deep pluralism work; the worldview of a Christian fundamentalism that has been politically supported by a neoconservative political order has no interest in coexisting with other worldviews. In the following sections, we deal with this premise of pluralism while highlighting the Christian fundamentalist worldview on humanism and its role in political life, its rationale for rejecting humanism (which does not differ much from poststructuralism's rejection of it.). In addition, we will highlight the important role of neoconservatism as an ideology that explicitly links domestic politics to foreign policy for the guaranteed political outcomes we have associated with the influence of fundamentalism in the U.S. This will mean explaining the role of the Iraq war in theological terms as well as ideological ones.[6] This is a just and romantic war, according to neoconservative promises made to Christian fundamentalists. Finally, we must highlight again for the reader that the concept of "Middle East" is itself an American creation, as is "democracy" and "freedom" in current usage.

"Because Humanity Repeatedly Fails....."

This part of the Christian Right belief structures merges and enhances the apocalyptic overtones throughout American society, whether secular, indifferent or technologically-minded. Belief in the "end" is not limited to nor is it produced by evangelicals or the militant political wing of fundamentalist Christians on the Right. "Endism" is a properly American ideology that captures religious belief in the "endtimes" as well as technological faith in the end of the human body and perfection of experience through technology. Endism is also endemic in American political thought in that it signifies the end of ideology through the perfection of political form in democracy and capitalism (Fukuyama) or utopianism as that which differs from idealism in its belief in "the harmony and perfectibility of human experience" by which "evil can be rooted out of human experience through social planning" (Boyle, 2004, pp. 95 and 97 respectively). As the model for political development the U.S. also considers itself the ultimate end state of political perfection. Endism is also featured in public and foreign policies whose ultimate goal is to satiate experience once and for all; no where else on earth is policy criticized for failing to produce *eternal* results. This orientation accounts for the repetition in demands for policy and ideas for political institutions; even those on the Left or progressive side of the spectrum cannot imagine a domestic security policy that does not resemble the New Deal programs of the 1930s and stubborn ignorance and belief in the uniqueness of American experience stops their ears against proposals tried in other countries. Citing the continuous waves of immigration throughout the nation's history as proof that everyone else in the world agrees with this assessment, "settled" American's fail to see the immigrant's utilitarian view of American citizenship (see Webber; forthcoming). Instead of viewing immigration as a sign of the success of liberal humanism, specifically as it has been expressed in twentieth century America, or as the virtue of the U.S. as a model country for development, immigrants view it on instrumental terms, as the last space not completely ruined economically by development. As Appadurai has argued,

> They seek opportunities as facts, not opportunity as a norm. Here is the slip, really the chasm, between official or indigenous patriotism and the more pragmatic desire for the good life that many would-be migrants to the United States seek. And here is where the practical pleasure in life in the United States – or the aim to enter it – can be consistent with a deep moral resentment of American polity and the American government as global forces," (Appadurai, 2006, p. 126).

What immigrants feel normatively toward the U.S .is not positive (and it needn't be; it's instrumental) but they see it as the only route to improving the lives of their families since there are no opportunities in their own countries, usually due to failed development policies imposed by one of the U.S. created and sponsored agencies, the World Bank, IMF (International Monetary Fund) or the United Nations. All of these post-WW2 agencies have been created and controlled by the U.S. and while other nation-states have representatives to these institutions studies have shown that policies do not get created unless the U.S. supports them (Foot, MacFarlane & Mastanduno, 2003, pp. 265–272). These institutions are an expression of U.S. political culture in its utopian and religious overtones as missionary like agents doling out relief and the promise of development throughout the twentieth century. The appointment of John Bolton as the U.S. ambassador to the United Nations and Paul Wolfowitz as Chairman of the World Bank reflected the neoconservative transformation of these institutions. Both saw as their mission the quest to transform these institutions according to the utopian vision of capitalism and sought to replicate domestic plans into international frameworks because unlike their foreign policy predecessors, whether realist or idealist, they see no clear dividing line between the two spheres of politics, the domestic and the international. As one scholar of neoconservatism writes,

> Defining itself in opposition to academic abstraction, neoconservatism is able to contrast its claims to those of a distanced foreign policy elite which it

CHAPTER 4

opposes, paradoxically allowing neoconservative foreign policy elites to claim a powerful anti-elitism in political discourse. More broadly, it is able to link the question of foreign policy directly to issues in domestic politics, and to place concerns about social and 'moral' decay within a vision of politics as a whole (Williams, 2005, p. 320).

How Americans *feel* about welfare is identical to how they *think* about international development. Religious beliefs and theologies find correspondence with political ideologies and their institutionalization in policy frameworks. Corresponding belief structures of the New Deal era include a postmillennial optimism as well as religious humanism that captured progressive political projects such as legislation for desegregation and civil rights and the belief in the equality of women and their importance to life in the present and future American polity. It is often forgotten that the origins of almost all progressive movements to take root in the United States were religious pacifists and staunch moralists about prohibition, crime and juvenile delinquency. Often these movements were conservative in nature by hoping to restore a kind of normalcy on citizens (usually immigrants) according to their salvationist worldviews. They generated the tremendous American faith in the righteousness of fighting fascism on the other side of the Atlantic and Pacific Oceans and many have remarked of the close similarity between Woodrow Wilson's religious foreign policy (based in Kantian notions of pacific peace) which is a reductionist version of religious Enlightenment ideals. Others have argued that utopian religious thought pervades American culture:

Like a word transplanted into another language, utopianism has blended into American life to such an extent that it is now almost an unrecognized part of the political vocabulary of the country. Therefore the neoconservatives in the Bush administration can employ this language and reasoning when formulating foreign policy while at no point losing their points of reference with the American people. Precisely, because it is a powerful trace element in America's political-religious tradition, it can be drawn out and emphasized with relatively little notice at relatively little cost, (Boyle, 2004, p. 95).

Often we hear media pundits and editorialists asking why the Christian Right doesn't care for the quality of life or "right to life" of adults or those already born in the United States in their sometimes single-issue politicking on abortion. The revelation in polls that pro-life supporters also favor the death penalty as a crime deterrent and nuclear weapons use as a viable foreign policy option is equally confusing to most moderate or liberal onlookers. However, what they fail to see is that the Christian Right rejects an idea so cherished by most progressives (here I mean people who, whatever their ideological affiliation, see change in the material world, sometimes for better sometimes for worse) that humans are the center of the universe and that promoting their interests above all else should be the primary goal of politics. That each potential human be given a chance at life is where the buck stops for pro-life citizens, the majority of whom fall into the fundamentalist or Catholic religious categories. Their strategy is to extend the rights of personhood to fetuses by amending the constitution. Ultimately, the rights of the unborn will be given the right to "be," because the pro-life movement is "less concerned with the epistemology of life than with the ontology of it," (Black, 2003, p. 315). Further, studies of the right to life movement's visual campaign have concluded that the proliferation of medical obstetric ultrasounds have cast pregnancy (and women's autonomy) completely out of the viewer's conception of the abortion debate. These representations work well with American political and cultural predilections for images:

> The autonomous fetal patient is a product not only of a voyeuristic medical culture and a media-savvy 'pro-life' movement but also of a society saturated with liberal individualist political discourses, according to Pechesky and Hartouni. The fetus represents 'man' in his natural condition; a protocitizen trapped in a state of nature vis-à-vis a pregnant woman. The mass distribution of obstetrical images urges the public to bring this little guy out of the state of nature and into civil society, (Schrage, 2002, p. 67).

Petchesky, by the way, is the abortion scholar to first notice the growing change within the right to life movement in the early 1980s circa Reagan to represent the abortion issue as one of viability and a misunderstanding of how nature works rather than simply an issue of religion, morality or conscience. Once again, using the secular ground of nature, the right to life movement has shifted the general public's perception of the abortion debate to the fetus and away from women's rights or voluntary motherhood. And, seeing the "little guy" as trapped within the woman's body transposes the issue of the state of nature as a punishment for original sin, making pregnancy, quite literally and only, the woman's responsibility. This has interesting implications for the Christian and conservative right-wing's preference for patriarchy and the geopolitical rationales they deploy to characterize it as a *national interest*.

A recent article in *Foreign Policy*, the country's mainstream journal of American strategy and analysis, contains just such an argument where progressives and countercultural radicals who have had fewer children are said to be undermining American national security. Not to worry, according to its author, Longman, the newer generations will adopt more conservative values from the older generation and this will ensure the "return of patriarchy" where patriarchy is imposed from government through the dearth of welfare policies concerning the aged; they will need offspring to take care of them when elderly. Further, the new patriarchy will be a variation of Roman patriarchy where men are cajoled into taking an interest in their children because they (conjugal children) ensure paternity and inheritance and have the potential to confer honor onto their father's name.[6] More children will be born because men will want sons and they'll have as many children as they can until the desired sex is sired (son preference is assumed in his analysis, not interpreted according to culture or other reasoning). Why is population declining? Well, because of abortion which is to the Christian Right's mind the subsequent policy outcome preferred by an entire generation opting out of having children because women have become careerists and men prefer leisurely pursuits and hanging out with other men to women's companionship. To a traditional conservative,

CHAPTER 4

as to a neoconservative or a member of the Christian Right, the point is that gender roles have become unhinged from their "original" (natural, Biblically –ordained) places within the nuclear family structure. It is the family structure, legally enforced through heterosexual marriage and the larger structure of patriarchy that, to their minds, guarantees appropriate sex role conduct for men and women. To them, this is the natural order of society, and any secular humanist interference by the state, is a sign of decadence. They all agree that the symptom of (liberal) secular humanist society is any deviation from a set of gender constructions and norms created by Victorian society where men are flawed (thus the attempt to "save" men from gay re-programming to boot camp) and women who originally flawed them in original sin have — as their mission as *superior moral beings* — the penance of fixing them. If the women fail, it is always because they haven't worked hard enough to overcome the taint of this original sin since having undergone that conflict they should have the moral strength to fix the inherently innocently wayward men of their society. For Longman, the task in mainstream periodicals such as *Foreign Policy*, is to use generic amounts of objective language combined with secular analytic categories, such as population, to guide the uninitiated or moderate thinker onto the Christian right path of righteousness. His entire argument is presented as a concern for lowered population rates in advanced industrializes societies (practically racist), but his veiled concern is normative: blame women for the decline of the "West." Ultimately though, the entire argument rests on the assumption that population is power; that it is the national interest to promote increased child bearing to counter the more populous countries the U.S. and Western Europe will have to compete with in the global economy and in military excursions abroad. This is the new argument of the Christian Right as it attempts to capture liberal humanist and secular rhetoric.

What Longman fails to explain, however, is that the U.S. can barely employ the work force it has today, and at a wage rate so low that, he concedes finally, couples believe they cannot afford children. The population equals power thesis also does not sustain scrutiny when superior technology in warfare and workfare require less labor and therefore workers, and the growing acknowledgement that the environment cannot sustain increased population growth. The quality of these proto-generations lives will be low. The central point is that patriarchy is defined for Longman as fatherhood encouraged by government coercion. Now, there's some social experimentation that is never named as such. It is true that governments have used population as a form of power. The Iraq-Iran war during the 1980s was said to have lasted as long as it did (8 years) because of the large populations both countries could mobilize to confront one another in ground warfare. In this case, population acts as a buffer zone between the actual government and the enemy forces in the absence of extensive territorial bunkers. What most analysts note, however, is that both Iran and Iraq, neither being particularly wealthy or developed politically were using war to decrease population and the drain it caused on government expenditure. Unless the U.S. is poised to fight a ground war with Mexico or Canada to decrease its own population in the future, the whole endeavor seems pointless from a strategic point of view. The implicit argument however, is that women's ultimate role is motherhood, indeed forced motherhood and that abortion itself is the culprit. It is a perfect specimen of the neoconservative attempt to use strategic international thought to accomplish a domestic political victory. Here is a veiled reference to it in Longman's text.

> To be sure, some members of the rising generation may reject their parents' values, as always happens. But when they look around for fellow secularists and counterculturalists with whom to make common cause, they will find that most of their would be fellow travelers were quite literally never born," (Longman, 2006, p. 65).

So, human life is valued as long as it is allowed to "be" but that being is not associated with the good life of the individual but is hailed forth to act as a centerpiece of foreign policy. It's as if the neoconservative movement anticipated the moral need for more troops in Iraq to accomplish a domestic policy objective for their Christian right base, all the while knowing they were outsourcing most of the war to contractors who could circumnavigate international law and the rules of war to accomplish some of the most outrageous war profiteering in the history of the human race. Trading on the popular, but unfounded belief, that population rates are responsible for the lack of troops deployed to Iraq and Afghanistan and the military failures in those spaces, however, it has been argued that theses problems could easily be rectified by a political solution of a sensible draft policy or higher pay for those already enlisted in the war on terror (Jervis, 2005, p. 356). The right to life does not ensure a long life (unless you're suffering on life support) but is the current government's way of ensuring that life will be used for *biopolitical* purposes. Similarly, the coincidence of right to life with death penalty fans can only be explained through a biopolitical lens. As Agamben puts it "the life that may be killed but not sacrificed" is precisely that of the soldier, the prisoner, the detainee. To the Christian Right, people who benefit from secular humanist society (when they break its laws) deserve to die because they've broken God's laws, not because they've broken real ones. Recently, federal authorities have requested the ban on medical testing on prisoners be revoked (Urbina, 2006, p. A-1). Thus, the human life on earth is only valuable to the extent that it serves the purposes of the government, who, in turn, serve corporate interests. Neoconservative foreign policy parts ways with traditional conservatism in that it doesn't seek to restore a past form of moral and political order but instead seeks to resurrect important American political symbols and notions of virtue to counteract the negative effects of liberal modernity: its rationalism and tendency to promote nihilism in individuals and institutions. Neoconservatism, unlike conservatism, accepts the "political logic" of the modern era as "progressive and forward-looking" but views it within the context of nationalism (Williams, 2005, p. 317). This is an important distinction as it does not rely on past greatness or the blood and soil nationalism so often associated with twentieth century fascism, but is founded on a nationalism of character bounded by morality and religion. American nationalism, child of the Enlightenment, is a natal form of nationalism, whose political form rests less on

CHAPTER 4

ties to land or ideas about racial and ethnic purity than on birth itself, the very condition of American citizenship.

Life or Quality of Life: Natal Fascism?

> "For the task of politics is not, as in earlier times, to provide a safe home for human life in the house of nature and nature's law but to provide a safe home for nature in a human house built of human law,"
>
> Jonathan Schell, "A Politics of Natality" p. 467.
>
> "This impulse to resolve the ambivalence of good and evil and jump over one's shadow into absolute positivity is a utopia,"
>
> (Baudrillard, 2005, p. 51).

The Christian Right pro-life stance has been to seek federal protection for the unborn through constitutional amendment. Alongside theses efforts are unmentioned grassroots organizing to limit abortion providers (only 15% of U.S. counties have abortion services), ban certain methods of abortion, force a decision about rationale and intention for the procedure, and censor public education about contraception, proscribe its distribution by pharmacists and through the increasing policing functions of the FDA (Federal Drug Administration), allowing insurance providers to continue to limit women's rights and access by refusing to cover birth control, abortion, only providing paid leave for pregnancy as sick leave, limiting clinical trials for medical testing to men only[7]. Recently, the CDC (Centers for Diseases Control) has issued a statement, endorsed by several prominent physicians and medial associations, that all women between the ages of 13 and 55 should consider themselves "pre-pregnant." This means they should be regularly taking folic acid, maintain ideal body weight, and refrain from cigarettes and alcohol and begin exercising (Payne, 2006). New films feature plots with women in the "West" suffering from an infertility crisis, and tabloids are rife with news of every celebrity's new baby, overemphasis on the role of motherhood in child development and sensational stories about the 'bad' mothers who kill their babies. American culture is obsessed with fertility and fetal life at present. We argue that it may even rival imperial motherhood in the late nineteenth century where white upper class women were encouraged to populate America as a maternal duty at the same time an aggressive U.S. military was annexing territories from Spain to take on "the White Man's Burden" as requested by Kipling. At that time a similar debate was popular in the country as to the "free love" movement which basically meant only a wife's right to refuse sex and choose the spacing of her children with her husband on a reasonable principle (Gordon, 1973). Now, the debate is whether or not a woman has the right to abort a fetus in the event of pregnancy (marriage is not really an issue here except where moral panics erupt) and whether or not she has the right of access to affordable, safe, reliable birth control options. Indeed, as Caryl Rivers has argued, "The attack on women's reproductive rights was one of the most undercovered stories of 2003-4, with not only abortion but contraception under attack. The FDA reversed its own expert panel to deny women over-the-counter access to emergency contraception," (Rivers, 2007, p. 11).

Roe left the main issue of abortion at the doorstep of viability; that is to decide when "life" begins. At each branch of the government, activists who oppose abortion are represented through specific judicial decisions and legislation, the first of which is the executive order imposed by President Bush on the funding of abortion or information about birth control on the thirtieth anniversary of the Supreme Court's *Roe* decision. Many intellectuals calling for a pragmatic approach to abortion debates see the two main parties exploiting the issue for electoral purposes, with the Republicans courting a hostile, unyielding pro-life side and the Democrats refusing to budge on the liberal feminist and established pro-choice lobby groups who view *Roe* as the issue in the abortion debate (Schrag, 2003). Evangelicals and other formerly religious groups disconnected from civic concerns and devoted to social gospel rather than political activism were drug out of the closet in the early 1970s not only by presidents who had begun to make abortion part of its legislation (Reagan's "Mexico City policy) but by Christian publications and radio commentators who urged them to take up politics here, "What changed was not just a matter of resources. Rather, a philosophical argument among evangelicalism's elites began to be won by those who wished to re-evaluate and criticize their tradition's sectarian inheritance. Ignoring opportunities to participate in the public arena (including the legal arena) was not longer seen as a virtue but as an abdication of Christian duty," (Hoover & Den Dulk, 2004, p. 25). For the activist then, not heeding the call to fight "evil" is falling down in one's duty, and evil is conceptualized much differently from the humanist version, which sees evil as misfortune (Baudrillard, 2005, p. 153). Instead, evil for the early activists such as LaHaye and Falwell, is attributed to people not to events or objects.

"Evil' people, on the other hand, are perceived as acting differently. Every evil that happens is perceived as the result of deliberate human agency; all effects of acts by 'enemies' are seen as intentional. The direct implication of the separation between good and evil is that it implies different concepts of the nature of persons and their motives. The primary virtue of 'good' people is sincerity, but 'good' people are susceptible to persuasion and easily misled by 'evil' ones. For this reason, the individual consciences of 'good people' are less important than the fact that they intend to do well," (Pearce et al., 1987, p. 179).

Like other issues that are the product of progressive political ascent (and with them the Democratic party) such as school desegregation, Title IX and VII legislation, and the defeat of the ERA, we have witnessed backsliding on the part of the population leading many prominent legal scholars to argue that perhaps these issues were forced on a reluctant (but slowly coming around) public through judicial action rather than democratic consent (Bell, 2005; Sunstein, 1997). Their arguments highlight a crucial debate is U.S. politics that is posed by the Christian Right through their activism and power. The Christian Right is indifferent to the *course* of humanity having already deciphered its *fate* in the Bible. This indifference to

CHAPTER 4

the quality of life of humans in the here and now and future generations is reflected in the many apocalyptic hues of their rhetoric and belief structure. As a social and political force pushing modernity forward the Christian Right can also be seen not as anti-human or pre-modern traditionalists (for whom time is said to stand still) but as posthuman. If we see the contemporary era has posthuman, we can begin to understand the futility of human rights campaigns whose language falls on deaf ears, when it does not outrage and offend those pushing their political agendas forward through particular religious interpretations, from Wahhabism to postmillennial Protestantism. One can begin to wonder whether or not the stalling tactics of liberals like Sunstein, who argue that in bypassing democratic consensus his comrades turned certain political issues into targets for right-wing attack, are not simply apologies for the electorate's indifference over the past thirty years (Baudrillard's "silent majorities") or a really strong case of *bad conscience*. In the case of the ERA (which failed) we would argue that we have a relevant comparison. When mainstream women's rights groups attempted to get the ERA (Equal Rights Amendment) passed (the text was written immediately after the 19th Amendment granting women the right to vote in 1920) for over 62 years, working through the democratic process by passing it in both houses of Congress then working through grass roots organizing to get the majority of states to ratify it, all it seemed to take was a well-oiled anti-feminist moral panic machine run by Phyllis Schlafly with a few extreme arguments about women in the military and sharing public restrooms to kill it in Illinois. Some have argued that women's groups slowed their organization and did not correctly anticipate backlash at the last minute (Berry, 1988). However, if we look to African American rights and constitutional protection we can see that the 14th and 15th Amendments have not encouraged the autonomy of African American citizens or empowered them to overcome many obstacles. While arguing that democratic consensus forges lasting political allegiance to enforcement of rights for women and minorities make good democratic sense, it does not make good political sense when faced with the strong arm tactics of the Christian Right. They don't see the Constitution as their limit, and neither has George Bush, so why do secular humanists continue to offer them the benefit of the doubt?

One way that pro-life activists have captivated audiences is by miming contemporary forms of advertising that sexualize women and by shifting the focus from the female form to the fetal one. Schrage has pointed out that the ubiquity of "disconnected fetal shots" in pro-life advertisements is pornographic in that they dehumanize the woman who is blotted out to show the fetus.

> "In these images, mass-produced by conservative Christian 'pro-life' groups, follow closely the conventions of traditional pornography, which [Annie] Sprinkle is also challenging when she defends he use of porn. Feminist critics of pornography have pointed out that porn tends to reduce sex to penetration and male orgasm –and reduce women to their sexed body parts. In a similar way, the free-floating fetus motif conflates reproduction with the fetal body and its transformations, implicitly treating women's bodies as insignificant and replaceable containers," (Schrage, 2002, p. 83).

Here we see the posthumanism of the Christian Right where women's bodies become "containers" for the central focus on the fetus. While the CR rejects cloning and the use of stem cells for biomedical research, it does not reject the use of advanced technologies to aid in human contraception and reproduction, including in vitro fertilization techniques. Humanism has been defined in many ways depending on the political project it serves or the developmental paradigm it supports. Since humanism promotes an ideology of positive change that can be observed in individuals who act in accordance with rationality over time, it works well with modern economic theories such as capitalism that stresses individual actors in the marketplace projecting their interests when buying and selling. It doesn't work so well with structural theories like Marxism, arguably humanism's largest critic to date. Other modern theories such as realism, have started with the Christian premise that humans are irrevocably flawed while they roam the earth as punishment for original sin, therefore, you will never see an individual act rationally for long before the sins of pride (Machiavelli) or vanity (Hobbes) poke through the artifice of reason. However, many of the modern realists tended not to view women in the way that the Christian right does; they were content to help men make their careers and proceed through the halls of power in Europe and the United States through their terrible ahistorical and uncritical Biblical analogies, but they never attacked women directly. This was because they kept the domestic and the international separate in politics and in political analysis; they had the luxury of doing so before globalization. The Neoconservatives keep them close together to effect one of the greatest institutional assaults in U.S. history, all while they corner the global markets.

One particular outcome of this way of thinking about human nature is that it justifies almost any construction of motive for conflict and aggression. Rather than seeing warfare as restricted by laws, Neoconservatives have "borrowed" the realist maxim that humans cannot overcome their condition of original sin and will always revert to barbarism; they have a cyclical conception of human history (the realists) and the Neoconservatives have traded on it to placate their Christian base because the pessimism that has always been a staple of realist foreign policy (think Kissinger here) is so close to endism in its political sentimentality that they can get away with using it in their rhetoric to conduct war abroad that serves their modernist capitalist desires, while placating their Christocratic base on the home front. This works well when the evil is explicitly delineated in presidential rhetoric as terrorists, leaders of foreign countries and unconverted citizens abroad (noncapitalist, non-Christian) and those who represent causes associated with cultural decadence at home (secular humanists, liberals). The two forms of evil are tied together in Neoconservative rhetoric because it relies so heavily on nationalist thinking about power: if we are weak and decadent at home how can we be strong enough to fight the evil enemy abroad? The effectivity of this logic is shown by the horrific protests staged by a Kansas family who oppose homosexuality by assaulting mourners at soldier funerals with the claim that U.S. soldiers die in war because of Americans' collective tolerance for the decadent evil of homosexuality. Another way that this logic consolidates the domestic and international is through the justification for torture and detention at Guantanamo Bay and elsewhere: if the

CHAPTER 4

other is so evil and barbarous, we Americans are justified in our inhumane treatment of them because they have already crossed a line in our collective imagination that says that nothing short of conversion will save them and whatever must be done to force it is justified by religious war.

In using this powerful rhetoric, the Neoconservative elites have, over the last decades of the culture wars, earned enormous amounts of political capital they have used to shape the public into pliable and Christocratic-friendly base they need to further their narrow international agenda. One central tool in the culture wars has been to exploit emotional backlash against progressive movements such as civil rights, and feminism. As Connell explains, backlash movements have not succeeded in completely reversing progressive political gains, but they have evoked a national conversation about "crisis" that enables them to back reform efforts that transform how the recipients of these progressive movements can *use* their rights. As he writes,

> Explicit backlash movements also exist but have not generally had a great deal of influence. Men mobilizing as men to oppose women tend to be seen as cranks or fanatics. They constantly exaggerate women's power. And by defining men's interests in opposition to women's, they get into cultural difficulties, since they have to violate the main tenet of modern patriarchal ideology – the idea that 'opposites attract' and that men's and women's needs, interests, and choices are complementary, (Connell, 2005, p. 1815).

Connell's point is that one – among many – interpretations for heteronormative attraction are exploited to benefit of the far right. Unable to take on feminism directly and argue for its reversal to an imagined patriarchy, the Christocrats have used the rhetoric of reform to discuss how to reshape women's roles within the larger society to benefit men. Thus, if women do not self-actualize into the caring and subservient roles laid out for them by the cherry-picked and loose Biblical interpretations of the Christocrats, they are choosing to be evil and any misfortunes they suffer are really their own fault and it is not the responsibility of "big" government to fix them. The reform rhetoric that follows backlash is where the political capital is accumulated; the backlash simply succeeds in making it known that a "crisis" is on the horizon (e.g. of the nuclear family, read women and gays; of boys, read masculinity and aggressive nationalism). Perhaps one reason the men's movement has waned since it crested in the 1990s is because of the overwhelming success of the media in limiting women's *visibility* and *autonomy* in American politics (Faludi, 2007, pp. 1–45). In other words, there is no longer any male anxiety about women's roles for fringe groups to exploit because the visible signs of female empowerment have been eclipsed by the Neoconservative ascendancy. Instead, women are urged to compliment men, even if the men are not able to be breadwinners (Gutterman & Regan, 2007). Now women should follow the lead of celebrity women and desire to stay home (Julia Roberts) or they are inundated with faulty social science research that argues women are "opting out" of careers to be stay-at-home moms. Momism has morphed into an ideology where women can voice political concerns so long as they disavow that they are citizens or professionals and still maintain a public voice.

James Dobson's Eharmony has shifted the narrative to fit this criticism in its commercials; where the original philosophy was to find one's "soul mate" who shared identical traits (hence the famous MeHarmony cloning skit on *Saturday Night Live* demonstrating the narcissism of this philosophy of attraction) they have now begun to focus on couples who are opposites and "compliment" one another. The Catholic Church is explicit about the issue of complimentarity when it limits women's human rights through doctrine and encyclicals to that effect. Bypassing the debate about equality altogether the Catholic Church asserts that men and women are different – equal only in "dignity" – and this difference accounts for separate gender roles and duties. Another line of reasoning asserts that women are already equal. Overlooking the fact that women still make 77 cents for every male dollar (and 12% of that spread is determined by sexism itself, studies have shown, not the wage assigned to certain tasks as John Stoessel would have us believe) and to re-iterate have no constitutional recognition as equal American citizens, neoconservative women's groups, such as the Independent Women's Forum (IWF) and Concerned Women for America (CWA) argue for a "sensible middle" for feminist goals (Spindel, 2003). This middle ground is deceptive if we consider how the ideological ground for women's rights has shifted to the far right. While many would claim that the "new right" has sought to take America back to some pre-progressive past, we would argue that they take advantage of progressive thought and discourse to produce change that is much different from past imaginings. They imagine a future where homosexuality is in the closet, women blame feminism for the miseries caused by their inequity and themselves for masculine unhappiness. America's only form of day care, public schooling, is now a privatized endeavor available to those who are wealthy enough to pay someone to tutor and look after their children, possibly the newly unemployed intellectuals? This production of modernity is often overlooked in most critical analysis of the role of the Christian right in American politics and it is politically expedient for the right to have its critics believe it wants to return to some past form of gender relating when humanism did not exist and the Bible dictated all of our conduct. It may be necessary to jettison humanism but that doesn't mean an abandonment of politics or humane treatment. It means there is a desperate need for imagination, for people who see the present political context for what it is and how it will change and begin to propose new ways of ensuring that people are not left behind in a post-secularist, posthumanist U.S.A.

Producing Modernity

Against claims that fundamentalists nurture a nostalgia for an imaginary past and seek to restore it with conservative policy agendas, a few insightful commentators have urged that it should be thought of as producing modernity; a new hybrid form of epistemology that rests less on rationality and objectivity and more on emotion and methods of producing and sustaining political sentiments rather than positions

CHAPTER 4

on issues as related to individual self-interest. Key to this understanding has been to view the Christian Right and its political representatives, which form a cross cutting cleavage across religious denominations and political affiliations as being against secularism and humanism while promoting their varied interests at the grassroots level as they pertain to these larger political and cultural issues. Central to consolidating their electoral victories every four years is a "uniter issue." For Bush, the one that works best is the very same one that's worked for all eternity: the central problem of evil in the world as viewed by the pessimist. Unlike liberal humanist versions of evil, for these political supporters evil comes from an extra-worldly source and is *not produced in the world but for the world, as a challenge to the good*, and in extreme cases, the Godly. This produces the now pervasive notion of testing; of faith, of democracy, of military prowess, of masculinity. Hence the Bush administration's preferred use of school metaphors in political rhetoric, "America will never seek a permission slip to defend the security of our country," (quoted in Jervis, 2005, p. 358)[7]. Trading on the image of the evil principal or school counselor as the United Nations or world opinion, Bush cashed in politically for the sake of the good which Baudrillard has outlined as operating according to a planetary logic that encapsulates all the symbolic strains of Tran signification.

The logic of testing corresponds to two main approaches handy while shepherding the flock of domestic public opinion and support, pastoral power and pastoral governance (Young, 2003 and Callahan, 2006, respectively). As a policy-oriented shift in affect and style, it trades on the American public feelings of inferiority toward the continent of Europe with its democratic history and comparative advantage in elite culture (more on this below). England is an important ally in that it symbolically approves of American simplicity and common sense. Recall that "Man takes his enjoyment neat." No words were ever more correctly spoken about American political culture and the neoconservatives have tapped this sentiment in a new fashion: whereas Clinton represented it and was a mirror to the American public and found himself an object of a love/hate projection by the American electorate (Rubenstein, 2008, p. 18), Bush became/performed a parody of the public itself knowing irony will be mistaken for sincerity, a much more effective way of drawing the electorate into his rhetoric without the fear that they will examine the process. Clinton reflected American common sense and its flaws with an ongoing attempt at self-improvement; in a word, he was human. Bush adopted the rhetoric of common sense and transforms it into a wholly new discourse of self-congratulation for apathy; he was a puppet. This produces a new concept of modernity when combined with ideas and policy choices of the Christian Right that is interested in the future as a continuation of a contested past. All institutions revered by Christian Right politicians, such as the family (Santorum's newest book mimes Hillary Clinton's earlier attempt to shift childcare policy, *It Takes a Family*) become the primary modes of ensuring the future, as is the War on Terror which seeks to protect such institutions from harm afar. Similarly, marriage must be protected for future generations as is the sanctity of religious belief that is considered to be "under attack" from public education and universities.

The pastoral form is incorporated into governance and surveillance strategies, where the authorities provide guidance as they incarcerate individuals for increasingly minor infractions, such as drug use and newly designated "illicit" commerce, in addition to the new layer of criminal activities added by Homeland Security surveillance. Echoing a late Foucault, Callahan asserts that pastoral governance, rather than being replaced with secular forms of governmentality in the seventeenth century, was supplemented by the tension between the sacred and the secular in both Britain and the U.S. and produced the nation as a sacred political community. This tension acted out simultaneously between agents of the state and agents of the church exemplifies Foucault's pastoral power, according to Callahan, to reinscribe that "the task of the art of government is to establish *continuity* between different spaces of activity," (Callahan, 2006, p. 400, emphasis ours). As we saw in the last chapter, Goldberg's analysis of the rise of mega churches throughout the United States shows how they take on functions that in earlier eras were regarded as the state's prerogatives, and how the specific form of these churches, as spaces of conversion to Christ (rather than institutions serving communities established by birth and identity (e.g. Catholic, Jewish, Muslim). Conversion, Callahan argues, works well with the concept of national humiliation as a ritual that forges the sacred political community because it trades on the idea of humiliation of the individual person as an event that incites self-examination and improvement, rather than the contemporary understanding of "hurting someone's pride" (Ibid. p. 400). He even asserts that a singular event such as the national humiliation day can provide widespread conversion in the span of twenty-four hours and that temporal modes of territorial states differ significantly from the transcendental world order of religion yet continues to "overlap" (Ibid, p. 397). National sin becomes an opportunity for national salvation through conversion and self-examination. Juridical powers conjoin with local centers of meaning-making and conversion (e.g. mega churches and their national curricula) to establish the continuity of the practice of national identity making that is constituted through the triad sin-humiliation-conversion. What is lost in the transformation of self to new member of the sacred political community is the earlier notion of the human individual that takes responsibility for what are considered self-contained acts (e.g. not provoked by circumstances or relationships) instead the new community member is absolved for taking responsibility by placing Christ at the center above all others; an Old Testament God, a jealous one. This is where Callahan's examination of national humiliation days in the past parts ways with contemporary pastoral power that is also formed by the threat/risk of the Other and the forms of security that come into play to protect the sacred community. Individuals are only responsible to Christ, (and converting others) whereas the centralized forms of government will take on the responsibility for anticipating threats from others (certainly not from natural disasters, which are of course, God's will) who are jealous of our "freedom." Supporting a muscular foreign policy such as the war on terror, which anticipates further threats to the security of the sacred political community, is the logical choice for those who have converted to the community of Christ and nation now bound together inextricably in a missionary foreign policy that perceives itself to be asserting the "good" against "evil," and a

CHAPTER 4

domestic policy structure that continuously forges the community in the private space of religious activity. People now beat addiction by converting to Christ rather than undergoing to the process of rationalizing behavior through steps designed to separate them from the object of seduction—yet they still call it therapy. The hierarchy of power is transformed along gender lines as well. As protectors, men are designated a new role as the leaders of domestic spaces to protect to the reproducers of the good (women) and the future (children) (Tickner, 2002; Young, 2003).[8] Central to making this community at the domestic level has been to view women as having been cast out of their privileged role as moral exemplars for children and men, and neoconservatism and religious interpretations restore that role assigning women a new pride of place in the sacred political community. These are the arguments of groups such as Concerned Women for America, the Eagle Forum and Ann Coulter. As for the new role of men as leaders, it conveniently comes on the heels of the "masculinity crisis" and the "boy crisis" of the late 1990s as a solution to the lack of prestige awarded to them and disproportionately and undeservedly heaped on women who "humiliated" them by doing their own thing under humanist and human rights interpretations of women's equality (Webber forthcoming).[8] Thus, humanism is responsible for alienating women from their true role in society and this in turn alienated men from their role as leaders and protectors. Despite the fact that humanism and liberalism have both been forms of political thought relatively impervious to feminist critique, they are feminized by an even more robust conception of manly measure by neoconservative thought, which stresses not only restoring the traditional notion of family with a male headed household and polity but also transforming that relationship into a permanent state of patriarchy more on line with the "regime of the brother" than with Oedipus (MacCannell 1990).

The "good" now attached to the seemingly eternal feminine is mobilized at the domestic space for biopolitical purposes, as well as the corporate sector for efficient workers (Momen, 2004). In this new modernity, women are the best workers because they are constructed as being morally superior to men and attend work at higher rates, are thought to have bodies ideal for piece rate work and can more easily be controlled by corporate managers (Ngai, 2005; Sassen, 2002). Yet, as Baudrillard has argued the good cannot proceed without producing an analytic form of evil; hence no morality or religiosity can abolish this bind. "If there is nihilism, then, it is not a nihilism of value, but a nihilism of form. It is to speak of the world in its dual, reversible form," (Baudrillard, 2005, p. 162). Where we were earlier concerned about the neoconservative insistence that the problem of politics is to reverse the social decadence and nihilism that is produced by liberalism, we must remember that they still confess to operating in a logic of modernity that is progressive and interested in transforming the future through the good, through visions of freedom tied to democracy and happiness, this is no different in form from the liberalism that seeks to promote happiness through individualism and self-interest. What neoconservatism has done to transform this progressive narrative is to make the good dependent upon the feminine, instead of a denatured concept of the human, and to make being the essence of existence, rather than exchange value. For Baudrillard then, we cannot extinguish evil, whether we are neoliberals or neoconservatives:

> What we need, then, is an irrevocable presence of evil, an evil from which there is no possible redemption, an irrevocable discrimination, a perpetual duality of Heaven and Hell, and even, in a sense, a predestination of evil, for there can be no destiny without some predestination.
>
> There is nothing immoral in this. According to the rules of the game, there is nothing immoral in some losing and others winning, or even in everyone losing. What would be immoral would be for everyone to win. This is the contemporary ideal of our democracy: that all should be saved. But that is possible only at the cost of a perpetual inflation and upping of the stakes," (Baudrillard, 2005, p. 148).

At the international level, men are reinscribed as protectors of American values abroad and of women and children there too, especially when these peculiar male tyrannies form in weak states and harbor the terrorist organizations whom one would think were the only men on the planet that are hostile to women. This Orientalism has always existed in European colonialism and American imperialism where as Spivak has noted "white men are saving brown women from brown men," (Spivak, 1987, p. 296). The evil produced in this march of good moral exemplars in the form of women is exploited by commercial parties (witness the increasing number of commercials and ads that adumbrate a virile, unthinking masculinity, that can be easily transferred to women through consumer objects: the burger that turns women into farting men with their hand down their pants, the miniature men at Burger King who promise to 'manage your meat" and the zoo keepers who entice men from their enclosures to eat Dairy Queen cheeseburgers). Susan Faludi describes this situation as our "terror dream" where as a response to 9-11 the population blamed women's liberation for "feminizing our men and leaving the nation vulnerable to attack," (Faludi, 2007, p. 23). Clearly, there is a polarizing anxiety about sexual and gender identity in the U.S. that is exploited by the Christocrats for their own causes. In particular, there is a very negative and regressive production of masculinity taking place in the contemporary scene that works well with social science analysis that predicts the end of biological men's contribution to society, and puts them up for public scrutiny as examples of scorn or fear. But, don't' worry: the Christian right has a plan to save them, and it involves women and the *Bible*. And yet, all this religious thinking and control is not about repression, it's about production.

Commentators have tried to place this neoconservative foreign policy within the framework of realism but it fails if we recall the political strategies of the Christian Right and the neoconservatives over the past two decades: to advance a radical agenda through the language of the status quo, or what they call "bourgeois populism." Using human rights rhetoric to establish the sanctity of life for the fetus is no different than using the language of realism to promote neoconservative foreign policy. Whereas some take the architects of the war on terror at their word that they are realists (Nuruzzaman, 2006, p. 249), we argue that this declaration is simply designed to put the public and other potential critics at ease, especially since

CHAPTER 4

realists came out as the main critics of the Iraq war, and even Henry Kissinger has parted ways with the administration's decision to intervene, and come around to agree with the Iraq Study Group, and the outcome is tragic (Klein, 2007, p. 376). A cursory explanation of the fundamental differences of opinion between realists and neoconservatives can shed valuable light on the neoconservative critique of humanism and secularism that is guiding the present inquiry. Further, it can explain why this foreign policy approach is so satisfying to the security concerns of the Christian Right. Any realist, whether structural, traditional, defensive or offensive views the balance of power as a central analytic tool for understanding conflict between states. Since the present conflict is between a non-state actor and a large imperial state, the parameters are somewhat different; however, a realist analysis would see the particular problem of terrorism as a regional issue involving the balance of power in the Middle East, not a problem of isolated states, weak states or rogue states. While these latter concepts may come into play in the analysis, since they form the discursive terrain of international policy following the Cold War, a realist does not pass normative judgment on any of them and sees each agent as a potential balancer in any conflict situation. Many early realists concerned with the U.S. invasion of Afghanistan, saw in the language of neoconservative policy-makers a confusion between the language of grand strategy (where a state attempts to supplant its vision of the world on the rest) and strategic balancing (the prudent statecraft of offensive realists). Thus, Henry Kissinger a traditional realist saw promoting the balance as more important than the judging the human rights abuses of individual states the U.S. might form temporary alliances with to alleviate full scale conflict. Central to realist thought is its impartial mode of inquiry; realism analyzes adversarial paradigms and attempts to subvert them, it does not participate in them as a partial actor. Neoconservative foreign policy begins with the assumption of an adversary that cannot be deterred by any traditional means coupled with a self-righteous hostility claiming they must "go alone." They are therefore anticipated as a threat to the security of the state (U.S.) because they act as the hostile target, leading the adversary their way to fight the heroic good fight. This is not "human, all too human" nor is it the objective "scientific" realism of Morgenthau; it is closer to the partisan Christian realism of Niebuhr.

Pragmatism and Anti-Intellectualism

Neoconservatives, as well as evangelical activists, have come to view American institutions as dominated by the logic of humanism and rationalism with debilitating effects on American character and virtue. For them, rationalism itself expunges any motivation for action other than selfishness, which leads to decadence, and finally, nihilism. Drawing upon the progressive logical form of the contemporary period, they seek to inject these virtues into the domestic scene of politics by forming a missionary foreign policy. As Williams has argued, they draw upon American tradition and founding as inspiration for contemporary action designed to transform the future, as a means of producing the form of modernity they desire. As was argued earlier, seeing no difference whatsoever between the foreign policy agenda and the domestic policy agenda, neoconservative elites benefit from an alliance with evangelicals against liberal humanists, the most obvious targets being in the universities. These groups would agree with our critique of the university as a bureaucratic neoliberal institution (as argued in the introduction) but for different reasons. For evangelicals and other Christian Right denominations, the war against the university is a war over the ideas and purpose of human life, as well as the funding of religious forms of education, a battle they have been slowly winning through legislation and policy in the form of tax breaks, vouchers, and the curtailment of academic freedom. For the neoconservatives, this it is a convenient way to silence foreign policy elites and discredit their analysis of the war in Iraq and Afghanistan in addition to other mistakes. Aware of the dearth of political, historical and strategic knowledge of the professional media the neoconservatives can control their messages to the public more effectively about strategic maneuvers.[9] By keeping the public mired in discussions about whether or not Kofi Annan is anti-Semitic for comments about UN peacekeepers bombed by Israeli Defense Forces, the U.S. media forecloses more important and objective questioning about the balance of power in the entire region, a question immediately relevant to traditional foreign policy analysis. This is a marked departure from historically American foreign policy views and it has gone relatively unnoticed by the public, no doubt due to the rhetorical strategies deployed by neoconservatives but also by the amplification by the media of the Christian Right's endorsement of it.

To accomplish this, Neoconservatives use language games to convey their messages. The main forms of belief transmission and argumentation: anecdote and aphorism (Pearce et al., 1987, p. 180). As a rejection of scientific observation, aphorism corresponds to unformulated comfort "truths" that reinscribe traditional gender relating, as mentioned above in the commercials for burgers. Hollywood and advertising have capitalized on these forms of representation and consumption producing less dramatic form featuring women as lead role, and commercializing on essentialized gender identities that naturally exclude queer representations. Trading on what Halberstam calls "reproductive time" the aphorisms produced by and for the Christian Right are aimed at reinscribing the traditional notions of family and kinship as heteronormative, an assumption that has been subject to scrutiny (Butler, 1999). They become therapeutic by helping "alleviate the burdens of modern life" by replacing them with naturalized interpretations of behavior ("that's the way men are" "women are biologically determined"). A corresponding romantic world-view is supplied by an overarching and simple portrait of a world that is believed to be no different from the past (except for those instances of evil that must be resisted). Several commentators note the repeated theme that rural areas are "idyllic" and provide protection from larger urban areas (Darbeyshire, 2002; Shaefer, 2004; Goldberg, 2006). Aphorisms also reassure their audience that things do not change in their rhetorical insistence on timeless truths about troubling social contradictions and complexities. Twinning aphorism with anecdote (the revelation of personal experience or even witness) works well in American political culture where there is resistance to intellectual arguments about complex social events or rights. Only when Americans can experience a social idea can they confirm it whereas

CHAPTER 4

in other political traditions the notion of going outside one's realm of experience to formulate rights or universal truths is championed as valuable.

The resistance to the idea of social change and human agency was replicated in Bush's neoconservative foreign policy approach where there is no conception of a type of governance or economy beyond democracy and capitalism; they are the end state that is sought through the international "conversion" experience and the Middle East is the ground for this bounded experiment (Boyle, 2004, p. 98). Boyle further notes that there is virtually no foreign policy toward Latin America as it has already been converted; Hugo Chavez represents one of these instances of evil or a testing of Latin America's faith. The belief that market fundamentalism lays the groundwork for peace on earth is perhaps most ardently found in America's neighbors. This romance extends to military affairs where neoconservative military ideals include a view of campaigns as heroic endeavors with elites claiming fame and praise for military exploits. As some scholars of romantic warfare have argued most military conquests by imperial powers were not waged for strategic purposes but for acclaim. Those who would argue that the U.S. invaded Iraq for oil or money interpret it as a political and economic calculation on the part of the administration but others have persuasively argued that the U.S. did not need access to Iraqi oil (Mearsheimer and Walt, 2003) and still others have confirmed that the U.S. "interests' in the Middle East do not correspond to liberal ideas about rational interests nor to realist imperatives of national interests (Williams, 2005). Instead the national interest in synonymous with domestic politics and in this case the romance of war enhances the romance of the nuclear family unit by creating uncertainty at war that heightens the perceptions and realities of uncertainty in domestic life.

> The crucial point is that Christians today, just as at the beginning of the twentieth century, cannot allow the dominant thought of the nation to be controlled by ideas that are alien to Christianity. In the pluralistic setting we find ourselves in today, we are on the verge of gaining wide recognition that it is inconsistent for mainstream cultural leaders to claim that the best intellectual life must be uniform in its commitment to exclusively naturalistic views of things. On similar grounds we should also challenge the other widespread assumption of both modern and postmodern thought – the assumption that humans are the creators of their own reality. For such challenges to be made, however, Christian communities will have to build first-rate intellectual centers where Christian scholars can work on such issues, (Marsden, 2003, p. 63).

The institutionalization begins; always a hallmark of social movement strategy to ensure the longevity of one's beliefs and goals. Central to disrupting the predominant narratives about apocalypse and also responding the to the Christian rejection of modern and postmodern thought, both important for understanding contemporary reality, is the need to demonstrate how tying one's fate to a militant political group's ideas about salvation forces an entire society to give up on its larger contribution and legacy to humankind for a short term political project that serves very narrow corporate interests. And, while it may be worthwhile to give up the worship of all things too human, it is also wise to place the critique of humanist ideology in a context that produces a tension to push history forward cautiously rather than a polarizing binary that collapses into an apocalyptic form that motivates both sides of the spectrum to widen, to the right and left. It seems that what the indifferent middle or silent majorities would like to hear is that there's a plan for the future rather than endism of all varieties, including environmental.

However, it seems unclear that given its anti-intellectual past and current forms, evangelicals and Christian Right politicians-as-preachers will find it difficult to sustain their message and create viable intellectual institutions without relying on the very conformity they criticized in humanist forms of public schooling. Indeed, the Christian Right has already adopted most of its mainstream philosophical interpretations from the Catholic Church, specifically those encyclicals penned by Pope John Paul II with respect to abortion and complimentarity; the most important ones restricting women's freedoms (*The Gospel of Life* 1995, *On Social Concerns* 1985). Although Catholics form a major coalition with protestant Christian churches at the United Nations as well as domestically over such issues as abortion, cloning and women's rights, they do not share its position on war or the death penalty, and many Christian right Protestants certainly would part ways with the Catholic Church's main (anti-capitalist) organizing trope: the meek shall inherit the earth. Perhaps they do agree; they see the meek (as those not saved) as burning in fires on earth while they are to be "raptured" (teleported to another place) and saved from the ill-fated planet's destruction. In this way, they share something significant with technological idealists who also view the end of humanism as a positive development: they see the limitations of humans as a hindrance to the opening of an even larger milieu navigated by technological vision. As Wendy Brown has argued, the religious beliefs that accompany neoconservatism act as a fertilizer for the neoliberal value system that underpins the entire American ideological spectrum (with the exception of some traditional conservatives) to hollow out democracy. Indeed, Brown argues that the reason Americans are left with such a narrow conception of civility and democratic practice is due to the convergence of these two value systems that overlap leaving little in the form of democratic practice (Brown, 2005).

Beyond Flesh

Humanism is a critical ideology about how humans can overcome their defects and vulnerabilities, why else would the authors of the *Manifesto* mention "hygiene?" Humanism has its origins in Western orientalist thought; from its inception it has designated zones of protection and privilege for those labeled human and misery or non-existence for those outside its self-definition. This is the essence of identity politics. We can understand why many people raised on secular humanism might be reluctant to let it go, but the institutions that protected it and nourished it are now on the verge of extinction. It is time to re-think a progressive politics through new vistas, perhaps even re-thinking them through religion. There is no official rulebook for any religion that says that women cannot go to work or that people cannot love whomever they like as religions are human-made systems of meaning that prescribe conduct. They can be altered and they have been altered. Like any other system of meaning they are challenged by language and by the social changes that engender new ways of thinking about life in the here and now. Mostly this will mean moving beyond conceptions of politics that begin with the primacy of the flesh and begin to think about how to use technological idealism to empower the meek to speak truth to power in religious America[10].

CHAPTER FIVE

THE LAND OF A THOUSAND CHURCHES

Part I: The Ex-Confederacy and the Resurrection of the South

In the weeks after the 2004 presidential election, a redrawn map of North America circulated on the internet, prompting wry amusement along the northern rim of states that had opposed George W. Bush. The various Canadian provinces, joined by the regions that had voted for John Kerry, were renam0ed the United States of Canada. To the south, the pro-Bush states congregated in another geopolitical entity: Jesusland (Phillips, 2006, p. 133).

The South had turned out to be not America's insular kingdom of the eccentric, forlorn, or exotic, but a place that had managed to maintain its identity while putting its fingerprints on almost every aspect of the nation's soul from race, to politics, to culture, to values (Applebome, 1996, p. 22).

In the twentieth century, with the SBC becoming the largest Protestant denomination in the United States, it became increasingly apparent that the white southerners had lost the war but won the peace (Harvey, 1997, p. 3).

As these quotations demonstrate there is a perception among Southerners, certainly, and the rest of the country that the South is a place and the rest of the United States, north, east, and west are simply directions. Before exploring and mapping the interconnections between the civic gospel, right–wing ideology and the South, it is important to define the political geography of the South. The map of the South as a cultural region would include the states of: Virginia, West Virginia, Kentucky, Tennessee, North Carolina, South Carolina, Georgia, Florida, Alabama, Mississippi, Louisiana, Missouri, Southern Oklahoma, and Texas. This cultural region has as its base the original eleven states of the Confederate States of America (Alabama, Arkansas, Florida, Georgia, Louisiana, Mississippi, North Carolina, South Carolina, Tennessee, Texas and Virginia). Interestingly enough if you overlay a map of the states in which the Southern Baptist Convention (SBC) is the strongest dominant Protestant Church, the map almost perfectly coincides with the exception of West Virginia, in which the SBC is one of the top four religious denominations (Phillips, 2006). The Southern Baptist Convention has also been called the Church of the Southern Cultural Memory (Phillips, 2006, p. 156). The South is the most churched region in the country with the rate of churches at 15.4 per 10,000 residents. So, the conceptions of Southern cultural memory, Christocratic religion and politics are explored in this section of the chapter. First we can explore how the South is personally experienced.

Bill was raised in Rochester, New York the son of a father that worked in a white collar office position at Taylor Instrument Company for forty years and a mother who worked off and on as a factory-line worker for various companies. Rochester, New York is a fairly conservative/Republican area. Monroe County where Rochester is placed, however, voted democratic in 2000 and 2004. In the November 2000 election, Monroe County narrowly supported Al Gore. Countywide, 141,266 people voted for Bush and 161,743 voted for Gore. Nader received 11,520 votes. According to unofficial vote totals for 2004, Bush received 158,856 votes and John Kerry received 166,355 votes. Rochester and its suburbs, despite the fact of narrow democratic victories in the past two Presidential elections, is a place where the major industry, Kodak has never had a unionized workforce. So, while being a very ethnically diverse area it is fairly conservative. Bill received all of his education in the Rochester area. While at the University of Rochester, during the early 1980s he was immersed in the study of the literatures of the reconceptualization of curriculum (Pinar et al., 1995), as well as Marxism, phenomenology, and post-structuralism. After graduating with a degree in Curriculum Theory from The University of Rochester and versed in these perspectives he went to teach at various institutions in the Midwest. He taught at the University of Wisconsin-Stout (Menomonie, Wisconsin), Oklahoma State University (Stillwater, Oklahoma) and Purdue University (Lafayette, Indiana). He found the Midwest, particularly Indiana much as Julie did. The climate and the psychic feelings were both cold. These Midwest places were predominately white, intellectually stifling and hopelessly conservative. In fact The Southern Poverty Law Center has confirmed the existence of twelve hate groups in Wisconsin, sixteen hate groups in Oklahoma and sixteen hate groups in Indiana. Interestingly enough, one hate group that appears in all the states is a Neo-Confederate group, the League of the South. In the League of the South's Core belief statements we find this reference to a Christian Nation agenda (Southern Poverty Law Center, 2006).

> The South still reveres the tenets of our historic Christian faith and acknowledges its supremacy over man-made laws and opinions; that our Christian faith provides the surest means of securing the welfare of all mankind; and that our primary allegiance is to the Lord Jesus Christ and His Holy Church (Vindice & Hill, p. 5).

This hate group's beliefs can combine Christian faith and racial bigotry which will be discussed later in the chapter. At this point the interesting phenomenon is that these confederate hate groups exist in states that either played a small part in the confederacy or actually fought against the confederacy. The fact is that traces of the South are felt across the United States and not just with extremist groups such as the League of the South. This notion is one of the main theses of this chapter. The South is a dominant force in American culture and politics. It may be that the actual conflict as continuously denoted by the mass media as red state and blue state conflict could actually be a conflict of blue and gray.

Bill moved next to Southeast Georgia to the town of Statesboro. A town made famous by the Allman Brother's Band song Statesboro Blues.

> I woke up this morning, I had them Statesboro blues,
>
> I woke up this morning, had them Statesboro blues.

Well, I looked over in the corner, and grandpa seemed to have them too (McTell, 1991).

Statesboro, Georgia manifests interesting and many times infuriating contradictions. There is still a downtown with the white domed county courthouse and the requisite statue to honor the Confederate dead. There was a small skirmish outside Statesboro with Sherman's army as it marched to Savannah about 50 miles away. But, of course, this was part of the larger lost cause. Statesboro has both a Statue to the Confederate dead and observes a Confederate Memorial Day. The Confederate Memorial Day is observed on April 26 in Alabama, Florida, Georgia, and Mississippi; on May 10 in North Carolina and South Carolina; on May 30 in Virginia; and on June 3 in Kentucky, Louisiana, and Tennessee. These memorial days are extremely important in maintaining the lost cause sentiments. Cash discusses this lost cause romanticism.

> Ironically, post-Civil War Southern nationalism was at least as powerfully felt, as that of the Confederacy. In the fashion of Poland and Bohemia, the former Confederate states nurtured feelings of resentment and mourning. They staged "Lost Cause" commemorations and parades of decrepit veterans; many old Rebels were elected to office (Wyatt-Brown in Cash, p. xviii).

David Goldfield discusses these statues in his book, *Still Fighting the Civil War: The American South and Southern History* (2002).

> The metaphors white southerners marshaled to re-create their past explicitly depicted their struggle as a religious movement. The war assumed a sacred quality, its heroes were martyrs and even its outcome reflected God's grace. Pastor's preached, 'He loveth who He chastiseth,' and congregations brandish this message into their souls. The generic portraits of Confederate soldiers, wan and doomed, that graced white southern homes in the decades after the war resembled Jesus in gray. As medieval townspeople erected statues to the saints, white southerners built monuments to their southern heroes. By 1900 scarcely a southern town existed without a statue or memorial to the Confederate soldiers as a permanent reminder of the heroic conflict (Goldfield, 2002, p. 29).

This connection between the religious and the War of Northern Aggression still waifs through the pines in southern Georgia and the rest of the south. After arriving in Georgia the first question asked was, "What church do you attend?" and then not receiving an answer after several months the question morphed into, "Have you found a church yet?" The questions first were experienced with shock and then annoyance. Bill figured out that since no one was sitting on the massive front porches that surround many southern homes old and new that everyone must be at church or at a Sons of Confederate Veterans meeting.

Most infuriating is the overt racial divide that is encountered in the south. One can drive through towns in the south and still witness almost exclusively economically depressed black areas, black gasoline stations, black grocery stores, and the like. It is not just in the division of labor, but in the everyday places of commerce and living as well. And it is outgrowth of the larger fear of what we described as not necessarily of the latte drinking liberals but of people of color in general. There is the constant controversy of the Confederate battle flag on courthouses and state flags. There are football teams named the rebels whose band marches out in gray uniforms flying the confederate battle flag. There are town festivals where small confederate flags are handed out to the parade watchers. This is in addition to Dixie Outfitters, who produce Southern Pride t-shirts and The CSAnet the E-Voice of the Olde South (a website that sells books, tapes and other nostalgic artifacts of the South). In addition there is the organization, Sons of Confederate Veterans and its sister organization Daughters of the Confederacy. It is interesting to read the introductory paragraph of their website.

> The citizen-soldiers who fought for the Confederacy personified the best qualities of America. The preservation of liberty and freedom was the motivating factor in the South's decision to fight the Second American Revolution. The tenacity with which Confederate soldiers fought underscored their belief in the rights guaranteed by the Constitution. These attributes are the underpinning of our democratic society and represent the foundation on which this nation was built. (http://www.scv.org/index.php).

Again we see that the issue of slavery is not the reason for war. This Civil War according to this page and others was about states' rights. A search of the website for information concerning slavery results in finding information on how there were Blacks who fought for the confederacy and the notion that it was Lincoln that brought the whole issue of slavery into the war. This is yet another example of the romanticizing of the "southern cause."

This romantic nostalgia becomes much more evident when the political shift is toward the radical right in America. John Ashcroft of Missouri was Attorney General of the United States 2001–2005 and Gale Norton of Colorad was Secretary of the Interior from 2001–2006. Both of these Bush Cabinet members praised the ex-confederacy despite its association with slavery. Ashcroft had this to say to *The Southern Partisan* magazine, which thinks of itself as part of the neo confederate movement described above. This magazine also issues a Scalawag Award in each issue to politicians who support politically correct actions (a Scalawag was a Southern white who joined the Republican Party in the ex-Confederate South during Reconstruction). Ashcroft thought it was important to defend "southern patriots" like Jefferson Davis and Robert E Lee.

> Traditionalists must do more. I've got to do more. We've all got to speak up in this respect, or else we'll be taught that these people were giving their lives, subscribing their sacred fortunes and their honor to some perverted agenda (Kettle, 2001, p. 1)

Apparently slavery was not a perverted agenda. In 1996 Norton's defense of the confederacy came when she was told a conservative group in Denver.

> "We lost too much when the south was defeated in the civil war of 1861-5. We certainly had bad facts in that case where we were defending state sovereignty by defending slavery," Norton told the Independence Institute. "But we lost too much. We lost the idea that the states were to stand against

the federal government having too much power over our lives (Kettle, 2001, p. 1).

This blends well with the Republican emphasis on states' rights. Most Black Americans and many White Americans as well would see praise for the confederacy as support for slavery. The hope, of course, is that praise and nostalgia for the confederacy was being replaced by concerns for equity and justice in terms of race. But that is not the case. In their book *Divided by Faith and the Problem of Race in America* (2001) by Emerson and Smith, religion and race are discussed. Their notion is that a Christocratic agenda in actuality supports the maintenance of the status quo, particularly when it comes to issues of racial inequality (the addition of Christocrats is ours).

> Racial inequality challenges their [Christocrats] world understanding, and it challenges their faith in God and America. And insofar as it does, it is capable of arousing impassioned responses, for they are now dealing not just in mundane policy matters, but with issues of cosmic significance. To these respondents, race especially the black race, is one of America's thorns in the side. If only blacks would 'catch the vision' change their habits, stop trying to shift blame and apply themselves responsibly – in short, act more Christian, as they define it – racial inequality would be a memory (Emerson and Smith 2001, p. 103).

The idea is that the lack of progress for blacks pivots on notions of individual responsibility. As we demonstrate in the next section, two key points in the Republican agenda are the importance of individual responsibility in solving social problems (self-help) and the suspicion of federal-management of governmental programs like welfare.

We are discussing the South and the ways in which its ideas have permeated the nation's identity. In all of the discussion with the white southern Christocratic Republican agenda there is no complicated conversation of slavery, segregation and violence associated with the South. The picture that is painted is that of the lost cause and the martyrs of the southern army and its almost God-like generals. The current notions of the South, on the part of the Christocratic/Republicans, are reminiscent of the Civil War paintings of Mort Kunstle. Always in the mist is Robert E. Lee riding Traveler the confederate battle flag gently flowing in the slight breeze – heroic nobility. It is Jesus with a gray uniform and beard riding on a gray horse. When the South becomes Republican and the country is southern, the issues of race are not discussed (even openly avoided) and lie for the most part just below the surface except in times when they emerge or explode because of a national scandal or disaster like the Rodney King event, the Jena 6, the lyrics of Hip Hop or Hurricane Katrina. And, as we will discuss, racial policy more than any other reason accounted for the shift in the south to the Republican Party. Racial policy and the policy towards homosexuals remains a key factor in the southernization of America. These policies help to maintain the so-called red state, blue state divide.

CHAPTER 5

The South Becomes Republican

How did the South become Republican and eventually exert its finger print on the rest of America? To understand that we have to look at the administrations of past Democratic Presidents and how they lost the South. Perhaps, the preeminent reason for the turn to a Republican South and the white voter exodus is race and the ways in which various Democratic Presidents have dealt with issues of race. Truman who desegregated the military caused the 1948 revolt of the Dixiecrats. "The party sprang into existence on July 17, 1948 when it held its national convention in Birmingham, Alabama. It was the formal expression of a growing sectional and civil rights revolt against the national Democratic Party. Dixiecrats organized in response to President Harry S. Truman's proposed 1948 civil rights package, understood by many whites as the greatest threatened federal intrusion into the South since Reconstruction. The package consisted of four primary pieces of legislation: abolition of the poll tax, a federal anti-lynching law, desegregation legislation, and a permanent Federal Employment Practices Committee (FEPC) to prevent racial discrimination in jobs funded by federal dollars" (Alabama Department of Archives and History, p. 1). South Carolina Governor J. Strom Thurmond and Mississippi Governor J. Fielding Wright were nominated, respectively, for president and vice-president in the 1948 election.

There was also dissatisfaction with Truman's handling of the Korean War. This unease with bungled war management would continue into Johnson's handling of the War in Vietnam, Carter's bungled rescue attempt of 53 American hostages in Iran and Clinton's anti-Vietnam stance, his attitudes towards gays in the military and his "wag the dog" war to divert attention from his sexual liaisons.

However, it was Lyndon Banes Johnson, more than any other democratic president who alienated the South. A southerner himself he proposed the most sweeping civil rights legislation that the country had seen. He signed the Civil Rights Act of 1964 and the Voting Rights Act of 1965. This, of course, magnified Southern reaction to the Democratic Party. Johnson was aware that this would, no doubt, deliver the South into Republican hands for a long time to come. But, dissatisfaction with Democrats continued. "Jimmy Carter, himself from Georgia and a born-again Southern Baptist managed to irritate even his fellow Southern Baptists with his various positions" (Phillips, 2006, p. 180). William Jefferson Clinton managed to breed vehement hatred and solidified the cultural and moral disenchantment with the Democratic Party.

> The Democrats crowning problem lay in the deepening mismatch with the cultural and religious viewpoints of their erstwhile bastion, the white South. When the Democratic administrations were in office, Washington was as much at odds with the southern white majority as the carpetbaggers of old, which helps to explain the resentments unleashed (Phillips, 2006, p. 180).

The Republican Party with its perceived agenda of anti-integration, ingrained individualism, suspicion of government, Christian values and resentment of taxes remained appealing to the majority of southern white voters.

The voting records of southern states in the 1992, 1996, 2000 and 2004 is an indication of the shift of the South to the Republican Party and how the South was crucial to the determination of the politics of the country. In 1992 the Bush/Quayle ticket took the states of Virginia, North Carolina, South Carolina, Alabama, Mississippi, Florida and Texas. In 1996 Virginia, North Carolina, South Carolina, Georgia, Alabama, Mississippi, and Texas all were in the Dole/Kemp corner. The Bush/Cheney ticket captured Alabama, Arkansas, Florida (not without a prolonged debacle), Georgia, Louisiana, Mississippi, North Carolina, South Carolina, Tennessee, Texas and Virginia. Finally in the 2004 election the reelection of Bush/Cheney was assured by carrying all the same states again. So by the 2004 election the solid South was solidly Republican and secured the Republican hold on the White House and the nation.

> Southerners – in alliance with pro-business conservatives and the religious right (intersecting but not identical categories, of course) – have, since 1968, shifted the American nation sharply to the right. The South lost the War but won the peace. The American nation lost; the nation has 'gone South' (Pinar, 2004, p. 235).

Not only has the Nation gone South and Republican, but the Republican Party has become America's first religious party.

> By the second administration of George W. Bush, the Republican Party in the United States was on the road to new incarnation as an ecumenical religious party claiming loyalties from hard-shell Baptists [SBC] and Mormons, as well as Eastern Rite Catholics and Hasidic Jews. Secular liberalism was becoming the common enemy (Phillips, 2006, p. 182).

In *The Rise of Baptist Republicanism* (2000) Oran Smith details the historical development of the ties among the South, the SBC and the Republican Party. In fact Smith makes the claim that, "the terms (SBC conservative leadership and the conservative bloc [Republican]) are interchangeable" (p. 207). This SBC is the historical outgrowth and development of the Moral Majority of Jerry Falwell, the one time SBC member and now Pentecostal Pat Robertson and the separatist fundamentalist Bob Jones. All of these we would classify as early Christocrats. Certainly not all SBC members are Christocrats with a civic gospel agenda, but many Christocrats are SBC members. The Christocrats and the Republican Party are indistinguishable. Smith helps us to further distinguish the Christocrats. He is discussing fundamentalists here but it is possible to substitute the word Christocrats.

> Fundamentalists [Christocrats] are much more Baptist dominated, much more participatory, and more likely to translate their religious conservatism into political conservatism than are evangelicals (Smith, 2000, p. 101).

So, the nation has gone south, gone Republican and gone Southern Baptist.

CHAPTER 5

The Christocrats, the Southern Baptist Convention and the South

> One of the biggest changes in politics in my lifetime is that the delusional is no longer marginal (Moyers, 2005, p. 1).
>
> ...the last two presidential elections mark the transition of the GOP into the first religious party in U.S. history (Phillips, 2006, p. vii).

The focus of this book has been the inextricable link between Christian-Right religion and Neo-Conservative politics in the United States. The strongest link remains the South. If we analyze the connections and examples of the role of religion in this phenomenon, we must look to the Southern Baptist Convention (SBC) or the "Church of The Southern Cultural Memory" (Phillips, 2006, p. 156).

Since its organization in 1845 in Augusta, Georgia, the Southern Baptist Convention (SBC) has grown to over 16 million members who worship in more than 42,000 churches in the United States. Southern Baptists sponsor about 5,000 home missionaries serving the United States, Canada, Guam and the Caribbean, as well as sponsoring more than 5,000 foreign missionaries in 153 nations of the world (SBC website, p. 1).

The SBC is the fastest growing Protestant denomination in the country and the preeminent Church in the South. Its president is Dr. Frank S. Page, a mega church pastor from Taylors, South Carolina. According to a seventy-one page report issued by the Mission Board entitled, *Comparison of Changes in Population, Southern Baptist Churches and Resident Members by Region and State 1990–2000*, SBC churches increased in number by 9.2 % in the period. 80% of the churches and 70% of the net gain were in the South. But California, Maryland and Pennsylvania were in the top 15 states both in numeric and percentage growth in churches. The largest number of churches remained in the South as did the most increase. As mentioned earlier the South has the distinction of the having the most churches per capita and they seem largely to be SBC. The largest number of SBC churches as of 2000 are in Texas, 4,973; North Carolina, 3,717; Georgia 3,233; Alabama, 3,148 and Tennessee, 2,972 interestingly enough all states in the original Confederacy and all that celebrate Confederate Memorial Day. This should mislead us to think that only the Southern states have SBC churches. They have a heavy presence in the Midwest the second most devoted region next to the South. Northern and Western states also witnessed an increase in SBC churches. Pennsylvania had an 86.6% increase and Massachusetts had a 58.7% increase and California was in the top five states with increases in SBC churches. Even though the heart of SBC is the heart of Dixie it has extended its influence into the all areas of the country. As of 2000 there were 41,514 SBC in the United States. The point of citing these demographics is to make clear that the SBC is an extremely influential force in the United States and though predominately located in the South. In 1996 they were in major leadership roles in the United States. Bill Clinton, Al Gore, Strom Thurmond, and Newt Gingrich are all SBC members (Stanley, 2000).

The ties among the SBC's beliefs and agendas and the close ties with the Republican agenda are clear. The SBC has a very Republican series of beliefs and resolutions. The SBC has an extensive website where the uninitiated can find a plethora of information. Careful examination of these ideas will demonstrate how the Church of the Southern Cultural Memory or the SBC is indeed interchangeable with the agenda of the Republican Party.

First the SBC is firmly and unquestionably pro-life. They firmly believe that life begins at conception. "Procreation is a gift from God, a precious trust reserved for marriage. At the moment of conception, a new being enters the universe, a human being, a being created in God's image. This human being deserves our protection, whatever the circumstances of conception. The Republican Party Platform of 2004 agreed with this stance. It states that the Republican Party opposes abortion, funding for organizations involved in abortion, school-based clinics that provide referrals, counseling, and, related services for contraception and abortion, using public revenues for abortion, oppose using public revenues for abortion and will not fund organizations which advocate it, partial birth abortions (Republican Party Platform, 2004). The other major point in the platform concerning abortion is the Republican commitment to appointing judges with a pro-life stance. The SBC's statement on abortion is clear.

> We reaffirm our belief that the *Roe v. Wade* decision was an act of injustice against innocent unborn children as well as against vulnerable women in crisis pregnancy situations, both of which have been victimized by a "sexual revolution" that empowers predatory and irresponsible men and by a lucrative abortion industry that has fought against even the most minimal restrictions on abortion (SBC, 2007).

Another issue closely tied to the issue of abortion is that of sex education. The Republican agenda in this area can be reduced to one word: abstinence. The SBC issued its resolutions centering on sex education, which, of course are closely aligned with the Republican Platform. The SBC advocates adopting a particular curriculum for the schools.

> Adopt curricula that teach sexual abstinence before marriage and fidelity in marriage as the only acceptable lifestyle in terms of public health as this is the best and only sure way crisis pregnancies and sexually transmitted diseases can be prevented; Refrain from distribution of condoms and other contraceptive materials; and Oppose the establishment of school based clinics which provide sexual counselling (SBC, 2007).

The preoccupation with peoples' conduct is evident here as it is with the issues of gay marriage in what follows. And, this concentration on conduct is in evidence in Republican and Christocrat agendas for school curriculum. They desire to have only the virtues of abstinence taught in sex education classes in schools. The agenda is in some cases called Abstinence Only Programs.[9] The point is that there is an attempt to stress and monitor purity (as defined by the Christocrats and their political party). As Webber will discuss in a forthcoming book there is a return to a type of Victorianism (Webber, forthcoming). It was a Victorianism that stressed a direct emphasis on conduct. Phillips (2004) stress that "moral pretension became a second British Flag, just as it later became a second American flag" (Phillips, 2004, p. 225). There are clear echoes here of the culture war. The reference to the sexual revolution clearly points to the era of critique in the1960s and 1970s which the SBC, Christocrats and Republicans have been fighting since the election of Richard Nixon. The conservative restoration as Ira Shor (1984) dubbed it was/is making sure to promote a political, economic and social agenda that prevents anything like that period from happening again. Actually most of the agenda of the right is geared toward that very purpose. Particularly in education many Christocrats believe that school policy is determined by a group of liberal counterculture activists whose values are outside the mainstream.

> Patrick Buchanan got great cheers from Christian Right activists by railing against policymakers from the Department of Education who wore 'beads and sandals,' a reference to the attire of hippies of the 1960s. Because liberals are seen as dominating the educational establishment, activists believe that it essential that Christian parents get some control of local school boards (Wilcox and Larson, 2006, p. 146).

Consistent with this preoccupation with people's conduct is a second point in the SBC agenda. They are opposed to Hate Crimes Legislation because it creates special protected classes like homosexuals and the transgendered. This is part of a larger opposition to gays and lesbians as we have illustrated in the previous chapters and is a major focus for the Christocrats and the Civic Gospel. In *Onward Christian Soldiers: The Religious Right in American Politics* (2006) the authors express the fact that the Christian Right has made opposition to gay and lesbian rights a central part of their policy agenda and a key theme in their direct-mail and fund-raising efforts. It has manifested itself in the debates on gay marriage. In the Republican Platform it is not a directly stated opposition to gay marriage, but appears as a statement that the Republican Party supports the tradition of marriage, meaning marriage between a man and a woman. This coincided with the Christocratic agenda and moved it to the top of their efforts.

> Many saw same-sex marriage as undermining the very fabric of civilization and in the words of Dr. James Dobson, hurtling the nation toward Gomorrah. Christian Right activists interpret the Bible to say that God destroyed Sodom and Gomorrah for their rampant homosexuality (Wilcox & Larson, 2006, p. 147).

In 2004 the gay marriage question was on the ballot in eleven states. The ballots were phrased such that a yes vote would only recognize marriage between a man and a woman. The ballot recognizing only "traditional marriage" passed in all eleven states. The South was well represented in these ballot initiatives. The states included; Arkansas, Georgia, Kentucky, Michigan, Mississippi, Montana, North Dakota, Ohio, Oklahoma, Oregon and Utah. Nine of the states that passed this legislation voted for Bush in the election. Michigan and Oregon voted for Kerry. The most interesting state in this case is Ohio where the ballot on gay marriage, most political observers agree, put the state in Bush's column although not by any wide margin. Bush received 2,858,727 votes and Kerry received 2,739,952. This is a difference of only 118,775 votes. Ohio was pivotal in Bush's reelection. This homophobic SBC/Christocrat/Republican agenda helped win an election. Juxtaposed to this anti-gay rhetoric are the actual incidents that occur. One recent case is an example. On November 4, 2006 Ted Haggard the 50 year old pastor of a large mega church (which we discussed earlier in the chapter), was forced to "resign from his leadership position at the 14,000 member New Life Church in Colorado Springs Colorado, which he started in his basement 20 years ago" (CNN, 2006). He also resigned from The National Association of Evangelicals representing more than 45,000 churches with 30 million members (CNN, 2006). Why did he resign? It was because he allegedly purchased methamphetamine and massages from a Denver man, Mike Jones. Haggard's response was that he did not have sex with him and threw the drugs away. Jones said that their relationship was, indeed, sexual and emotional and that they had met over three years ago and had monthly encounters. On November 6, 2006 a letter from Haggard was read to the congregation of the New Life Church in which Haggard confessed to being a liar and a deceiver. In the letter he said, "There is part of my life that is so repulsive and dark that I've been warring against it all of my adult life." (Denver Channel, 2006). The irony of this case is that this pastor was one who was most vociferous in his attacks on gays. In the film *Jesus Camp* (2006), Haggard discusses homosexuality in a sermon.

> So, we don't have to have a debate about what we think about homosexual activity it's written in the Bible. I think I know what you did last night (laughs from the audience). If you send me a thousand dollars I won't tell your wife. If you use any of this, I'll sue you. (Haggard in Ewing & Grady, 2006).

Just before the film's release Haggard disowned it claiming it had misrepresented evangelicalism. Another important aspect to this story is that Ted Haggard has important Republican connections. In an interview conducted with Richard Dawkins, author of *The God Delusion*, Haggard claims to have had weekly phone conferences with George W. Bush. This demonstrates that tie between Christocrats and the Republican Party.[11] Although Haggard was not in the SBC, he was/ is an important voice in the Christocratic movement. And, consistent with our discussion of homosexuality in Chapter 2, there exists a cure for Haggard's homosexuality. James Dobson, of the California-based Focus on the Family and one of the most prominent pastors in the Christocrat tradition said in a Larry King interview that he could cure Haggard... Dobson said that he was asked to serve on a three person restoration panel for his friend Haggard. He indicated that the purpose of a planned panel was to restore Haggard from being gay to not being gay. He also indicated that he didn't have time because the process could take four or five years. Apparently Dobson was incorrect about the required length of time. This cure is consistent with Focus on the Family's conversion plan for homosexuals. "Focus helped to sponsor a large campaign to change public opinion about homosexuality

CHAPTER 5

and to promote the 'conversion of gays and lesbians to heterosexuality" (Wilcox and Larson, 2006, p. 71). In February of 2007 after three weeks of intensive treatment at an undisclosed Arizona treatment center, Haggard emerged into the sun and claimed that he was completely heterosexual. This story brings the issue of homosexuality and the Christocrats full circle. Homosexuality is not only wrong, but completely curable.

There is a larger SBC/Christocrat/Republican movement against science, which is clarified in a book, entitled, *The Republican War on Science* (2005) by Chris Mooney. Mooney states that his book attempts to explain how "our nation gave rise to a political party movement whose leaders, to put it bluntly, often seem not to care what we in the 'reality-based community' know about either nature or ourselves (p. 13). A principle voice in the anti-global warming agenda, part of the war on science, is James Inhofe, a Republican senator from the state of Oklahoma. Interestingly enough Inhofe received, in the 2002 election, more contributions from oil, gas and electric companies than from any other source and he is somewhat famous for his extreme statement amongst others that the Environmental Protection Agency was "Gestapo bureaucracy." He is the chairperson of the Environment and Public Works Committee of the Senate and when Gore testified before Congress on global warming was his chief adversary.

> As I said on the Senate floor on July 28, 2003, "much of the debate over global warming is predicated on fear, rather than science." I called the threat of catastrophic global warming the "greatest hoax ever perpetrated on the American people" (Inhofe, 2005, p. 1).

Inhofe also thinks that the separation of church and state is a hoax played on the American people and he sometimes refers to global warming as the second biggest hoax next to the church and state hoax. But, they are both hoaxes none the less. This rhetoric has earned him the title of theocratic from the mainstream Baptists. Inhofe is a Christocrat in the United States Senate.

This doubt about global warming is consistent with the SBC and their weariness about global warming euphemistically dubbed climate change. This is expressed in one of their belief statements about CO_2 emissions as a significant part of the global warming issue. Recently the Christocrats have softened their stance on environmental issues. There are, however, a number of the Christocrats who believe that Man has the right to rule over the natural world and use it as he sees fit. In this group Armageddon fever has caught hold as it has with many of the Christocrats. They believe the End Times are near so what does global warming matter?

> [This] leads some to believe that either there is no need to take care of the environment, or, alternatively, that actively exhausting the environment will speed the Second Coming (Hendricks, 2005).

The slogan that is derived from these beliefs is, "the faster it burns, the sooner Christ returns. It is the belief "that global environmental annihilation is a divine requirement for Christ's return" (Hendricks, 2005, p. 21). Even the SBC is not to that point. But, it is one view held by the Christocrats. The SBC has a carefully worded statement that demonstrates that science is questionable and the concept of global warming maybe doubtful

> We consider proposals to regulate CO2 and other greenhouse gas emissions based on a maximum acceptable global temperature goal to be very dangerous, since attempts to meet the goal could lead to a succession of mandates of deeper cuts in emissions, which may have no appreciable effect if humans are not the principal cause of global warming, and could lead to major economic hardships on a worldwide scale; and further its influence nation-wide (SBC, 2007)

On the issue of global warming (climate change) there is a Christocratic/SBC/Republican agenda. Of course, this agenda is tied to economic goals and to the oil, gas, electric, and coal lobbies.

As we mentioned in the Introduction section the Christocrat Civic Gospel is to remove the separation of church and state. The SBC agenda is in line with that objective. Again, this is from their belief statements.

> That the messengers to the Southern Baptist Convention meeting in San Antonio, Texas, June 12–13, 2007, urge our pastors to preach the whole counsel of God, not only passionately inviting people to Jesus, but also prophetically declaring biblical truth concerning the burning moral issues that are being debated in the culture and government; and be it further we encourage pastors to model and promote informed and active Christian citizenship among the membership of our churches; and be it finally that we support our pastors as they lead their congregations to engage their communities, our culture, and our nation as salt and light, showing the way to the only hope for America and for the world, who is Jesus Christ. (SBC, 2007).

Jesusland, indeed.

The Southern Nation – To Jesusland and Beyond: A Faith-based War

> As in Britain nearly a century earlier, evangelical religion, biblically stirred foreign policy and a crusader mentality ill fitted a great power decreasingly able to bear the rising economic costs of strategic and energy supply failure (Phillips, 2004, p. 262).

> You're either with us or against us in the fight against terror. (Bush, 2001, p. 5).

The missionary zeal of the Republican Religious Party is not without its consequences. Although we don't think that the Republican Religious Party is out to develop a Theocracy, there is as we have demonstrated a push to make the United States a Christian Nation through witnessing and other more political means. It is evident in many indirect and not so indirect biblical allusions in speeches by various Republican Party officials including the President. Thus, for us or against us is a not so subtle reference to Christ's words. "He who is not with me is against me, and he who does not

CHAPTER 5

gather with me scatters (Matthew 12:30, New International Version). What it has led to is the New Crusade. The shields of white with red crosses have been replaced by desert camouflage. Bush actually called the War on Terrorism a crusade but quickly backtracked in his rhetoric after intense reaction in the United States and abroad. But, his words are, perhaps, more true than we want to believe. Reminiscent of the lost cause (although there may be more similarities there then we are want to admit) we are now engaged with a Noble Cause in a so-called "just war." Bringing democracy, corporate capitalism and the Christian God to the rest of the world are the foundations of the New Crusade. The military invasion of Iraq was a precursor to the next phase of the Crusade; the coming of the faith-based aid organizations. This also can be viewed as happening simultaneously. They have descended upon Iraq and will continue to come. They will come with food and assistance in one hand and Bibles and tracts in the other. Faith-based organizations were the centerpiece of the Bush domestic agenda and have the possibility of becoming one of the major forces in the War on Terrorism. In the war with Iraq Christocrats and Latter Day Saints provide a reservoir of support for the Bush policy (Wald and Calhoun-Brown, 2006, p. 201). The SBC wire service was in support of the War in Iraq and the possible religious opportunities. "American foreign policy and military might have opened an opportunity for the Gospel in the land of Abraham, Isaac, and Jacob. Franklin Graham, the son of Billy Graham, and Marvin Olasky, the inventor of Bush's "compassionate conservatism, agreed" (Wills, 2006, p. 8). Bush promised his Christocratic followers faith-based social services, which he called compassionate conservatism, "he went beyond that to give them a faith-based war, faith-based law-enforcement, faith-based education, faith-based medicine, and faith-based science" (Wills, 2006, p. 1). There are also other larger dangers in this faith-based war.

There is a particular danger with a war that God commands. What if God should lose (Willis, 2006)? That is unthinkable to the Christocrats. "They cannot accept the idea of second-guessing God, and he was the one who led them into war. Thus, in 2006, when two thirds of the American people told pollsters that the war in Iraq was a mistake, the third of those still standing behind it were mainly evangelicals (who make up about one third of the population). It was a faith-based certitude" (Willis, 2006, p. 11).

And the New Crusade can be carried out largely by privatization. The United States military provided boots on the ground and guns, but the majority of other wartime functions were carried out by corporations. Corporate contractors, such as Halliburton provided functions such as medical support, food service, and most surprisingly other functions usually provided by United States fighting men and women. Embassy protection, diplomatic protection, and actual front line battle were provided by mercenaries. The complexity of the connections between the Christocrats, the Bush Administration and private contractors are clarified when we analyze one military corporation, Blackwater.

> Today, Blackwater has more than 2,300 private soldiers deployed in nine countries, including inside the United States. It maintains a database of 21,000 former Special Forces troops, soldiers, and retired law enforcement agents on whom it can call on at a moment's notice. Blackwater has a fleet of more

than twenty aircraft, including helicopter gun ships and a surveillance blimp division. Its 7,000 acre headquarters in Moyrock, North Carolina is the world's largest private military facility (Scahill, 2007, p. xviii).

Scahill's book presents an extensive analysis of this mercenary organization. For the purposes of our interest in the Christocrats and the crusade that is Iraq we turn our attention to the connections with Christocratic groups and the acknowledged former leader of Blackwater, Eric Prince. This, once again, demonstrates that the Jesusland is a global issue not just an American issue. There is a definite connection between the executives of Blackwater and a "Christian supremacist agenda." (Scahill, 2007, p. xxv).

Eric Prince one of best known of the founders of Blackwater is a conservative Catholic and has donated millions of dollars not only to right-wing Republican candidates, but to Christocratic causes and organizations as well. Prince has donated large sums of money to organizations such as Focus on the Family, Council for National Policy, and Catholic Answers (an extremist Catholic fringe organization). He has "supported Jesse Helms, Ollie North, Richard Pombo, Spencer Abraham, Dick Chrysler, Rick Santorum, Tom Coburn, Tom DeLay, Jim DeMint, Mike Pence, Duncan Hunter and others" (Scahill, 2007, p. 13). And, of course, he was/is a supporter of George W. Bush. So, there is a mercenary army doing service in Iraq and in the United States led by a right-wing politically conservative Christocrat. Blackwater provides services such as the protection of diplomats and officials such as Paul Bremer. Increasingly they were also engaged in direct combat operations. The important point is that this private army is part of the larger crusade for Iraq lead by Eric Prince.

> Prince would soon draw on his father's ideals and money to build up an army of soldiers who would serve on the front lines of a global battle, waged largely on Muslim lands, that an evangelical President Prince helped put in the White House would boldly define as a crusade (Scahill, 2007, p. 24).

The Blackwater invasion was a simultaneous phase of the Crusade with the coming of the faith-based aid organizations. They have descended upon Iraq and will continue to come. They will come with food and assistance in one hand and Bibles and tracts in the other. Faith-based organizations are the centerpiece of the Bush domestic agenda and had the possibility of becoming one of the major emphases in the War on Terrorism. "In the war with Iraq Christocrats and Latter Day Saints provide a reservoir of support for the Bush policy" (Wald and Calhoun-Brown, 2006, p. 201). The SBC wire service was in support of the War in Iraq and the possible religious opportunities. "American foreign policy and military might have opened an opportunity for the Gospel in the land of Abraham, Isaac, and Jacob. Franklin Graham, the son of Billy Graham, and Marvin Olasky, the inventor of Bush's "compassionate conservatism, agreed" (Willis, 2006, p. 8). Bush promised his Christocratic followers faith-based social services, which he called compassionate conservatism, "he went beyond that to give them a faith-based war, faith-based law-enforcement, faith-based education, faith-based medicine, and faith-based science" (Willis, 2006, p. 1). There is also a larger danger in this faith-based war.

CHAPTER 5

The former deputy undersecretary for defense intelligence, General William (Jerry) Boykin—a man leading the search for bin Laden—has made headlines during the Iraq war with a slide-show lecture he gave in churches. He appeared there not in his dress uniform but in combat gear. When he presented his slide show he also discussed the enemy as he showed slides of Osama bin Laden.

> The battle this nation is in is a spiritual battle; it's a battle for our soul. And the enemy is a guy called Satan.... Satan wants to destroy this nation. He wants to destroy us as a nation, and he wants to destroy us as a Christian army (Willis, 2007, p. 512)

Boykin also advocated that people needed to join God's army to defeat this enemy (Satan).

Appointments to leadership positions in Coalition Provisional Authority in Iraq also reflected this turn toward a faith-based war. One example is that of James Haveman. He had been responsible for operating a Christian adoption agency meant to discourage women from having abortions. He was appointed to the Iraqi Health Services Directorship. His objective, after his appointment, was a plan to help Iraqis quit smoking while the health facilities in the country went downhill and were left unstaffed. There have also been numerous Bible study group in the Green Zone.

The agenda of the Southern Republican Religious Party and the course of not only domestic policy but those of international import continued as the 2008 election approached. The party was at that point losing even some of the most devoted of Christocratic followers. The Christocrats became somewhat disillusioned with not only Bush but the party as well and their slate of candidates for the presidency. It is not surprising. After all the rhetoric on abortion, same-sex marriage, stem cell research and God, there has been little action taken. In fact after the 2004 election, which, as has been demonstrated, to have been won with the support of the Christocrats, Bush's first agenda item was the privatization of social security. And Christocrats feel much lip-service has been paid to the other issues. And, Hell hath no fury like a Christocrat scorned. On September 30, 2007 James Dobson, probably one of the most powerful Christocrats, met in Salt Lake City with other like-minded Christocrats to discuss the 2008 elections. At the conclusion of the meeting a statement was issued:

> If neither of the two major political parties nominates an individual who pledges himself or herself to the sanctity of human life, we will join others in voting for a minor-party candidate. Those agreeing with the proposition were invited to stand. The result was almost unanimous (Dobson, 2007, p. 2).

This is a reaction to not only, we believe, the issue of abortion but other disappointments the Christocrats have experienced at the hands of the Republican Party and what were the possibilities for 2008. As we will discuss in the concluding chapter the Christocratic agenda is even making its way into the Democratic Party when the Democratic candidates made statements of their relationships with God.

Obama, Clinton, Edwards, and others have made statements about their religious faith. It has become a political necessity.

We would like to conclude this portion of the chapter with a quote from Christopher Hitchens' book, *God is not Great: How Religion Poisons Everything* (2007).

> At the time [9/11], the United States had an attorney general named John Ashcroft, who had stated that America had 'no king but Jesus' (a claim that was exactly two words long). It had a president who wanted to hand over the care of the poor to 'faith-based' institutions. Might this not be a moment where the light of reason, and the defense of society that separated church and state and valued free expression and free inquiry, be granted a point or two ? (Hitchens, 2007, p. 32).

We would say yes.

PART II: THE MYTH OF THE COMMON CULTURE, RUSTBELT RELIGION & RIGHT-WING POLITICS

> The values people vote for are not necessarily the same values they live by. No region of the United States has a higher divorce rate than the Bible Belt. (The divorce rate in these southern states is roughly fifty percent above the national average). In fact, eight of ten states that lead in national divorce are red, whereas the state with the lowest divorce rate is deep blue Massachusetts. Even if people consider themselves conservative or vote Republican, their political ideals may be just that: reflections of the way they *wish* things were in America, rather than a product of the way they actually experience it.
>
> Ariel Levy *Female Chauvinist Pigs* (Levy, 2005, p. 29).

In examining the role and influence of evangelical Christianity on contemporary politics and schooling, this section examines the political impact of the myth of common culture that has operated in the rustbelt U.S. states. Several recent books have alerted publics to the significance of the new religious and right-wing trend (*What's the Matter with Kansas,* etc.) Also, this section will show how another common assumption, that the Midwest is a place that wishes it could live the morals it votes for, is a little misplaced and perhaps more appropriate when applied to the rural south (Levy, 2005). Rather, this chapter concludes by examining how the assumption of common culture worked on both sides of the political aisle (left & right) to produce confusion over the substance of a so-called "common culture." Indeed, it argues that for both ideologies it was the dearth of common civic practices, public spaces and educational understandings that produced a polarized rustbelt public searching for answers to common democratic problems from unlikely sources (corporate bureaucracies, Washington politicians, preachers?). Drawing on Wendy Brown's (2006) theorization of neo's (liberalism and conservatism) this paper will detail the ways in which these two ideologies nourished the myth of a common

CHAPTER 5

culture while destroying what might be left of a modified utilitarianism (e.g. J.S. Mill).

Using Grumet's (1988) conception of "common culture" and juxtaposing it with theories that rely upon the notion of nostalgia for the "sacred canopy" (Berger, 1967/1990) and applications of it to questions of the public sphere (Habermas *The Structural Transformation of the Public Sphere, The Divided West*) we examine key points of conflict in rustbelt politics that are animated by the growing attraction to evangelical religious belief.

As the above quote by Levy suggests, it is the American south that idealizes an American family life serving up a wholesome American dream while its demographics serve as a continuous disappointment and stark reminder of the effects of classic underdevelopment on a territory within a largely wealthy nation-state. Levy's analysis could also be taken to describe the "Midwest" which is the territorial and ideational space we now examine in the next several pages. Our aim is to highlight the distinguishing features of the Midwest in relation to the larger themes of the present study of religion and education. There are significant differences. If the south represents what we refer to as the Bible Belt, then the Midwest represents the family values said to suture the entire American experience together into a cohesive narrative of national progress. Family values are also an aspiration of voters rather than a reality in the Midwest, as is the imaginary community living said to keep families together in these states. It has the last affordable big city in the country: Chicago. People who visit the Midwest frequently compare it to parts of continental Europe *sans* mountain ranges and rivers. The region stretches from the upper Midwestern "lakes" states like Wisconsin, Minnesota and Michigan though the central plains of solidly blue Illinois, Ohio and solidly red Indiana onto the western plains states like the Dakotas, and Iowa, with gatekeepers like Missouri and Kansas providing the country with a view to the Midwest strongest example of fundamentalist politics to date. Several years ago, Madeleine Grumet confronted what was popularly known in curriculum studies as the "common culture" an alienating term for the way bureaucratic mindsets composed school policies that did not address value conflicts between the school and the home. Setting up school policy to deliver an education to "the little nobodies that go no where" was an efficient way to avoid confronting the fact that students obtain most of their cherished beliefs outside the classroom, and often at home. These conflicts enlarged as the years went by, and as has already been addressed in the introduction of the book, the politics of the "culture wars" pushed this conflict to a startling head; the misunderstanding that Grumet had identified had turned into a full-scale war on public education led by what Frank calls the elites of the backlash politics: people who spent their free time anguished over the lack of values in American society began spending their free time working for causes that attacked the existing institutions of American society as fundamentally flawed because of their public character. One of these institutions was the school because it produced this common culture that did not address their personal values. Grass-roots movements orchestrated by the ever increasing number of Christian and far Right radio forums questioned the compulsory character of public schooling, the content of the curriculum and the lack of religious piety in school spaces. Grumet's misunderstanding, one that she urged educators to address earnestly, had fallen on deaf ears and had spiraled into a political movement that sought to take control over the education of children and produced such outcomes as NCLB, charter schools, vouchers, Christian camps and promoted policies within existing schools that banned sex education, encouraged chastity and policed the speech and content of curriculum. These political conflicts dominate Midwestern schools and municipalities and make the political elites who seek high office highly attentive to their concerns. One reason the Midwest is featured in this chapter is because these fundamentalist politics have come to shape its identity and through that shaping have impacted their electoral preferences. These electoral preferences though largely ambiguous have given backlash elites the support they need to push through "reforms" to education at the highest levels, and begin to dismantle public institutions like universities and public schools, by arguing that academic freedom means something like consumer preference. These are the policies of groups like ACTA (American Council of Trustees and Alumni) who, using seed money from federal grants with support from the leaders of federal grant agencies such as NEH and NSF, have argued for such things as a "student bill of rights" on university campuses. In effect, domestic dissatisfaction with public institutions for reasons *de-linked* from present conservative agendas has been unjustly used to dismantle curricular freedom.

Indeed, all of the political wing of the fundamentalist message that is linked to the larger mission of the Conservative Coalition and earlier Moral Majority find their overwhelming support in Kansas, with Missouri a patchwork of strong support in rural zones. Taken together this area is a mix of red and blue, to put it in electoral terms, and it is precisely the contrasts between populations and their differing political and social demands (or rather reluctant admissions of "perceptions" of them, which is all polls can measure) that makes many of these states critical target areas for presidential candidates. Holding large numbers of electoral votes and presenting to both right and left, republican and democrat a portrait of opportunity to sweep the nation with their votes, the Midwest is attractive because of this political bipolarity. Such contrasting political views do not clash with one another very often because the people who subscribe to them self-segregate and contain each other to knowable places. Most have at least heard of Jonathon Kozol's depiction of East St. Louis for example, where poor and working class kids attend underfunded schools deprived of a tax base for support by what is often called "white flight" to the suburbs. Race, culture and religion are predominant factors that determine who lives where and gets what, where and how in Midwestern states. The legacy of Lincoln's support for ending slavery provides much of the self-satisfaction of Midwestern identity as "not racist," even though segregation by race and class is among the highest in the country in public schools and neighborhoods throughout the region (Rau, Shelly & Beck, 2001). Erased from the memory of Midwesterners is the overt racism practiced by its forebears in the likes of Henry Ford and others.[10] Read an entry from Ida B. Wells Barnett's autobiography of the account of a lynching and ask Midwestern students where they believe it takes place and they'll all answer the South, but when you inform them that it is Pekin, Illinois ten miles from where they sit, they refuse to believe you. Because Illinois license plates read "Land of Lincoln" that somehow absolves its residents of historical knowledge about race (and therefore class) issues that inform the present.

They may even hate you for telling them and this brings us to a major cultural point about the Midwest: it lacks irony. Jokes among American studies students go something like this: in the Midwest it is BYOI (Bring Your Own Irony) or that the Iron Curtain of Irony closes down on the Mississippi River. Irony—though it should be a staple of Midwestern culture given the enormous social contradictions that underwrite its identity and existence is actually banned from the Midwest and one finds strong social sanction for using it publicly. Like liquor on Sundays, an unwritten Blue Law exists in the Midwest that demands each person be forthright with their demands, hardworking and refrain from commentary on the social contradictions produced by demographic changes or the glaring injustices that linger in the form of informal segregation of schools and housing, the abandonment of public spaces such as community centers, libraries and town halls, to only the poorest of the poor who use them for their information technologies, to pay bills, apply for menial jobs or self-educate themselves to obtain them. This is the Midwest described by Thomas Frank through the experience of Kansas where self-righteousness and contempt for "liberals" is part of the everyday discourse of work, family and church life (even though many of these same critics happily enjoy state subsidies for small business, tax breaks and public schooling paid for by state lotteries). Its contradictions are exposed in the larger parts of the liberal media and distorted by the conservative media to effect what Frank refers to as the "backlash culture" throughout his book, a curious mix of pop psychology and humor peppered with an autobiographical attempt at explaining the way the contradiction works: how working class people come to hate an imaginary liberal, intellectual professionalized order to the benefit of the corporate class and republican party elite. Julie's experience is much different, as is her so-called liberal conversion narrative: born in Pontiac, Michigan and raised as the daughter of a mid-level engineer for one of the big three automakers, she moved to Indiana and stayed there for ten years as a student finally earning a Ph.D. in Political Science before obtaining an assistant professor job at Illinois State University in Normal, Illinois a republican town housed in a blue state. Having experienced the "rust belt" phenomenon first-hand (the very first bumper sticker she could read went like this: "The last one out of Detroit, please turn out the lights!") growing up with disdain for unions she could not define and then moving to the reddest of red states to find answers to the contradictions that formed her childhood by accident (She went to Purdue University to be an engineer to be able to do her part to one day salvage the auto industry) stumbling across political sanity in an introductory American politics class where the professor blared 2LiveCrew before his lecture on free speech, she found Indiana stifling compared to Michigan. When she looks back on it, suburban Detroit had its class contradictions and growing up in a division of labor does not predispose one to understanding simple Marxist terms like contradiction, and alienation but she did, unlike Frank, find her teenage experiences mirrored in the family of movies centered around a "transcendent dick joke"—*American Pie* was her adolescence, more or less. Small town, IL was another matter: there was no city, no diversity and she wasn't moving there for college so she could no longer ignore the parts of the culture she resented: the unfair prejudices applied to intellectuals, the barely contained suspicion of Catholics and Jews (She grew up in Catholic Detroit, so she did not meet the fear until Indiana), just the stifling culture of anomie. Unlike a major city where one finds the anomie relaxing because people are carrying on and doing different things the anomie of the Midwestern city is unbearable because it is as if no one is home in any house you pass, no one is outside doing anything, talking to anyone. People are contained to their associations, the various churches and business groups that breed the backlash culture that Frank examines. Advice to Julie upon hearing she was moving to small town, Illinois was "Be sure to make friends quickly, so that you don't "Die on the vine over there." This is the criticism of not liberals, but outsiders, to the 'heartland": it may be paradigmatic of American values, but nobody really wants to be forced to live them!

However, what is unique about the Midwest is its ideational power in the national imaginary. The Midwest signifies for the rest of the country its center of moral rectitude and this is disturbing. The one space that Hollywood rarely messes with is the Midwest as it makes up most of their audience. The Midwest is a space of refuge from the bustling life of the big city or the slow, rural backwardness of the south. The great benefit in the minds of the American public is that it does not disturb but provides a space of repose: if all else fails move to the Midwest and settle down. Settle down. This is the ideational power that the Midwest provides in midst of great shifts in capital and power under globalization. The weather won't remind you much about global warming: it's always gray, except in summer. The culture won't challenge you to rethink your place in the world because the Midwest vigilantly opposes all evidence that change is taking place. Elections in the Midwest confirm that it is a referendum on American presidential support: "In the end, the Midwest region exit poll shows that Bush won the Midwest by the same margin with which he won the nationwide popular vote, 51-48 percent. No other region came close to mirroring the outcome of the nation more than the battle for the Midwest," (Rankin, 2005, p. 164). Further, the author notes that the key states where this battle was won were the de-industrializing lake states such as Ohio, Wisconsin, and Michigan.

One trend in the Midwest developing over the last thirty years has been the decline in the industrial base, with a corresponding decline in the representation of working class interests. This is the so-called "rustbelt" label from the chapter's title which signifies the rusting of the railways that moved raw materials and goods between factory cities that "staked their fortunes to an industry and suffered greatly for it," (Mellon, 2002, p. 6). The flight of factories from the Midwest to parts of the south and other countries has meant that those buildings and the identities of the people who worked in them, has vanished or become transformed into something new. This has meant a decrease in traditional values associated with urban, (often Democrat) non-Protestant working class and often immigrant citizens. Instead of the promotion of what Ignatieff has called the heroic national identity whose self is produced by the synchrony between factory work and school set to reproduce the nation as an industrial machine where values like loyalty and sacrifice were rewarded

CHAPTER 5

by industrialists and championed by politicians, the new identities of corporatism in the Midwest are supported by the work ethic and values of companies such as those affiliated with telecommunications, drug sales and manufacturing, and laboratories. Such companies tend to find homes on the outskirts of cities, near the "exurban" areas described by Goldberg in one of our earlier chapters. As such, these growing cities of the Midwest that replace the old industrial centers are built alongside the rusting railways. Hardly anyone living in these cities can ignore the fact that a trip on the freeway from one city to another forces you to drive parallel to the railways that are now largely defunct. Service roads buffer the freeway and the railway and increasingly become zones of commercial building sites for the new professional classes who flock to the homes that seem as if they've been cloned, almost overnight.

Though the term exurban was first used by Stanley Greenberg and called "exurbia" to signify the very fast growing communities outside of cities composed of citizens who were displaced by them (Rankin 2005, 162), these communities best capture the phenomenon of religious and political blending that is the objective of this book for study. Largely Republican, these communities are challenging the Democratic vote in the cities where most poor and disenfranchised voters still reside. They are strongly religious and pro-business accounting for one-fifth of the country's manufacturing base, despite the rustbelt fear-mongering. What was displaced was the importance of political interests supporting the concept of a social wage in the form of unions, civic groups and guild associations, public funding for daycare and schooling largely supported by the state through increasing the burden on the tax payer. These communities are characterized by their attractiveness to state-level political candidates that offer shifting the tax burden away from the state and allowing the privatization of social forms of security, including welfare, childcare, healthcare, prisons and higher education. Even though the burden of cost is shifted to the consumer, instead of the taxpayer, (that is to say, the same person) most of these exurbans, as consumers, favor them because they allow them choice. As political liberty comes to be associated solely with consumer choice, it shouldn't be surprising that privatization becomes popular. The increasing values associated with this demographic of white collar professional sales are associated with a different kind of national identity than the one so celebrated during the twentieth century.

The persons who inhabit these growing cities in the suburban and rural Midwest seek community in a different manner. Following the logic of privatization and choice they seek spaces of congregation that reinforce the values of corporate America, the Walmart-inspired philosophy of bigger is better, one-stop shopping organized to maximize their options without taxing their leisure time or weighing down their psyches. This is a growing class of Americans that want religion and culture lite in the sense that they have ontological baggage attached to them. Rejecting previous Midwestern generation's self-sacrificing mentalities, these exurbans desire culture and religious experiences that resemble what they already know while at the same time discouraging them from being reminded of what they've past rejected. This is a weightless identity, not a throwback to conservative moral values. The vacuousness of the values espoused in these spaces must be sufficiently airy enough to expand

and fill the vast architectural spaces they frequent: the shopping mall, the Wal-Mart mega center, the rock concert hall, skating rink and mega church. These weightless values do not sink to the level of moral integrity but much more closely resemble the ethical values criticized by curriculum scholars as forming the basis for a curriculum that deals blandness to other people's children (Grumet, 1988, p. 164–182). Think of NCLB as a kind of genetic code or formula as the basis for the design of every mega church.

A Midwestern Mega Church

> Big is beautiful…Any church in a large, growing community that is practicing the 'Great Commission' cannot keep from growing. To criticize a church for being big is to imply disbelief in Christ's commission…A church gets big because its spirit is big…Nobody ever started a business without hoping that someday, if he or she worked hard enough, it would be a big success. That is the American dream, isn't it? (Thumma, 2006, p. 2).

One cannot help but see the growing evangelical mega church phenomenon as another bland expression of the fascination with big in American culture: big boobs, trucks, big defense spending, big confidence, big oil, big corruption cases, big fries, big tobacco, big time lawyers, big cars, etc. The most satisfying expression of this is big bombs, mostly representing American big presence in other regions like the Middle East. As a matter of fact: recall the MOAB? Mother of All Bombs detonated in March of 2003 just prior to the "possible" war in Iraq? A CNN report describes the device as a psych-ops one developed by the Air Force for possible use in Iraq, but looking back on it one has to see that the psychological operation was really intended for the American psyche. To nurture the awe inspired by bigness would hopefully lead to widespread psychological comfort with the march to war and the anxieties created by the war on terror. The images in Nina Berman's celebrated mega church series demonstrate this bigness, as well as its fundamental relationship to the development of children and the use of technologies merged with the physical body. In these images she has captured the essence of the mega church phenomenon, experienced by all those who prefer it as a space of worship. To some, it may look reminiscent of the stadium style meetings of the 1990s group the Promise Keepers, and in many respects the mega church does grow out of that grassroots moral sentimentality (Brickner, 1995). Some take Jesus into their lives as a personal savior, some make the commitment to Christ, which means spreading the Gospel to all the unconverted, and still others see the contemporary focus on religion for what it is: a way to recover a sense of community in a time when traditional sources of it are shrinking alongside the public sphere. Most contemporary protestant churches rely on a conversion to Christ, and several of the faith-based services require it before a patron can receive assistance. Central to this growing religious movement is an emphasis on conversion that is protected by policy through faith-based initiatives from the federal government under Bush, although the Clinton administration would have liked to have devolved state responsibilities in a similar fashion.

CHAPTER 5

Any outsider to the conversion narrative cannot understand the concept of the mega church; its form and lack of ornamentation are off-putting to the uninitiated. Several scholars have attempted to make sense of this utilitarian style for outsiders. Some see the non-denominational Protestant mega church as a direct descendent of the Calvinist meetinghouses built in the seventeenth century (Loveland & Wheeler, 2003) but there are sufficient reasons to doubt this claim, including the autobiographical portraits of church ministers who see the mega buildings as expressions of the decline in ascriptive identity in the latter half of the twentieth century. In response to this decline, many theories are offered relating to the identities of the mega church goers as rationale for their size, style and public offerings. As early as 1996, one researcher citing the famous Osting for authority, argued that mega church identity corresponded to the kinds of institutions that the prototypical believer already grew up in and found comfort: the mall, the consolidated high school, the corporation in the office park, and the food warehouse (Thumma, 2006, p. 14). Unabashedly stating that the typical congregation is composed of middle class baby boomers that are at "home" in such large and anonymous environments, most coverage of mega churches do not disavow what to outsiders seem their garish, plain and corporate-style, insisting that they mold their churches as best they can to meet the needs of believers with comfort. According to Thumma, the decline in ascriptive identity makes possible the modern, Enlightenment-oriented identity of the typical megachurcher as they desire to make their own personal choices and commitments concerning religion rather than have them determined by birth or familial affinity.

This intriguingly modern conception of church going jives well with our previous understanding of the Bush administration's claim to be "producing modernity" and that the more societies move away from dependence on fated or determined futures, a window of opportunity opens to make change throughout the world and in individual lives. Importantly, to make use of this opportunity in time, one minister remarked on the architecture of the mega church as "friendly and accessible, determined to banish the sense of otherworldliness that has long been a very heart of Christianity," (Hofman, 2001, p. 2). Thus, the church should be a constant reminder in architectural form of the present moment as one unique to the believer over all future indemnities. The aura is also seemingly banished in the mega church, although some might argue that the aura shifts from ornament and objects to the practices of spirituality convened in "large volumes of spaces that enhance worship," (Ibid, 2). As one group of business and political advisors put it, the mega churches are not communities of 10,000 but 1,000 communities of 10," thus they resemble the high school experiences highlighted for the public in Columbine except these are the adult cliques that meet to worry about college tuition for children or strategize about community development. One of the most interesting congruencies between new evangelical churches and their seventeenth and eighteenth century forebears is the fetish for prefixes to otherwise ordinary activities such as "Christian aerobics" or "Christian basketball" that seemingly have no connection to religion other than their participants being brought together through the fellowship of the mega church where the activities are sponsored. As Hindmarsh describes, in the seventeenth century the prominent prefix or adjective to activities of people who had self-described conversions was "Gospel.' Today, such a phenomenological experience is captured in the Christian adjective, but does it signify a change in one's life similar to those evidenced in the autobiographical conversion narratives described in Hindmarsh's dense academic portrait that outlines the sociological and historical form of Christian confessional narratives from St. Augustine through to the seventeenth century Methodists, like Winthrop? Is the contemporary evangelical conversion narrative a genuine religious experience, like those preferred as objects of study by William James or is it as many who attempt to "sell" this new culture to undecided and "anxious" publics claim: an opportunity to find meaning in a changing world whose seismic demographic shifts seemingly threaten the integrity of family life? (Sosnik, Dowd & Fournier, 2006, p. 95). If one accepts the latter depiction that is based on the evidence provided by mega church leaders themselves, those who study them and eminent business strategists such as Peter Drucker, than the growing popularity of mega church culture is made possible by its powerful recognition of people's changing lifestyles. These are lifestyles that are expressions of a changing world rather than a world that wishes to remain unchanged; for the commentators argue that what they wish to retain in changing lifestyles is their family connections and the mega church provides a space for them to reproduce the new family norms in the retreat of state-centered attempts to do so. One of the massive changes that the authors of *Applebee's America*, a book whose title depicts the kind of privatized meeting space where family values are reproduced, note is the increasing number of women in the workforce (Sosnik et al., 2006).

Neoconservative vision can be shared by Jews and Christians alike because it inheres not to a conservative reality, where conservation means retaining aspects of European and other (m)other cultures but creating politics and belief systems that seek to actively distinguish themselves from them. By isolating what is uniquely American, mega churches are cultural expressions of a new political ideology: conversion.

Another aspect of the non-denominational mega church believer is the growing interest in autobiographical conversion narrative. Corresponding directly to the Baby Boomer fad of "finding one's self" whether through genealogy, the rock concert, mass street protest or gang bang, personal therapy, consumerist self-fashioning or phenomenological research, this kind of autobiographical identity structure grooves with American individualism (Cushmann, 1995). Where the "rationality of the individual is often feared lost in mass culture"[12] particularly of the big variety, it can be refound through the conversion narrative format. What individualism is lost in translation to mega institutions is gained in the reconstitution of the self through Christ. The individualism that is lost is the one previously fashioned out of privacy provided by liberalism's respect for the separation of spheres of private/public, sacred/profane, church/state, where the individual could leave citizenship and national identity at the door of public buildings to enter the sacred private space of the home to carve out a separate (personal) identity with self-chosen and selected persons or things.

CHAPTER 5

Common Culture

If anything unites Midwestern culture it is an outward disdain for the very sexual commodities so oddly and abundantly found in the rural American south: porn shops, XXX truck stops, movie theaters and strip clubs: the overt raunch culture found in the South. Guns are prevalent throughout the Midwest but their use is severely limited by different types of state gun control laws. For example, in Illinois a homeowner could shoot a trespasser with impunity until a bill was introduced by newly minted Illinois state senator Barack Obama and passed through with little public outcry. Though the Midwest does have these amenities so popularized in the south, it has purposefully secluded them to the edges of town, the poorer areas of small cities and along the freeways that connect one direct line of corporate chain restaurants to another. As a common disavowal these amenities, sex and guns, exist as reminders of a past America founded on wilderness territory, lawlessness and trading. These small, decaying shops are the remnants of "freedom" in the Midwest, and they signify a mercy option to the degraded outcast populations while they remain problematic for the poor and working class within the cities trying to raise their families in environments characterized by violence that surrounds such shops.

In the Midwest, new growth business cultures spark interest in optimistic worship formats. Trading on the industrial misery suffered here by unemployment, recessions and layoffs, new growth industries, like waste dumps and prisons, are readily welcomed here for the few jobs they might provide. And these optimistic houses of worship match their sermons to the business ethos of the new growth. Like the "Successories" stores that pepper Midwestern shopping malls offering consumers an opportunity to purchase catchy phrases superimposed on plaques, mugs and wall hangings for offices, the Successories chain is the best example of this business culture that morphs into the mega church style: "Each day thousands of organizations and leaders from all walks of life demonstrate that the use of motivational media to communicate corporate culture is an effective organizational tool," (Successories website). Churches use similar motivational media with 93% of music composed by electric guitar bands (there's no off-putting organ music found here).

While it has been accepted for a long time that the U.S. is dominated by one religion and one racial group: white Protestants, a newer development of commonality occurs along the lines of ideology. With so many choices for politicians these days it would seem as if they would be presenting the public with a great diversity of programs and choices. But, as we have seen so far in the book, many of the policies made real under W were desired policy outcomes of the Democrats that preceded them to the White House in 2001. Similarly, we do not find that many differences between Republicans and Democrats in Congress, nor are there many creative options for politics coming to the forefront from the grass roots or highlighted by the mass media. Instead, all political solutions, those that are the domain of the state are steadily coming under the rubric of privatization through corporations. Though corporations should technically present innovation and therefore choice, what we find under the eminent domain is a rather common set of options for politics and contemporary civic practices. This is not merely the convergence or feeding loop between neoconservative policy and neoliberal policy but is the overall result of a market culture with a tendency toward uniformity and standardization.

The critics of this new common culture found in Applebee's and mega churches are mostly former and current native inhabitants. Curtis White describes the dilemma perfectly in the following quote:

> In the end, evangelical Christianity conspires with technical and economic rationalism. In the end, they both require a "duty" that masks the unspeakable violence and injustice. In the end, the Muslim whose legs are being reduced to a pulp by his American tormentor doesn't care if he's being murdered because he's despised by Christianity or an impediment to economic rationality. He understands far better than we do how the two became one at the end of the torturer's rod. The predator missile, product of American scientific ingenuity, that homes in on his head is both self-righteously and arrogantly evangelical and meanly pragmatic. It is the empire that the rest of the world reads in George Bush's smirk. As John Ruskin understood 150 years ago, "The only question (determined mostly by fraud in peace, and force in war) is "Who is to die, and how?" (White, 2006, pp. 34–35).

Rustbelt Religion

"Changed lives" (Lampman, 2006, p. 3). If there is anything the Midwest seems to suffer from politically it is a lack of changed lives, at least for the better. Corporate culture and the mega church phenomenon that nourishes it give many people who feel abandoned by industry and politicians a way to conceptualize their lives *as changed* on terms they can say are of their own choosing. This is important. While many quibble with the notion that the decline of industrial production has meant little by way of a degradation of living conditions, they fail to see that the new growth industries in the Midwest do not employ the same folks downsized by the capital flight of rustbelt corporations. Those who work for the new industries are not usually indigenous to the Midwest but form a part of a white collar middle and upper class college educated demographic that have flocked to the Midwest from elsewhere in the country. If there was ever a truly rustbelt religion it was composed of an industrial working class ethos that maintained a strict separation of church and state; the workplace was a space of national reproduction in that it constructed patriotic identities that envisioned their labor as contributing directly to national wealth, prestige and power. Now that connection between the working class and national production is severed and the new white collar classes are products of the changing demographic whose identities are not based on the sacrificial model of sweat and labor for the family and nation but the flight from such weighty concerns to suburban and exurban living associated with rural lifestyle choices. It is not that this flight to the rural has meant an acceptance of agrarian values but that new cities are growing in the previously grid-marked cornfields described by novelist David Foster Wallace. This common culture is corporate culture and it is as Georgio Agamben puts it "not life, but death in motion," (Agamben, 1997, p. 186).

It gets stickier in Missouri, where the origins of all things fundamentalist seem to converge: Jesus Camp, mega churches, marriage bans in the state legislature. Indeed, Missouri is the gateway to Kansas that gives the road traveler along Route 66 a tiny bite of Christian culture to whet the appetite before the Whopper is served up in Kansas. Thomas Frank's book stimulated controversy for its overestimation of Kansans as the prototypical Bush voter, as well as his larger argument about this support verging on false consciousness.

Other People's Children

Grumet's analysis is focused on the teacher's point of view in relation to the curriculum and its supposed "ethics" which are, as she argues, defined as the morals that apply to strangers; moreover, they should be applied dispassionately (Grumet, 1988, p. 167). She further speculates that all weight holding down those who seek progressive lives for their children – for them to "master and commit to forms of being," they consider as un-performed in their own lives—comes in the form of this abstract curriculum that decides meritocracy and evaluates developmental achievement.

One of the criticisms of public schooling is that its curriculum contradicts the values of the home, especially those that relate to religion, with our notable examples of evolution and free speech challenges by religious witnessing. The home-schooling movement, flight to suburbs (urban schools are no longer the educational powerhouses celebrated by John Dewey) school choice in the form of vouchers and an overarching federal policy, NCLB (No Child Left Behind) that capacitates these – usually state-driven consumer/policy choices- leads to the dismantling of the semi-sacred canopy[11] of education that Grumet analyzes. Yet there are two mediating structures implied here: the one that corresponds to the nostalgic time when teachers taught the Bible as the main component of curriculum, (before they took God out of the schools!) the one that inheres to the professionalized demands criticized by every curriculum scholar as an alienating product of Taylorism and efficiency (after they took meaning out of education). Both, in their own ways, are championed in the present era as forms most suitable to promote and nourish the *nomos* of American democracy. Yet each of them is a product of the exact same critical tendency and shared sentiment concerning a lack of meaning in public education. What we need is a third, wholly new option that does not flow directly out of criticisms from either camp as they both stem from political demands made by adults in the name of children's rights. They are the fullest expression of what Julie calls the new (unquestioned) political movement to influence policy through nontraditional avenues that flow from playground to politics (Webber, forthcoming). This was first criticized by Arendt in a controversial essay concerning the de-segregationist efforts in Little Rock, Arkansas (Arendt, 2000, [1959]). While Arendt's concern was delimiting the child's zone of protection and responsibility against a zealous mature population from harm, she argued that this precedent opened to door to what we now know of as "children's rights" where children are conceptualized at the species level for rights we extend to racial minority citizens in relation to autocratic govermentalities, and animals, cells and plants. Rights have been devolving to the molecular level over time without referencing the original purpose to which rights are addressed: the naturalized assumption that the strong should have power over the weak (Mill, 1989, p. 124). Children are not a separate species or race onto themselves, they are a subset of the human race and therefore should be seen as subsumed under parental rights as having merely achieved "non-age" as Mill puts it. It is one of the most glaring examples of the shift from a disciplinary society (school as developmental institution that targets the formation of habit and routines conducive to an eventual public life in mature liberty) to a biopolitical one: individual sovereignties extended to children to protect them from harm at the level of their species. Who are they being protected from? Adult humans. The abstract extension of rights to children is nonsensical because the enforcer of those rights is presumed to be the state except in most cases where it is argued these rights are most needed the state is either in retreat or works together with the violator of child rights, usually corporations. So, who is to enforce these children's' rights? Under the sacred canopies of both religion and the curriculum we assumed it was the parents or state protection agencies that enforced rights on behalf of their minor children. However, now the assumption is that children need protection from families. How did a tangible public problem in the form of child abuse or neglect get transformed into an opportunity to dismantle curriculum and policy for the sake of partisan adult political agency?

Another contradiction emerges: these same adult interests who use minor children to challenge the separation of church and state (on either side of the aisle) also tend to support political agendas of delegates who oppose the extension of children's rights at the international level (Buss & Herman, 2003, pp. 83; 87) It is similar to the way one political theorist described the citizen self awareness promoted by Ronald Reagan's presidencies, "not as an instance of hypocrisy or of self-conscious mendacity but an evidence of neurotic splitting, the moral equivalent of a stroke, in which the right hand doesn't know what the left hand is doing," (Weinstein, 1991, p. 221).

As newly empowered children cognizant of their "rights" seek to proselytize in school (even during classroom periods) they challenge the common culture that seeks to offend nobody, and attract no one. "Other people's children" now pose a challenge to some people's children by bringing their conceptions of family and religious and cultural meaning into the school to sell it to others. Yet, by far the greatest challenge they pose is to the curriculum itself by challenging its generic ethics. Posting the 10 Commandments in schools following school shootings was an initial attempt to foist religious home-based values into school settings, and one can certainly question the values inherent in them for their relevancy to pertinent social issues, as Bill Maher recently did when he questioned an interlocutor as to whether he really thought not swearing and refraining from Sunday work were more important than sanctioning pedophilia. However, the curriculum resists any attempts to reclaim public space for private purposes, as its focus can never be specific or target practical social and political problems in a satisfying way, even Christian ones. And the curriculum of the mega church cannot either as it seeks to attract everyone and reject no one. It is modeled on a typical school curriculum: formulaic to an extreme degree, standardized, pre-packaged with directions for use and built-in scripts that leave no room for criticism. It is slick, technological, organized and entertaining. This is daycare for adults.

Maybe we are just jealous—those of us who cannot free ourselves from our ascriptive identities and languish in a political purgatory that is suspended between the heaven of participating in the American dream without guilt (if it's Christ's commission then the guilt is moot) and the hell of the same: popular culture scripted for our entertainment or shock value (such as the latest blockbuster movie or Starbuck's frozen smoothie) that shoots for a normalizing effect: enough titillation to arouse controversy over some presumed "value" that it can be explained away on Sunday by a charismatic church leader wearing a Hawaiian shirt who makes us feel cool for rejecting a progressive message. So much so that we refuse to think outside our large, airy boxes moving from one to another passing alongside those rusting railways, ready for nothing to change and everything to be presented as possible. This is one way to deny the "shredding of the sacred canopy" although one might see as a re-building of the canopy through faith-based initiatives. One central argument that those who favor faith-based support for social services is that the very de-humanizing ethics demanded by governmental (read secular and profane) policies and agencies fail to address the individual who is experiencing a soul struggling ordeal trying to pay the rent or feed their children.

Other people's children are doing the necessary political proselytizing to make it possible for many children to go without adequate public services. And other people's parents now serve in the role of *in loco parentis* for children who are unnamed yet threatened by the generic values that bolster both capitalism and democracy. These parents who attend mega churches embody the contradictions in Midwestern corporate capitalism and at the same time stand for family values contradict one another and preside over the dismantling of a state structure that guarantees their constitutional right to oppose school curricula and promote their own agendas. These are the big bodies that go no where.

EPILOGUE

THE STORIES WE TELL OURSELVES

This is what we are up against. Christian nationalists worship a nostalgic vision of America, but they despise the country that actually exists – its looseness, its decadence, and its maddening lack of absolutes (Goldberg, 2006, p. 210).

The issues we have addressed in this book are part of a complex attempt to rewrite the stories we tell ourselves. Not only our private stories but our national stories as well. Perhaps, the real struggle that the civic gospel and the Christocrats are part of is the great effort to determine who gets to tell our stories, what our stories say and the ways in which our stories determine us.

The latest phase of this process ignited when the cultural wars were inflamed with the reelection of Richard Nixon in 1972. This reelection of the "law and order" candidate signified the beginning of the end of the period of critique that the nation and the world had experienced up to that point. The Civil Rights Movement, the Women's Movement, the Anti-War movement, and the ecology movement were strong voices of the critique. These were/are voices that are hard to silence. They remain in the hostile rhetoric of red and blue states which while not a new phenomenon it is a rather simple way to gloss over the complex divisions and stories that have swirled around in this country for some time. It is part of a larger political, historical, economic, religious, gender, and racial story that is being constructed. It is the story that is moving toward a restoration, re-establishment, restitution or reinstallation of a wholeness that never existed. This story is filled with nostalgia and ressentiment as we discussed in the initial pages of this book. The story is accomplished through the rhetorical strategies examined in chapters three and four and find material home in the geographic areas of the Midwest and South examined in chapter five. Certainly there is the attempt to dismantle the economic and social dispositions of Franklin D. Roosevelt's New Deal and its Keynesian economic story. In the new metanarrative altruism is seen as weakness, greed as strength. "The three major programs of economic retrenchment in the alternative Friedman neoconservative economic agenda are cutbacks (particularly in social programs), deregulation, and privatization" (Klein, 2007, p. 57). But, even these very specific monetary measures are disguised or viewed as secondary in importance next to the cultural imagery. In fact, it is not so much about political agendas or economic programs as it is about the stories that gloss over these realities. These stories we are told and the ones we tell ourselves contribute to a perceived national identity. They favor an assured type of rhetoric that serves to obfuscate reality. Of course, it is a constructed identity and we wish to deconstruct that identity some in this final chapter. It is about the contribution of the Christocrats to that American imaginary. We would like to pursue as part of the deconstruction, how the imaginary is constructed and how it operates.

The Beginning of the New/Old Story

To the "greatest generation" (Brokaw, 1998) the turbulent 1960s was an anathema.

> For many, the war years were enough adventure to last a lifetime. They were proud of what they accomplished but rarely discussed their experiences, even with each other. They became once again ordinary people, the kind of men and women who always have been the foundation of the American way of life (Brokaw, 1998, p. i).

This characterization of the pre-1960s generation is part of the creation of the larger story and an element in a larger yearning for certainty.

Part of the development of the new/old story is that there is nostalgia. Boym (2001) elucidates the concept nostalgia which appears particularly after or during a period of uncertainty. "Nostalgia inevitably appears as a defense mechanism in a time of accelerated rhythms of life and historical upheavals." (xiv). But what in the early 21st century comprises that nostalgia or the desire for the story? There is yearning. Although, according to Boym it is difficult to determine exactly for what we are yearning. Aspects of the yearnings, however, can be articulated. The desire is for "another time, or a better life" (Boym, 2001, p. xiv). Now with the Christocratic influence coupled with this look backwards there is also a look forward. The Christocrats have perpetuated a desire for the end times. These yearnings are a crucial part of the development of the present mythology or narrative. There are many interconnected contributors to the present nostalgic story. We have elaborated many of these contributors in previous chapters. The creators of this particular symbolic order include, but are not limited to the Republican Party, the Christocrats, the neoconservatives, and the media (including journalists, musicians, political pundits and writers). The struggle over this symbolic order is more commonly referred to as the culture war. The important aspect of this struggle over the symbolic order is that those who determine the parameters of the symbolic order determine how we view ourselves. More importantly the symbolic order inscribes the debate and the issues that are important to a society. So, the story that "wins" allows only those aspects of the narrative that allows that story to function. Oppositional or counter strategic narrative strands are considered superfluous. They are considered by an order of bourgeois populists, to use Kristol's phrase. When the order that evaluates them is solely based upon moral precepts, then the opposing story is deemed immoral or amoral. Foucault discusses these stories as discourse. The presence of the Christocrats within the struggle takes the struggle to that level. The story that the Christocrats (read also Republican right-wing) has both a nostalgic and forward-looking themes.

Marriage

First and foremost it is a heterosexual story and an anti-homosexual one. As Puar (2007) states it is a heteronormative story. The assumptions behind this necessity of the family are both moral and political. As the argument goes, if there is no basic unit of society with an intelligible power structure, then society will turn chaotic. Rather than reconceptualizing the basic unit, the dominant story has reinforced the notion that the nuclear family (itself an invention of the nineteenth century West)[12] is 'natural' and under attack, in need of protection. That is one of the fundamental themes in this story. There must be a nuclear family. Homosexuality threatens marriage because it undercuts the historical primacy of patriarchy, where the husband is the leader of the family and the wife is subservient to him. Christocrats find a practical confusion here: who will be the man in a gay marriage? Therefore, marriage, of course, must be between a man and a woman to avoid confusion. This is why Bush never called for the equality of women or the empowerment of women in any speech he gave about domestic or international policy. He speaks instead of the "respect" for women which means the restoration of their place as a victim in need of protection from a masculine agent of power; in a word, a man, any man. That is one of the fundamental themes in this story. There must be a nuclear family. Marriage, of course, is a "law and order" solution to an open moral, economic and societal question. James Dobson, a preeminent spokesperson for the Christocrats has a lot to say about this portion of the story. Dobson has written a new book centering on this portion of the story entitled, *Marriage under Fire: Why We Must Win this Battle* (2007a). In an article on the Focus on the Family web site entitled, "Same-Sex 'Marriage' and Civil Unions (2007b) Dobson's contribution to the story goes like this

> Marriage is a sacred, legal, and social union ordained by God to be a life-long, sexually exclusive relationship between one man and one woman. Focus on the Family holds this institution in the highest esteem, and strongly opposes any legal sanction of marriage counterfeits, such as the legalization of same-sex "marriage" or the granting of marriage-like benefits to same-sex couples, cohabiting couples, or any other non-marital relationship (Dobson, 2007b, p. 1).

As we have shown the Republican Platform also supports this concept of marriage as part of the story. The 2008 Republican Party candidates for president also continued the construction of the story. The former governor of Massachusetts, Mitt Romney supported a Federal Marriage Amendment defining marriage as between one man and one woman. The Former governor of Arkansas, Mike Huckabee stated on his website that he supports "covenant" marriage.

> I support and have consistently supported passage of a federal constitutional amendment that defines marriage as a union between one man and one woman (Huckabee, 2007a, p. 1).

EPILOGUE

Although former Governor Rudy Giuliani supported partnerships he supported the notion that marriage is between a man and a woman. Senator John McCain's website provided his stand on marriage.

> The family represents the foundation of Western Civilization and civil society and John McCain believes the institution of marriage is a union between one man and one woman. It is only this definition that sufficiently recognizes the vital and unique role played by mothers and fathers in the raising of children, and the role of the family in shaping, stabilizing, and strengthening communities and our nation. (McCain, 2007, p. 6).

Former senator and actor Fred Thompson also supported the story of marriage as one man and one woman.

> Fred Thompson believes marriage is the union of one man and one woman, and that this institution is the foundation of society. As such, he supported the Defense of Marriage Act when he served in the Senate. He supports a constitutional amendment to prevent activist judges from misreading the Constitution to force same-sex marriage on any state and on our society (Thompson, 2007, p. 2).

The major candidates for the Republican nomination for the presidency were all supporters of the rhetoric of this portion of the metanarrative. Interestingly enough the Democratic candidates for president in 2008 also opposed same-sex marriages. They had less strict opposition, however, when it comes to supporting same-sex rights. Senator Hillary Clinton supported same sex civil unions and opposed same sex marriage. But she was against a constitutional amendment defining marriage. Senator Barak Obama opposed same-sex marriage, but supported same-sex unions. He opposed a constitutional amendment that would ban same-sex marriage. Former Senator John Edwards opposed same-sex marriage but supported equal rights for same-sex couples. Edwards opposed a constitutional amendment that would ban same-sex marriage. The only candidate that varied from support of the story was Representative Dennis Kucinich who supported same-sex marriage and opposed a constitutional amendment that would ban same-sex marriage. With little opposition the conceptualization of "covenant" marriage, a basic component of the metanarrative was consistently supported regardless of political affiliation. And, of course, this theme in the story was completely support by the Christocrats as we have demonstrated earlier in this text. In fact, the late Jerry Falwell, Pat Robertson, James Dobson and a host of other Christocratic leaders have blamed the decay of the traditional marriage, and gay and lesbians with the woes are country faces at the present moment.

Traditional marriage as part of the metanarrative of the 21st century, particularly since 9/11, is a foundational element to the story. It is a reaction to the "sexual revolution" that is credited to the 1960s era. The era of "free love" is seen as part of a larger failed social revolution. The point of the new/old story is to completely eradicate from memory and from society the traces of that failed attempt, even though the decline in marriage is mostly attributed to the reform of divorce laws in states in the 1950s (Gordon, 1973), and to the declining wage status of new generations (Reed, 2001). There exists the desire to return to some imagined notion of a post-World War II environment of the 1950s when the greatest generation was clearly in control. Remember we say an imagined 1950s. As we said previously nostalgia for what never really was. But, there is a strong sense that times were better then. There was more certainty, more security, more traditional values and less critique. Popular culture, of course plays a large part in fostering this notion of a better time. There were so many popular television programs in the 1950s that helped to construct this imaginary. One of the best examples, of course, was/is *Leave it to Beaver* (1957–1963). There were 234 episodes. It is now widely seen in syndication on cable networks. This show was part of a genre of shows. It was similar to another ironically titled show for the construction of this narrative, *Father Knows Best* (1954–1960). In essence, the series was one of a slew of middle-class family sitcoms in which moms were moms, kids were kids, and fathers knew best.

The Cleaver family is all too familiar to baby boomers. It was Ward Cleaver (husband), June Cleaver (wife), Wally Cleaver (oldest son), and Beaver Cleaver (youngest son). It was the nuclear family. The Cleavers lived in Mayfield a typical 50s suburb. No state was ever mentioned. Mr. Cleaver had an office job with a secretary but no official job was ever mentioned, but it was clear it was a good middle-class occupation. Of course June Cleaver was a stay at home Mom. She was frequently shown cleaning, dusting, or preparing meals in time for Ward's return from work. This is ideal middle-class family and part of the imaginary of the new/old story. Though the media focus on the family has changed from the Cleavers to the Simpsons and it is clearly "more dangerous to leave it to Bart than to leave it to Beaver (Cantor, 1999, p. 738). *The Simpsons*, according to Cantor, "still provides elements of continuity that makes it more traditional than it may appear and they are more familiar to the millennial generation" (Cantor, 1999, p. 738). Still the older story persists in the current imaginary. The nuclear family, the marriage between one man and one woman with two kids, living in suburbia, the father knowing best and working outside the home to provide a family wage and the mother staying at home raising the kids and serving her domestic function. There is a yearning on the part of those perpetuating this mythic narrative to go back to this time. We may have drifted from this image in reality, but the story is part of the agenda of the Christocrats and the politicians. It is in the rhetoric of family values, character education, abstinence education, anti-abortion debates and anti-feminism.

Now *Leave it to Beaver* is preached from the pulpits of mega churches and the podiums of presidential debates. Pat Robertson in a 700 Club message discusses marriage as bedrock.

> Now that, ladies and gentlemen, is the basis of marriage. It is male-female, not male and male, not female and female. It is male and female. There is no way that two women can reproduce. There's no way that two men can reproduce. The whole concept of marriage is to bring forth a godly seed, to bring forth children who will grow up to serve the Lord. That's what marriage is about and it is about nothing else. It has nothing to do with these hedonists, self-absorbed hedonists, if you will, that want to impose their particular sexuality on the rest of America. They don't need marriage because marriage

> was the protection of men and women, male and female, for the bringing forth of children. That's what it's about, nothing else, bottom line. And if America goes the other way we will be flying directly in the face of the clear word of the Bible. (Robertson, 2004, p. 40).

And, the preachers are followed by the politicians, who in speeches and in their books foster the story.

> Whether or not our culture should accommodate persons of the same gender who wish to share hospital visitations rights, insurance benefits and so forth is an entirely different discussion, but to call anything and everything a 'marriage' is unacceptable because marriage means something specific – a permanent relationship between a man and a woman for life (Huckabee, 2007b, p. 146).

Of course, if you deviate from this script you are immediately labeled as a tie-dyed remnant of the 1960s or as anti-social, anti-American or worse. This marriage theme is closely followed by the reestablishment of manly men. Those men who benevolently rule the family, protect women, and serve patriotically when the nation is threatened domestically or globally. This, despite the fact that free market fundamentalism reduces all workers –men and women- to substandard wages, all the while encouraging them to consume products with inflationary prices.[13] This reestablishment was especially true after 9/11, but had been in and out of favor since the 1980s. Actually the notion of manly men is a thematic which haunts American history from the days of the mythical frontiersmen to the present day firefighters. (see Faludi, 2007).

Generational Politics

Another reason this story is able to be told and go without critical commentary is that anyone who remembers how the fifties actually transpired is too disenfranchised to tell it or simply no longer with us. The Republicans have used the ignorance of entirely "new" generation (in the Arendtian sense) to tell a different story. Critical scholars and teachers who would tell the documented and objectively verified story of sex, race and class in America have been burdened with No Child Left Behind, with increasing bureaucratic red tape, with under funding and with every assault one can think of on our public system of education, while they construct this new, cheap version of events in the media (which is the best way to get the message across) that people readily accept because it trades on the very feelings of insecurity and ignorance fostered by these same story tellers through their inept governing in disasters like 9-11, Katrina, the economy and health care reform. It is a cycle of abuse to poor and working people to tell them they must have faith while these same story tellers undermine any basis in reality for them to have hope for a better or even acceptable future. It is easy to tell men they can be protectors at precisely the moment in history that they are least likely to be in financial, moral or political control over their lives, and to tell women that they will be protected at a time when they are under direct attack for doing anything other than having babies and worrying about being married. This is the heteronormative story, and it is impossible to fulfill in any material sense of the word, so they construct it in fantasy and regulate it through normative censure. It is the story of manly men and the women they protect but it is also how more violence and injustice is reproduced.

Manly Men and the Women they Protect

> When an attack on home soil causes cultural paroxysm that have nothing to do with the attack, when we respond to real threats to our nation by distracting ourselves with imaginary threats to femininity and family life, when we invest our leaders with a cartoon masculinity and require of them bluster in lieu of a capacity for rational calculation and when we blame our frailty on 'fifth column' feminists – in short, when we base our security on a mythical male strength that can only measure itself against a mythical female weakness – we should know that we are exhibiting the symptoms of a lethal, albeit, curable, cultural affliction (Faludi, 2007, p. 295).

Along with the theme of the nuclear family and marriage as defined as between one man and one woman, the new/old story attempts to (re?) establish men as masculine he-men and not as feminized sissies. Susan Faludi in *The Terror Dream: Fear and Fantasy in Post 9/11 America* (2007) discusses the return of the macho-man. She cites a *New York Times* article which characterizes the desire or yearning to return to a time when men were manly.

> In contrast to past eras of touchy-feeliness (Alan Alda) and the vaguely feminized, takish man-child of the 1990s (Leonardo DiCapro), the notion of physical prowess in the service of patriotic duty is firmly back on the pedestal (Leigh Brown, 2001, p. 5).

The fear of feminized men has been a consistent theme in the reconstruction of the metanarrative. Fear arose before the dawning of the 21st century. In the 1980s with the election of Ronald Reagan the first cowboy president there was a hopeful return to macho masculinity. Reagan was the political embodiment of father knows best, a cowboy and an actor. The United States had endured, as the Christocrats would have it, four years of the malaise of the Jimmy Carter administration with sweater fire side chats, exorbitant interest rates, and a failed rescue attempt to free the hostages in Iran amongst other perceived failures. It was time for a manly man to be president and to return other men to their rightful place. Reagan was frequently pictured wearing cowboy boots and a cowboy hat riding his horse. He played the part of a man's man. And most of the country delighted in it. With his loyal wife Nancy by his side he wanted to return America to its greatness and part of that was the destruction of the aberration of the 1960s era consciousness. The popular culture followed his lead. Particularly in the area of films that returned macho men to the screen during the 1980s.

Many texts have contributed to our understanding of the emergence of the Reagan era films (Rubenstein, 1989; Rubenstein, 1990; Tasker, 1993, Tasker, 2004; Chapman & Rutherford, 1988). These analyses suggest that the 1980s was a time to readjust masculinity. The American people had elected a movie hero as president and it was time to return America and its men back to a rightful place of power and preeminence. Chapman and Rutherford (1998) suggested that the image of a tough muscle macho man:

> advertises a destructive machismo as the solution to men's problems. He is John Wayne with his gloves off., wildly lashing out at everything that threatens and disappoints him. He confronts a world gone soft, pacified by traitors and cowards, dishonorable feminized men. It is a world that has disrupted his notions of manhood and honor. It threatens his comprehension of who he is. And his attempts to recreate order, and subdue the forces that threaten him, degenerate into a series of violent actions (28–29).

Much of the muscle men action movies of the 1980s served to bolster masculine spirits after the debacle of Vietnam (Reynolds and Gabbard, 2002) and the consequent Vietnam Syndrome. In fact these muscular heroes helped to rewrite our memories of the politics of Vietnam and reconstruct a more "honorable" masculinity. Giroux has provocatively analyzed films about Vietnam and demonstrated certain aspects of the ways in which those macho men with "spectacular bodies" (Tasker, 1993) rewrote our memories and developed our identities in the Reagan Era (Giroux, 1999, 2002; Reynolds & Gabbard, 2003).

> At the height of the Reagan Era, Hollywood rewrote the Vietnam War in the image of an unbridled and arrogant machismo. Films such as *Uncommon Valor* (1983), *Missing in Action 2, The Beginning* (1985), *Rambo: First Blood, Part II* (1985), and the *Hanoi Hilton* (1987) used Vietnam as a backdrop to celebrate heroic rescues. Chemical Warfare, forced settlements, and the burning of villages on the part of the U.S. military were written out of the history, as Hollywood invented wooden macho men intent on saving the real victims of Vietnam, the MIAs, from the demonized Vietnamese (Giroux, 1999, p. 151n).

Giroux continues that what was at issue in this rewriting of history was a Reaganite construction of the image of masculinity that coincided with a conservative image of national identity and patriotism.

> Flashback (1980s) – the smoke clears, the fire flares, the ground explodes and out of the haze emerges the muscular body wrapped in a bandoleer of bullets – *Rambo: First Blood Part II* (1985) played by Sylvester Stallone or Arnold Schwarzenegger) with a long broad sword in *Conan the Barbarian* (1981) or as a cyborg in *The Terminator* (1984) or a host of other muscled men in the 1980s action films (Jean-Claude Van Damme, Bruce Willis, Clint Eastwood, and Chuck Norris) (Reynolds, 2007, p. 343).

The 1980s did try to reestablish that notion of the strong man. Faludi (2007) chooses John Wayne as the classic American archetype of the cowboy macho hero. And, perhaps, all of those "spectacular bodies" (Tasker, 1993) of the 1980s were mere beef cake versions of John Wayne with 80s angst. But, there was the attempt to reestablish masculinity in terms of violence. It also meant that men, white straight men in particular, would be the saviors of our civilization, even if they had to kill and destroy to do it. Blain the character played by Jesse the body Ventura (former governor of Minnesota) in the film *Predator* (1987), a film populated by other muscular men (Arnold Schwarzenegger, and Carl Weathers) epitomizes the macho men of the 1980s. After one of fellow soldiers of fortune informs Blain that he is hit and wounded, Blain's response as he spits chewing tobacco is simply. "I ain't got time to bleed" (Silver, & McAlpine, 1987).

It is an interesting side note that when Ventura ran for governor of Minnesota in 1998 he changed his slogan from Jesse "the body" Ventura (his pro wrestling handle) to Jesse "the mind" Ventura. Perhaps, this was indicative of the 90s change in perceptions of masculinity.

William Clinton came into the White House in 1992. He was not the greatest generation cowboy. He was a baby boomer allegedly who avoided the draft and smoked but didn't inhale marijuana. This transition had an effect on the masculine image. The 1990s witnessed the emergence of books such as Robert Bly's *Iron John: A Book about Men* (1990) and *Fire in the Belly: A Book About Men* (1991) by Sam Keen. These books appear at the beginning of the 1990s and were a type of reaction to feminism and the quandary of masculinity. They were seen as a move away from a necessarily macho masculinity and perhaps a feminized perception of men. This version of masculinity was occasionally given the appellation "new age man".

Iron John (1990) was the book that initiated the discussion in the early 1990s about men and conceptualizations of masculinity. It even gave rise to the men's group phenomenon of the 1990s, famous for men moving to a more primitive stance and beating drums. Bly the author is a major American poet. When contrasted to Ronald Reagan and Jesse Ventura it is interesting to observe that a poet was discussing masculinity in the 1990s. Bly wanted to promote a new characterization of masculinity based on allegory and myth. And, he advocated men talking with one another. Bly believed that there were eight stages to developing his "wild man or hairy man" (Bly, 1990).

> The Iron John story proposes that the golden ball [unity we had as a child] lies within the magnetic field of the Wild Man, which is a very hard concept for us to grasp. We have to accept the possibility that the true radiant energy in the male does not hide in, reside in or wait for us in the feminine realm or the macho/John Wayne realm, but in the magnetic field of the deep masculine. It is protected by the *instinctive* one who is underwater and has been there we don't know how long. (Bly, 1990, p. 8).

The transition to the discussion of the hairy man buried deep within the male psyche was a challenge to the notions of Rambo man. Of course, the writing of an allegorical poet weren't necessarily widely accepted by large numbers of American males, yet the book did have influence and created other 90s interpretations of masculinity.

Keen's *Fire in the Belly* (1991) posits a new masculinity. It must be detached from women.

EPILOGUE

> As weapons and pollution threaten our existence we approach an era in which the practice of science and technology, which has been the dominant source of masculine pride for nearly two centuries, must give way to some new vocation, some new mode of masculine identity (Keen, 1991, p. 106).

The question, of course became: what was this new mode? The text explores various forms of mythology that contributed to the image of masculinity we had up to the 1990s. It discusses man's connection with the environment, war, technology and various other influences. The new male that Keen envisions is neither devoted careerist nor self-absorbed New Age guy nor cool, detached "post-modern man." He is husbandman and steward of the earth–strong, vulnerable, with a capacity for moral outrage, empathy and wonder–whose right livelihood is consonant with ecological awareness.

Alongside this identity literature popular culture also was delineating a new age type of masculinity. Films were still showing tough heroes but their essential qualities changed somewhat. Likewise television paraded a new host of male characters. The male heroes still were semi-tough and saving the world, but in the 1990s some had a social consciousness about the environment and issues of race. Of course, women were still the object of the gaze and didn't fair much better in the 1990s. Although there were some tough female action heroes like Linda Hamilton in *Terminator 2: Judgment Day (1991)*, Susan Sarandon and Geena Davis in *Thelma and Louise* (1991), Jamie Lee Curtis in *Blue Steel* (1990), Sigourney Weaver in *Aliens 3* (1992), Kristy Swanson in *Buffy the Vampire Slayer* (1992) which also ran as a very popular and cult television series from 1997-2003, and a number of others throughout the decade of the 1990s. The interesting thing is that the women who portrayed these heroines were still clad scantily and remained objectified despite their powers on screen.

The male action heroes of the 1990s contributed to the overall imaginary of that period by demonstrating cracks in the armor of macho masculinity. Typical were the Bruce Willis character of John McClain. McClain appeared in *Die Hard* (1988), *Die Hard 2: Die Harder* (1990), Die *Hard: With a Vengeance* (1995), and Live *Free or Die Hard* (2007). The character of John McClain is very macho, but not quite as beefcake as a Sylvester Stallone. He does suffer from alcohol problems, smoking issues, marital problems, authority issues, and male identity issues. He is the prototypical 90s hero. He is broken. He does save everyone in the end, but he does have that 1990s male angst. So, for a period of time the macho male was challenged in the popular literature, film and television.

Some would say a new stereotypical image of men in the 1990s emerged. Cowboy boots were replaced on weekends by Birkenstocks. Men worked in climate controlled offices in Brooks Brother's suits. Men drove BMWs and Mercedes. On weekends they left hunting in the woods for stays at exclusive hotels, resorts or ski trips to Aspen or spent their time learning how to prepare a gourmet dinner. Of course, there were always men who detested that particular image. They were stereotyped as well. They were the NASCAR-loving, football watching, Budweiser drinking, pick-up truck driving, country music loving boys. The point is, however, that the

Birkenstock wearers were the popular fostered image. But with the election of George W. Bush and the incidents of 9/11 all that would change quickly.

September 11, 2001, according to Faludi (2007), had a tremendous impact on our story of masculinity and the American imaginary. The terrorist attacks of 9/11 gave renewed strength to the development of the new/old story. After the horrendous terrorist attacks, a return to a warrior macho male seemed appropriate. John Wayne returns to protect the vulnerable maidens of our country. The quintessential man of the new/old story was a fireman, rescue worker, policeman, and the Blackwater mercenary. Gone were the references to the non-gendered terms such as firefighter. The photographic image of a soot covered fireman carrying a limp body of a child or woman away from the destruction of the Twin Towers was burned into the American imaginary. And, we had as a president a new breed of cowboy. G. W. Bush is a windshield cowboy. He doesn't ride a horse but drives a four-wheel drive pick-up truck and cuts brush with a chain-saw. "He is God's Cowboy Warrior" (McLaren, 2005, p. 261).

> Ever since the myth of America as God's chosen nation ingressed into the collective unconscious of the American people, U.S. politics has been primed for the appearance of national savors and sinners. Without skipping an opportunistic beat, Bush has assumed the mantle of *jefe* global warlord, taken up the hammer of Thor, and is continuing to wield it recklessly, in blatant disregard for the court of world opinion (McLaren, 2005, p. 262).

It was/ is the tough guy story all over again. Tough men would protect weak and helpless women and protect the United States from all manner of evildoers with whatever force deemed necessary. And, the presidential rhetoric was storied and cowboy tough. "I want justice...There's an old poster out West, as I recall, that said, 'Wanted: Dead or Alive'" (Woodruff, 2001, p. 32).

This is the tough guy story – the return of the macho male to the White House and for the rest of the nation. The John Wayne American male was back, if it ever really left, in the American imagination. It is interesting to note, in this context, that plethora of Republican candidates were all male and tripping over themselves to be the toughest guy on the block. This is consistent with the new/old story of masculinity. Now, Birkenstocks and organic clothing are replaced by work boots, cargo pants, fire helmets, camouflage and the ever ubiquitous American flag.

Violence against Women

And this is not without consequences. The manly macho persona is seemingly undermined by all our politicians "proud" work on domestic violence renewing the *Violence Against Women Act* (1994, 2007), in intervention in Afghanistan to subvert the gender terrorism of the Taliban. Violence throughout the world has taken on explicitly gendered formations, from violence against women, children of both sexes and same sex participants in various cultures (not all countries have "gay" and "lesbian" movements, their same sex or bisexual community's histories are as varied as their languages, religions, national rhetorics and geographies). The response to these violences has been to issue legislation and regulation to "protect" these "victims." Problem is, rather than urging equality and the rights that empower these groups to defend and claim their own dignities, on their own terms, this legislation has largely reinforced the notion that these groups are by their very nature weak, and this leaves the masculine heteronormative protector to decide: will he protect them or will he destroy them? Does he have time to bleed? Or think? In either choice, the idea that heterosexual men are natural protectors capable of extreme violence and strength for good or evil remains, and often this protector will be Caucasian.[14]

Second, the idea of protection gives those who seek to militarize our societies a justification for more violence. What happens when the Violence Against Women Act is renewed? Are women empowered to take on more rights, benefits, education or freedom? Again, we validate a "law and order" solution to the problem of gender violence. No, the funding is increasingly funneled into surveillance technologies and policing efforts to track abusers and place them in prison. It also creates an enormous surveillance institution that sneaks a partisan morality about gender and childrearing (deciding who is a good mother and bad one) based on Americans almost cult-like concern for the "best interests of the child." These institutions have been justified because of the larger story we tell ourselves about women and girls representing "purity" and self-sacrifice in the name of the nuclear family. Are the women of Afghanistan free from forced child marriage, burkas or public beatings? No, the Northern Alliance (allies to the invasion forces) it turns out, have the same ideas about women that the Taliban did. Women in Iraq have been under house arrest since the 2003 intervention, such chaos surrounds the country that the middle and upper classes have left, including the women professionals whose existence gave reliable proof that Iraq had made significant progress compared to its neighbors on gender equality, as had Iran and others before U.S. interference. Gay and lesbian coalitions in the U.S. have been smart to frame local ordinances and other legal measures in terms of human rights, rather than simply as legislation that empowers the police to surveil them. Not only has the framing of protection hurt women but it has indirect effects on gays and lesbians as it creates a national dialogue surrounding family that celebrates the heteronormative – and hierarchical- coupling, and alienates anyone whose romantic status doesn't fit the picture, including singles. As Bumiller reports, such discrimination against gays and lesbians has been justified by proposals to protect women in marriage in other countries (Bumiller, 2006, p. 332).

And if these threats don't convince the public, there's always quiescence on global climate change by politicians and the increasing endism of the Christocrats to frighten it into abeyance with the heteronormative fiction, the abandonment of the Constitution and the blurring between church and state.

The End-Times – Christian Eschatology

But when our born-again president describes the nation's foreign-policy objective in theological terms as a global struggle against "evildoers," and when, in his recent State of the Union address, he casts Saddam Hussein as a demonic, quasi-supernatural figure who could unleash "a day of horror like none we have ever known," he is not only playing upon our still-raw memories of 9/11. He is also invoking a powerful and ancient apocalyptic vocabulary that for millions of prophecy believers conveys a specific and thrilling message of an approaching end – not just of Saddam, but of human history as we know it (Boyer, 2003, p. 3).

Many Christocrats feel that concern for the future of our planet is irrelevant, because it *has* no future. They believe we are living in the End Time, when the son of God will return, the righteous will enter heaven, and sinners will be condemned to eternal hellfire. "They may also believe, along with millions of other Christian fundamentalists, that environmental destruction is not only to be disregarded but actually welcomed – even hastened – as a sign of the coming Apocalypse" (Scherer, 2004, p. 11).

Another theme in the story is that of Armageddon or more euphemistically known as the end times. It is a theme within the larger new/old story. Just how many Christocrats believe or relate to the discussion or the quandary of the end times. Of course, the exact number is not known, but there are many who relate.

Although survey results vary, some 7 to 10 percent of U.S. churchgoers appear to be Pentecostals, and perhaps a quarter of churchgoers are full-fledged end-times believers, as opposed to the 50 percent or so who relate to the symbolism when holy wars or tsunamis dominate the news (Phillips, 2006, p. 106).

Perhaps, one the key elements of the resurgence of the end-times theme is a series of books written and the films based upon those books by mega church preacher Tim LaHaye's. The *Left Behind* series of 16 books, begun in 1995, has sold 65 million copies. This series begins in the initial book *Left Behind* (1995) with the rapture and believers disappearing, being pull/transcending out of cars, relatives disappearing only to have people recognizing they are entering the tribulation. The books basically follow LaHaye's version of the end-times all the way to Armageddon and the return of Jesus Christ.

Besides LaHaye's fictional accounts of being left behind, because that is what happens to non-believers, much of the current thinking of the end-times can be traced to John Nelson Darby. Although most current end-timers could not trace their theology back to Darby, his conceptualizations are certainly a base. Darby was the most prominent of the Plymouth (England) Brethren movement.

The Plymouth Brethren, when first organized, had two main distinctions: (1) theirs was an ecumenical movement, and (2) they sought to do away with an ordained clergy and anything which even resembled organization within the local church. They were opposed to music or any type of ritual in the church service. Darby's watchword, according to his biographers, was "the union of the children of God." The Brethren frowned on ordination as constituting a man-made ministry, and the very word "Brethren" was an attempt to get away from denominationalism. (Cox, 2007, p. 11).

EPILOGUE

Their beliefs are sometimes termed Darbyism. Darby had an order for Biblical and end-time events. This is called dispensationalism. Dispensationalism's definition or characteristics are somewhat disputed but the end-times are part of this dispensationalism so a brief delineation is helpful. Each dispensation is best looked at as an historical period. "Each period according to Darby situates man under a particular condition and with a responsibility to God. The various dispensations are: 1. Eden to the Flood; 2. Noah; 3. Abraham; 4. Israel; 5. Gentiles; 6 The Spirit; 7. The Millennium" (read end-times) (Enns, P. 1989 p. 516). It must be remembered, however, that this is Darby's interpretation of the book of Revelation in the Bible. His chronicle of events for the end-times is as follows. First, there is the Rapture. The rapture is when Christ will descend from Heaven with all the spirits of the saints and angels, even those that existed before his incarnation. Then the physical remains of these saints are transported to meet with their spiritual essences. Then all Christians that are alive on earth are transported to meet Christ in the air. They will have resurrection bodies, as does Christ. The timing of this event is contested in fundamentalist circles as to exactly when the faithful will transcend to heaven. When will the transcendence occur? Some believe it will be pre-tribulation and some believe it will be post-tribulation. The tribulation is a period of time when Christian believers will experience worldwide persecution and all manner of destruction. Darby sides with the pre-tribulationists. Darby's are not the only orientation to the end-times.

> True believers are suddenly pulled into the sky to be with Christ. Next follows the seven-year tribulation, when the satanic antichrist will arise in Europe and seize world power. At its end Christ and his armies will triumph in a great battle in Har-Megiddo, near Haifa in what is now Israel. From Jerusalem Christ will proclaim the start of a one-thousand-year reign of peace (Phillips, 2006, p. 253).

There are at least major three views of the end times. They have been labeled premillennial, amillennial and postmillennial. These are different ways of viewing the timing and sequencing of the final days.

Premillennial views suggest that the second coming of Christ will occur before Christ has a thousand year rule. This is the view of the *Left Behind* series. This means that the rapture will occur before the tribulation begins. Most Christocrats hold this view. The amillennial view holds that Christ will actually return but all of the premillennial views are merged into a millennial age. In this view Christ does not literally reign on earth but builds a church through his followers. There is a long time of struggle until the final judgment. The Roman Catholic Church and most Protestant (read non-Christocrat) denominations are mostly likely to favor this view. Finally, the postmillennialists generally agree with the amillenialist. That is postmillennialists think that believers are working toward a Christianized world which sets the stage for Christ's return (see Enns, 1989). It is apparent that if believers are wrapped up in end-times thinking political agendas that either work toward establishing a Christian Nation or bring about the end-times are compelling goals. These agendas would hasten the millennial age. This end-time thinking was alive and well specifically in the second term of George W. Bush.

Bush's continual references to good versus evil, the axis of evil, evil doers and crusades amplifies the connections with end-time thinking and helps to solidify this theme in the story. "Bush's public theology has shifted from talking mostly about a Wesleyan theology of "personal transformation" to describing a Calvinist "divine plan" laid out by a sovereign God for the country and himself' (Caldwell, 2003, p. 1).

> End-times prophecy fueled a fifth dynamic at work as the forces for the Iraq invasion gathered, because many Christian fundamentalists dismissed worries about oil or global warming out of belief that the end times were under way. The Bible lands were what mattered. Events were in God's hands. (Phillips, 2006, p. 95).

"One of the very many connections between religious belief and the sinister, spoiled, selfish childhood of our species is the repressed desire to see everything smashed up and ruined and brought to naught" (Hitchens, 2007, p. 57). The point of the end-time story is that while the faithful Christocrats are consumed in this imaginary story about the journey to the rapture, they do not have to spend time worrying about issues like global warming, violence against women, heteronormative practices, wars based on lies, senseless genocides and alike. After all, the end is coming and Christ is coming back to make it all right. So, why worry about it when you have all the answers. In fact if the unilateral aggression of the United States brings the end-times on faster so much the better. Along with the strict delineation of marriage and its requisite homophobia, the tough guy bravado, and the consequent objectification and violence against women, and the looming end-times these themes comprise the metanarrative. But the metanarrative is not reality. It is delusional. "That self-delusion, so deeply ingrained in our history, so heavily defended by our culture, calls out for refutation" (Faludi, 2007, p. 295).

Actually much of the rhetorics that have been constructed in the Bush years are not only delusional but assists in taking us away from the discussion of important issues. Frank (2004) makes the point that the Christocratic Republicans are very successful in the use of issues such as gay marriage. The rhetoric escalates and the debates become heated and the faithful go to the polls and vote conservative candidates into office. Once these candidates secure their elections and their offices and for the most part ignore these trigger issues. After Bush won the 2004 election based mostly on the anti-gay vote in Ohio, his first act of business was the attempt to privatize social security. This was a strategy that was certainly against the interests and well-being of the very people who voted for him. Not only are these types of moves frequent, but also there is little in-depth discussion of the real issues like the Iraq War. There is talk about Armageddon, not Afghanistan or Iraq. In a script from an episode of *Real Time with Bill Maher* (2007), Maher's guest Salman Rushdie expressed the nature of the discussions on issues like Iraq.

> Well, see, What I think is strange is it's like the Republicans, in order to not talk about the war, you know, any excuse not to discuss the actual war, mean you attack people who talk about the war in ways they don't like. So, you talk

about talking about the war [laughter] instead of talking about the war. You know you don't like Dan Rather because of the way he talks about the war. You don't like MoveOn because of the way they talk about the war (Maher et al., 2007, p. 13).

Delusional denial and the diversional characterize the present historical moment.

The Future of the Story

We have discussed in this text the past and the present concerning the Christocratic agenda and its consequences. We did so because we were both concerned and alarmed at the historical moment and what it presented as a possible future. We are living in a time that swirls in lies and the delusional and diversional. And, quick-fix strategies or stories for education, the environment, elections, and all the other interconnected issues will serve little purpose other than to exacerbate the problems. It is also alarming that even though there is a plethora of information available to American citizens they apparently are too consumed with consuming to really pay attention or get involved. And, when there is activism it is not reported by the mainstream media. Although the Christocrats and Republicans would have us believe that the media is some left-wing conspiracy. And of course, anyone who critiques the government or its agenda is labeled a terrorist. Dissent is not to be tolerated or given any coverage. The culture wars come with a price. And, it has consequences beyond whether you drink Merlot or Budweiser, live in a Red or Blue State, or drink lattes or Maxwell House, The culture war has a materiality as we have tried to demonstrate in this book. It enters into the struggles over privatization, homosexuality, health care, and military unilateralism. That materiality affects our everyday lived experience.

The 21st century is still young perhaps, there is a possibility of some type of challenge to the current milieu can be made. Faludi (2007) states that we need to attempt the challenge.

September 11 offers us, even now, the chance to revisit that past and reverse the long denial, to imagine a national identity grounded not on virile illusion but on the talents and vitality of all of us equally, men and women both (Faludi, 2007, p. 296).

After working through the intricacies of the cartography of Christianity and the civic gospel, we couldn't agree with her more.

NOTES

[1] The content of this disobedience is very different from Thoreau's, Grimke's or Ghandi's.

[2] While many in the men's movement joined in response to feminism and the way it altered relationships between men and women in public and acted as a reactionary force those that stayed in the movement have developed sophisticated critiques of masculinity and the way it harms men. Most of these critiques are similar to those made by feminists. I doubt we will hear of a critique of Christianity from the Christian Right unless they want to return to arguments about the imperialist Papacy although this would be entirely different from the men's movement as well.

[3] This phenomenon has also been applied to the war in Iraq and Afghanistan where private contractors act as a shadow army to the official one. See Jeremy Scahill. 2007. *Blackwater*. New York: Nation Books.

[4] By the way, for anyone who doesn't know the answer to "Why do they hate us?" The answer is righteousness, which Tocqueville said "exalts a nation" but he failed to mention that it doesn't win the nation any respect, friends or sympathy.3

[5] Karen Hughes, speechwriter, campaign expert and undersecretary for public diplomacy (2005–2007) has bragged publicly about how she managed to get 23 references to *Psalms* into George W. Bush's speeches following 9-11.

[6] Federally funded clinical testing was not required to test both men's and women's reactions to drugs and treatment as well as the effects of diseases until 1993, when Clinton used an executive order to force compliance against a recalcitrant congress. All trials before that were conducted only with men as test subjects.

[7] The disdain for the elderly is retained in the new modernity as they are unable to contribute in a biopolitical fashion. This means aged men (still retaining power) must demonstrate that they are in fact not old and pharmaceutical companies are more than willing to help stage this virile performance by devoting clinical research time to hair re-growth products, erectile dysfunction medications, etc.

[8] Witness the forced retirements of every news anchor and journalist with knowledge of Cold War strategy, the Vietnam War and U.S. policy during this administration. The promotion of women by news networks does not imply the promotion of knowledgeable newswomen but has been offered to the public as a concession for extinguishing criticism.

[9] At the time this goes to press, December 2007, a court ruling has made the Bush administration's claim that records of White House visitors be kept private null and void. Arguing that the records belong to the Secret Service instead. The public may soon find out the actual ties between the administration and these groups.

[10] Arjun Appadurai's *Fear of Small Numbers* is instructive on this point. His point about the loss of individual rationality is a serious one, in that the move to mass cultures we find backlash movements against them in the form of racism and anti-immigrant measures. But, Appadurai's central claim is that democracies fear "small numbers" meaning numerical minorities because of procedural reasons related to the concept of dissent, not difference. It is not the Other, per se, that is feared, but a difference of opinion, where the normative value from procedural minorities and temporary minorities is transferred to substantive ones (64).

[11] The semi-sacred canopy alludes to Berger's analysis by way of educational policy administration where authors argue that education in the United States possessed its own separate *nomos* largely designed to protect its practitioners, according to David Wiles. Citing Iannocone (mid-1960s) and Elliot (1959) he argues that the semi-sacred canopy slowly breaks down with the professionalization of education and the notion that educational policy can be studied by political scientists as any other governmental policy would. There is, however, still a bias in political science against studying educational policy: that someone is somehow not studying serious or real policy and it is often feminized just as the occupation of teaching itself was during the same period.

NOTES

[12] In most cultures, at varying times, family formation or social organization has shown remarkable diversity, depending on the type of production in that society. For some, extended families provide the kinship necessary to produce food and care for all members of families, in other times, marriage has been seen as a contract between men for the exchange of women. In the eighteenth century, the U.S. inherited marriage law as coverture from an interpretation of English Common Law made by Williiam Blackstone, who argued that women lost their legal personhood in marriage to their husbands, who were to represent them. While there have been reforms to this law, it has never been fulllly repealed and individual states monitor the contractual status of marriage in the U.S. See (Hoff 2007). The nuclear family is an invention of postwar prosperity in the U.S. See (Coontz, 2000).

[13] This strategy worked well for the patrons working the lafundistas in Central America, and apparently it works in a free and open democracy as well.

[14] According to a CBS News report, commanders in the field of Iraq and Afghanistan are looking the other way when soldiers get outed as gay or lesbian by their peers because the morale is so low and they can't improve recruitment rates. See (Stahl, 2007).

BIBLIOGRAPHY

Agamben, G. (1998). *Homo sacer: Sovereign power and bare life* (D. Heller-Roazen, Trans.). Palo Alto, CA: Stanford University Press.

Agamben, G. (2005). *State of exception* (K. Attell, Trans.). Chicago: University of Chicago Press.

About us-meet southern Baptists. In the about us section of The Southern Baptist Website. Retrieved October 10, 2007, from http://www.sbc.net/

Alabama Department of Archives and 1948. Retrieved December 12, 2006, from http://www.alabamamoments.state.al.us/sec54.htmlHistory. Dixiecrates-the states rights party

Allitt, P. (2003). *Religion in America since 1945: A History*. New York: Columbia University Press.

Ambrose, S. (2004, April). *Resisting market fundamentalism: Ending the reign of extremist neo-liberalism*. Retrieved December 18, 2007, from http://www.50years.org/cms/ejn/story/61

Altemeyer, B. (1996). *Authoritarian specter*. Cambridge, MA: Harvard University Press.

Appadurai, A. (2006). *Fear of small numbers*. Chapel Hill, NC: Duke University Press.

Applebee, P. (1997). *Dixie rising: How the south is shaping American values, politics, and culture*. New York: Harcourt Brace & Co.

Arendt, H. (2000). Reflections on Little Rock. *Dissent*, (6)1. Reprinted in *The Portable Hannah Arendt*. New York: Penguin. (Originally published in 1959)

Armstrong, K. (1994). *A history of God: The 4,000-year quest of Judaism, Christianity and Islam*. New York: Ballantine Books.

Armstrong, K. (2000). *The battle for God: A history of fundamentalism*. New York: The Random House Publishing Group.

Arreguin-Toft, I. (2005). *How the weak win wars: A theory of asymmetric conflict*. Cambridge University Press.

Baggett, D. (2000). On a reductionist analysis of William James's philosophy of religion. *Journal of Religious Ethics, 28*(3), 423–448.

Baker, S. (2000). *The postmodern animal*. London: Reacktion.

Barton Schwiger, B. (2004). How would Jesus vote? The prehistory of the Christian right. *Reviews in American History, 32*, 49–57. [Review of Gaines, F. M. (2002). *Moral reconstruction: Christian lobbyists and the federal legislation of morality, 1865–1920*. Chapel Hill, NC: University of North Carolina Press.]

Barkat, A. (2006). *Economics of fundamentalism and the growth of political islam in Bangladesh*. Retrieved December 17, 2007 from http://www.secularvoiceofbangladesh.org/article%20by%20Abdul%20Barkat.htm

Basu, A. (2004). The human and his spectacular autumn, or, informatics after philosophy. *Postmodern Culture, 14*(3). only/issue.504/14.3basu.txt

Basu, A. (2005). *Mantras of the metropole: Geo-televisuality and contemporary Indai cinema*. Unpubished doctoral dissertation, University of Pittsburgh, Pittsburgh.

Baudrillard, J. (2005). *On the lucidity pact* (C. Turner, Trans.). New York: Berg.

Baylor, C., Dougherty, K., Froese, P., Johnson, B., Mencken, F. C., Park, J. Z., et al. (Eds.). (2006). *American piety in the 21st century: New insights to the depth and complexity of religion in the US (Selected findings from the Baylor Religion Survey)*. Waco, TX: Baylor Institute for Studies of Religion and Department of Sociology.

Baum, C. (producer) & Kuzui, F. R. (director). (1992). *Buffy the vampire slayer* [motion picture]. United States: 20th Century Fox.

Beasley-Murray, J. *Deleuze, Guattari and a political philosophy of interest*. Retrieved September 10, 2005, from http://www.arts.uwa.edu.au/EnglishWWW/abstracts/10.html

Bell, D. (2005). *Silent covenants*. Oxford University Press.

Benjamin, W. (1969). *Illuminations*. New York: Schocken.

Bennett, W. J. (1992). *The de-valuing of America: The fight for our culture and our children*. New York: Simon & Schuster.

BIBLIOGRAPHY

Berger, P. (1990). *The sacred canopy: Elements of a sociology of religion.* New York: Anchor.
Bergson, H. (1996). *Matter and memory* (N. M. Paul & W. S. Palmer, Trans.). New York: Zone Books.
Berlant, L. E. (1997). *The queen of America goes to Washington City: Essays on sex and citizenship.* Durham, NC: Duke University Press.
Berry, M. F. (1988). *Why the ERA failed.* Bloomington, IN: Indiana University Press.
Bishop, D. H. (1972). William James and the humanist manifesto. *Religious Humanism, 6*(1), 34–39.
Black, J. E. (2003). Extending the rights of personhood, voice and life to sensate others: A homology of right to life and animal rights rhetoric. *Communication Quarterly, 51*(3), 312–331.
Bly, R. (1990). *Iron John a book about men.* Reading, MA: Addison-Wesley.
Boyer, P. (2003). *When U.S. foreign policy meets biblical prophecy.* Retrieved December 13, 2007, from http://www.alternet.org/story/15221/?page=3
Boyle, M. (2004). Utopianism and the Bush foreign policy. *Cambridge Review of International Studies, 17*(1), 82–103.
Boym, S. (2001). *The future of nostalgia.* New York: Basic Books.
Brickner, B. W. (1999). *The promise keepers.* Lexington, KY: Lexington Books.
Brokaw, T. (1998). *The greatest generation.* New York: Random House.
※ Brown, W. (2006). American nightmare: Neoliberalism, neoconservatism, and de-democratization. *Political Theory, 34*(6), 690–714.
Buchanan, I. (2000). *Deleuzism: A metacommentary.* Durham, NC: Duke University Press.
Bumiller, E. (2005, October 13). Bush criticized over emphasis on religion of nominee. *The New York Times.* Retrieved from http://www.nytimes.com/2005/10/13/politics/politicsspecial1/13bush.html
Bumiller, K. (2006). Freedom from violence as a human right: Toward a feminist politics of nonviolence. *Thomas Jefferson Law Review, 28,* 327–354.
Burrell, B. (1994). Campaing finance: Women's experience in the modern era. In S. Thomas & C. Wilcox (Eds.), *Women and elective office.* New York: Oxford University Press.
Burum, S. H. (Producer) & Kotcheff, T. (Director). (1983). *Uncommon valor* [Motion picture]. United States: Paramount.
Bush, G. W. (2001, August 8). *Character development.* Speech present to the YMCA Picnic, p. 1. Retrieved from http://www.whitehouse.gov/query.html?col=colpics&qt=values
Bush, G. W. (2001, November). *Press conference.* Retrieved October 2, 2007, from http://archives.cnn.com/2001/US/11/06/gen.attack.on.terror/
Buss, D., & Herman, D. (2003). *Globalizing family values: The Christian right in international politics.* Minneapolis, MN: University of Minnesota Press.
Chalcedon Foundation. (2007). *Chalcedon vision statement.* Retrieved December 18, 2007, from http://www.chalcedon.edu/vision.php
Caldwell, D. (2003). *George W. Bush: Presidential preacher.* Retrieved December 12, 2007, from http://www.baptiststandard.com/2003/2_17/pages/bush_preacher.html
Callahan, W. A. (2006). War, shame, and time: Pastoral governance and national identity in England and America. *International Studies Quarterly, 50*(2), 395–419.
Cameron, J. (producer) & Cameron, J. (director). (1991). *Terminator II: Judgement day* [motion picture]. United States: Carolco Pictures.
Canham, M. (2005, June 3). Evolution battle to flare up in Utah. *The Salt Lake Tribune.*
Cantor, P. A. (1999). The Simpsons: Atomistic politics and the nuclear family. *Political Theory, 27*(4), 734–749.
Cash, W. J. (1941/1991). *The mind of the south.* New York: Vintage Books Edition.
Chapman, R., & Rutherford, J. (Eds.). (1988). *Male order: Unwrapping masculinity.* London: Lawrence and Wishart.
Christocrat.com. *Had enough yet?* Retrieved December 18, 2007, from http://www.christocrat.com/Ads/newspaper%20ads%20for%20organizing%20groups/had%20enough%20yet.doc
CNN. (2005, January 14). *Judge: Evolution stickers unconstitutional markers in science textbooks violated church-state separation.* Retrieved December 20, 2007, from http://www.cnn.com/2005/LAW/01/13/evolution.textbooks.ruling/

BIBLIOGRAPHY

CNN. (2006, November 4). *Church forces out Haggard for 'sexually immoral conduct'*. Retieved December 20, 2007, from http://www.cnn.com/2006/US/11/03/haggard.allegations/index.html

CNN. (2007, March 4). *Coulter under fire for anti-gay slur*. Retrieved December 20, 2007, from http://edition.cnn.com/2007/POLITICS/03/04/coulter.edwards/

Cobb, J. C. (1999). *Redefining southern culture: Mind and identity in the modern south*. Athens, GA: The University of Georgia Press.

Cobb, J. C. (2006). *Away down south: A history of southern identity*. New York: Oxford University Press.

Colebrook, C. (2002). *Gilles Deleuze*. New York: Routledge.

Coleman, S. (2005). An empire on the hill? The Christian right and the right to be Christian. *Anthropological Quarterly, 78*(3), 653–671.

Columbia Journalism Review. *Who owns What?* Retrieved December 17, 2007, from http://www.cjr.org/resources/index.php?c=timewarner

Connell, R. W. (2005). Change among the gatekeepers: Men, masculinities, and gender equality in the global arena. *Signs, 30*(3): 1801–1825.

Connolly, W. E. (1999). *Why I am not a secularist*. Minneapolis, MN: University of Minnesota Press.

Connolly, W. E. (2005). The evangelical-capitalist resonance machine. *Political Theory, 33*, 869–886.

Connolly, W. E. (2005). *Pluralism*. Durham, NC: Duke University Press.

Coontz, S. (2000). *The way we never were: American families and the nostalgia trap*. New York: Basic Books.

Copjec, J. (2002). *Imagine there's no woman*. Boston: Massachusetts Institute of Technology.

The crafty attacks on evolution. (2005, January 23). *The New York Times*. Retreived October, 28, 2006, from http://www.nytimes.com/2005/01/23/opinion/23sun1.html?pagewanted=print&position.

Cushman, P. (1995). *Constructing the self, constructing America*. Reading, MA: Addison-Wesley.

Darbyshire, P. (2002). The politics of love: Harlequin romances and the Christian right. *Journal of Popular Culture, 35*(4), 75–87.

De Laurentiis, D. (producer) & De Laurentiis, R. (director). (1981). *Conan the barbarian* [motion picture]. United States: Universal Pictures.

Deleuze, G. (1983). *Nietzsche and philosophy* (H. Tomlison, Trans.). London: The Athlone Press.

Deleuze, G. (1986). *Cinema 1: The movement image* (H. Tomlinson & B. Habberjam, Trans.). Minneapolis, MN: The University of Minnesota Press.

Deleuze, G. (1988). *Bergsonism* (H. Tomlinson & B. Habberjam, Trans.). New York: Zone Books.

Deleuze, G. (1990). *The logic of sense* (C. V. Boundas, Trans.). New York: Columbia University Press.

Deleuze, G. (1991). *Bergsonism* (H. Tomlison & B. Habberiam, Trans.). New York: Zone Books.

Deleuze, G. (1994). *Difference and repetition* (P. Patton, Trans.). New York: Columbia University Press.

Deleuze, G. (1995). *Negotiations 1972–1990* (M. Joughin, Trans.). New York: Columbia University Press.

Deleuze, G. (2004). *Desert islands and other texts 1953–1974* (M. Taomina, Trans.). Cambridge, MA: MIT Press.

Deleuze, G. (2006). *Two regimes of madness: Texts and interviews 1975–1995* (D. Lapoujade, Ed., A. Hodges & M. Taormina, Trans.). Cambridge, MA: The MIT Press.

Deleuze, G., & Guattari, F. (1983). *Anti-Oedipus: Capitalism and schizophrenia* (R. Hurley, M. Seem & H. R. Lane, Trans.). Minneapolis, MN: The University of Minnesota Press.

Deleuze, G., & Guattari, F. (1987). *A thousand plateaus: Capitalism and schizophrenia* (B. Massumi, Trans.). Minneapolis, MN: University of Minnesota Press.

Deleuze, G., & Parnet, C. (1987). *Dialogues* (H. Tomlinson & B. Habberjam, Trans.). New York: Columbia University Press.

Delgado, R. (1977). Religious totalism. *Southern California Law Review, 51*, 1–99.

Dembski, W. A. (1999). *Intelligent design: The bridge between science & technology*. Downers Grove, IL: Intervarsity Press.

Devji, F. (2005). *Landscapes of the Jihad*. Ithaca, NY: Cornell University Press.

Denver Channel. (2006, November 5). *Ted Haggard's letter to New Life church members*. Retrieved from http://www.thedenverchannel.com/news/10250226/detail.html

BIBLIOGRAPHY

Dewey, J. (1929). *The quest for certainty: A study of the relation of knowledge and action.* New York: Minton, Balch and Co.

Dewey, J. (1997). *The influence of Darwin on philosophy.* New York: Prometheus Books. (Originally published in 1910).

Diamond, S. (1989). *Spiritual warfare: The politics of the Christian right.* Boston: South End Press.

Diamond, S. (1998). *Not by politics alone: The enduring influence of the Christian right.* New York: The Guilford Press.

Diamond, S. (2002). *Dominion theology: The truth about the Christian Right's bid for power.* Retreived December 12, 2007, from http://www.sullivan-county.com/nf0/fundienazis/diamond.htm

Dideon, J. (1994). *Leo Strauss and the American right.* New Haven, CT: Yale University Press.

Dideon, J. (2003, November 6). Mr. Bush and the divine. *New York Review of Books,* 81–86.

Dobson, J. C. (2007a). *Marriage under fire: Why we must win this battle.* Carol Stream, IL: TyndaleHouse Publishers.

Dobson, J. C. (2007b). *Same-Sex 'marriage' and civil unions.* Retrieved December 12, 2007, from http://www.family.org/socialissues/A000000464.cfm

Domke, D. (2004). *God willing: Political fundamentalism in the White House, the "War on terror" and the echoing press.* Ann Arbor, MI: The University of Michigan Press.

Doug. (2005). Judge throw book at Dover Board in rulling. *Secular Left.* Retrieved December, 15, 2007, from http://www.secularleft.us/archives/2005/12/judge_throws_bo.html

Dubuc, N., & Thompson, M. (Producers) & Ewing, H., & Grady, R. (Directors). (2006). *Jesus camp* [Motion Picture]. New York: Magnolia Pictures.

Duggan, S. (Producer) & Wiseman, L. (Director). (2007). *Live free or die hard* [motion picture]. United States: Cheyenne Enterprises.

Dunn, C. W. (2003). *Faith, freedom and the future: Religion in American political thought.* Lanham, MD: Rowman and Littlefield.

Eco, U. (1995). Eternal fascism. *Utne Reader,* November/December, 57–59.

Egan, T. (2006, June 4). In a solidly conservative state, a loyal core of support for Bush. *New York Times,* p. A-1.

Ehrman, J. (1995). *The rise of neoconservatism: Intellectuals and foreign affairs 1945–1994.* New Haven, CT: Yale University Press.

Elden, S., & Bailasiewicz, L. (2006). The geopolitics of division and the problem of a Kantian Europe. *Review of International Studies, 32,* 623–644.

Emerson, M. O., & Smith, C. (2001). *Divided by faith: Evangelical religion and the problem of race in America.* New York: Oxford University Press.

Emens, E. (2004). Just monogamy? In M. L. Shanley (Ed.), *Just marriage* (pp. 75–81). Oxford University Press.

Enns, P. (1989). *The handbook of theology.* Chicago: Moody Press.

Evangelicals for Social Action. *Chicago declaration of evangelical social concern.* Retrieved December 18, 2007, from http://www.esaonline.org/Images/mmDocument/Declarations%20&%20Letters/Chicago%20Declaration%20of%20Evangelical%20Social%20Concern.doc

Ewing, H. (producer) & Grady, R. (producer). *Jesus camp* [motion picture]. Magnolia Pictures.

Faludi, S. (2007). *The terror dream: Fear and fantasy in post 9/11 America.* New York: Metropolitan Books.

Feitshans, B. (producer) & Cosmatos, P. C. (director). (1985). *Rambo first blood: Part II* [motion picture]. United States: Carolco Pictures.

Feldman, G. (2004). *Dixiecrats – the states' rights party, 1948.* Retrieved December, 15, 2007, from http://www.alabamamoments.state.al.us/sec54.html

Fenn, R. K. (2001). *Beyond Idols: The shape of secular society.* Oxford University Press.

Flint, A. R., & Porter, J. (2005). Jimmy Carter: The re-emergence of faith-based politics and the abortion rights issue. *Presidential Studies Quarterly, 35*(1), 28–51.

Foucault, M. (2007). *Security, territory, population: Lectures at the college DeFrance 1977–1978* (G. Burchell, Trans.). New York: Palgrave.

BIBLIOGRAPHY

Fountain, J. W. (2001, February 15). Kansas puts evolution back into public schools. *The New York Times on the Web*. Retrieved September 28, 2006, from www.nytimes.com

Franks, T. (2004). *What's the matter with Kansas? How the conservatives won the heart of America*. New York: Metropolitan Books.

Fraser, J. W. (1999). *Between church and state: Religion and public education in a multicultural America*. New York: St. Martin's Press.

Friedman, B. (2005). *Mr Bush, specialist young would also like to speak with you*. Message posted to http://www.bradblog.com/?p=1772

Frontline. (2004). *The Jesus factor*. PBS Video.

Fukuyama, F. (1993). *The end of history and the last man*. New York: Harper Perennial.

Giroux, H. A. (1994). *Disturbing pleasures: Learning popular culture*. New York: Routledge.

Giroux, H. A. (1999). *The mouse that roared: Disney and the end of innocence*. New York: Rowman and Littlefield Publishers, Inc.

Giroux, H. A. (2000). *Impure acts: The practical politics of cultural studies*. New York: Routledge.

Giroux, H. A. (2003). *The abandoned generation: Democracy beyond the culture of fear*. New York: Palgrave.

Giroux, H. A. (2004). *The terror of neoliberalism: Cultural politics & the promise of democracy*. New York: Paradigm Publishers.

Gitlin, T. (2000, December 8). The renaissance of anti-intellectualism [Review]. *The Chronicle of Higher Education*, p. 7.

Glassner, B. (1999). *The culture of fear*. New York: Basic Books.

Glenn, C. L. (2000). *The ambiguous embrace: Government and faith-based schools and social agencies*. Princeton, NJ: Princeton University Press.

Globus, Y., & Golan, M. (producers) & Hool, L. (director). (1985). *Missing in action 2* [motion picture].United States: Cannon Films.

Goldberg, M. (2006). *Kingdom coming: The rise of Christian nationalism*. New York: W.W. Norton.

Goldfield, D. R. (2002). *Still fighting the civil war: The American south and southern history*. Baton Rouge: Louisiana State University.

Gorenberg, G. (2002). The left behind series. *American Prospect*, *13*(17), 23–29.

Gordon, L. (1973). Voluntary motherhood: The beginnings of feminist birth control ideas in the United States. *Feminist Studies*, *1*(3/4), 5–22.

Gordon, L., & Silver, J. (producers) & McTierman, J. (director). (1988). *Die hard* [motion picture]. United States: 20th Century Fox.

Gordon, L., Silver, J., & Gordon, C. (producers) & Harlin, R. (director). (1990). *Die hard 2* [motion picture]. United States: 20th Century Fox.

Goodstein, L. (2005, November 10). A decisive election in a town roiled over intelligent design. *The New York Times*. Retrieved November 10, 2005, from http://www.nytimes.com/2005//11/10/national/10dover.html?

Grumet, M. (1988). *Bitter milk: Women and teaching*. Amherst, MA: University of Massachusetts Press.

Halberstam, J. (2005). *In a queer time and place*. New York University Press.

Hardisty, J. (1999). *Mobilizing resentment: Conservative resurgence from the John Birch society to the promise keepers*. Boston: Beacon Press.

Hardt, M., & Negri, A. (2000). *Empire*. Boston: Harvard University Press.

Hardt, M., & Negri, A. (2004). *Multitude: War and democracy in the age of empire*. New York: The Penguin Press.

Harris, S. (2005). *The end of faith: Religion, terror and the end of reason*. New York: W.W. Norton & Company.

Harvey, P. (1997). *Redeeming the south: Religious cultures and racial identities among southern baptists, 1865–1925*. Durham, NC: University of North Carolina Press.

Hendricks, S. (2005). *Divine destruction: Wise use, dominion theology and the making of American environmental policy*. Hoboken, NJ: Melville Publishing House.

BIBLIOGRAPHY

Henning, R. J. (2004). *General information*. Retrieved November 28, 2007, from http://cardiovascular-research.org/default.aspx

Henriques, D. B. (2006, October 8). Religion trumps regulation as legal exemptions grow. *New York Times*, pp. A-1, A-22–A-23.

Hindmarsh, D. B. (2005). *The evangelical conversion narrative: Spiritual autobiography in early modern Europe*. Oxford: Oxford University Press.

Hitchens, C. (2007). *God is not great: How religion poisons everything*. New York: Hachette Book Group.

Hofstader, R. (1962). *Anti-intellectualism in American life*. New York: Vintage Books.

The Holy Bible. (2002). *New international version*. New York: Harper Torch.

Hoover, D. R., & Den Dulk, K. R. (2004). Christian conservatives go to court: Religion and legal mobilization in the United States and Canada. *International Political Science Review*, *25*(1), 9–34.

Huckabee, M. (2007a). *Marriage*. Retrieved December 12, 2007, from http://www.mikehuckabee.com/?FuseAction=Issues.View&Issue_id=10

Huckabee, M. (2007b). *From hope to higher ground: 12 STOPS for restoring Americas' greatness*. Lebanon, IN: Center Street.

Hurst, B. (2002). The plains vs. the atlantic. *The American Enterprise*, *13*(2), 36–39.

Iannaccone, L. (1993). Heirs to the protestant ethic? In M. Marty & R. S. Appleby (Eds.), *Fundamentalisms and the state*. Chicago: University of Chicago Press.

Inhofe, J. (2005, January). *Climate change update*. Senate floor statement. Delivered at the Senate meeting, Washington, DC.

Inglehardt, R., & Norris, P. (2003). *Rising tide: Gender equality and change around the world*. Cambridge University Press.

Jacoby, S. (2004). *Free thinkers: A history of American secularism*. New York: Metropolitan Books.

Jager, C. (2006). After the secular: The subject of romanticism. *Public Culture*, *18*(2), 301–321.

James, W. (1997). *The varieties of religious experience*. New York: Simon & Schuster. (Originally published in 1909)

Jelen, T. G. (2005). Political Esperanto: Rhetorical resources and limitations of the Christian right in the United States. *Sociology of Religion*, *66*(3), 303–321.

Jervis, R. (2005). Why the Bush doctrine cannot be sustained. *Political Science Quarterly*, *120*(3), 351–377.

Johnson, P. (1994). Martin Luther King, Jr., and the African-American social gospel. In P. Johnson (Ed.), *African-American Christianity* (pp. 159–177). Berkeley, CA: University of California Press.

Kagan, R. (2003). *Of paradise and power*. New York: Knopf.

Kaldor, M. (1999). *New and old wars: Organized violence in a global era*. Palo Alto, CA: Stanford University Press.

Kaplan, E. (2005). *With God on their side: George Bush and the Christian right*. New York: New Press

Katz, C. (2001). The state goes home: Local hypervigilance of children and the global retreat from social reproduction. *Social Justice*, *28*(3), 47–56.

Kaufman, A. (2006, October 3). Jesus is tragic. *In these Times*. Retrieved October 12, 2006, from http://www.inthesetimes.com/site/main/article/2837/

Keddie, N. R. (1998). The new religious politics: Where, when, and why do 'Fundamentalisms' appear. *Comparative Studies in Society and History*, *40*, 696–723.

Keen, S. (1991). *Fire in the belly: On being a man*. New York: Bantam Books.

Kettle, M. (2001, January). Echoes of slavery as bush nominees back confederacy [Electronic version]. *The Guardian Unlimited*, p. 1.

Kilde, J. H. (2006). Megachurches: Investigating the religious and cultural work of church architecture. In L. P. Nelson (Ed.), *American sanctuary: Understanding sacred space*. Bloomington, IN: Indiana University Press.

Kintz, L. (1997). *Between Jesus and the market: The emotions that matter in right-wing America*. Durham, NC: Duke University Press.

Kishwar, M. (1990). Why I do not call myself a feminist. *Manushi*, November/December, 2–8.

Kitzmiller V. Dover Area School District, No. 04cv2688 (MD of PA. December 20, 2005).

Klein, N. (2007). *The shock doctrine: The rise of disaster capitalism.* New York: Metropolitan Books.

Knowledgerush (2006). *Doublespeak.* Retrieved December, 12, 2007, from http://knowledgerush.com/kr/encyclopedia/Doublespeak/

Kristol, W., & Kagan, R. (1997). Towards and neo-reaganite foreign policy. *Foreign Affairs, 75*(4), 18–32.

Lampman, J. (2006, February 6). Megachurches: Way of worship is on the rise. *Christian Science Monitor.* Retrieved March 30, 2007, from http://www.csmonitor.com2006/0206/p13s01-lire.html

Lawless, J. L. (2004). Women, war and winning elections: Gender stereotyping in the post-September 11th era. *Political Research Quarterly, 57*(3), 479–490.

Leigh Brown, P. (2001, October 28). Heavy lifting required: The return of manly men. *The New York Times,* section 4, p. 5.

Levy, A. (2006). *Female chauvinist pigs.* New York: Free Press.

Lieven, A. (2003, June 19). The empire strikes back. *The Nation.* Retrieved October 11, 2005, from http://www.thenation.com/doc/20030707/lieven

Lively, S., & Abrams, K. (2002). *The pink swastika.* Sacramento, CA: Veritas Aeternea Press.

Longman, P. (2006). The return of patriarchy. *Foreign Policy, 153,* 56–60; 62–65.

Lorraine, T. (1999). *Irigaray and Deleuze: Experiments in visceral philosophy.* Ithaca, NY: Cornell University Press.

Loveland, A. C., & Wheeler, O. B. (2003). *From meetinghouse to megachurch.* Columbia, MO: University of Missouri Press.

Lutz, W. (1989). *Doublespeak: From revenue enhancement to terminally living: How government, business, advertisers, and others use language to deceive you.* New York: HarperCollins.

Maher, B., Carter, S., Grey, B., & Gurvitz, M. (producers). (2007). Episode 519 [Television series episode]. In B. Maher, S. Carter, B. Grey, & M. Gurvitz (producers) (Eds.), *Real time with Bill Maher.* Hollywood, CA: HBO Broadcast Company.

Marsden, G. (2005). *Fundamentalism and American culture* (2nd ed.). Oxford University Press.

Marty, M. E., & Appleby, R. S. (1995). *Fundamentalisms comprehended.* Chicago: University of Chicago Press.

Magnet, M. (2000). *The dream and the nightmare: The sixties' legacy to the underclass.* San Francisco: Encounter Books.

Malik, A. A. (2005). *With God on our side: Politics and theology of the war on terrorism.* Bristol, England: Amal Press.

Mansfield, S. (2003). *The faith of George Bush.* New York: Tarcher.

Marks, J. (1998). *Gilles Deleuze: Vitalism and multiplicity.* London: Pluto Press.

Marrapodi, E. (2006, November). *Evangelical confesses to 'sexual immorality' in letter.* Retrieved October 10, 2007, from http://www.cnn.com/2006/US/11/05/haggard.allegations/index.html

Martusewicz, R. A. (2001). *Seeking passage: Post-structuralism, pedagogy, ethics.* New York: Teachers College Press.

Marx, K. (1983). On the Jewish question. In E. Kamanka (ed.), *The portable Karl Marx.* New York: Penguin.

Matiasek, E. (2006). *What would Jesus do about the question concerning technology? An investigation of metaphysical contributions to democratic pluralism.* M.A. Thesis, Illinois State University (unpublished).

McCain, J. (2007). *Human dignity and sanctity of life.* Retrieved December 12, 2007, from http://www.johnmccain.com/Informing/Issues/95b18512-d5b6-456e-90a2 12028d71df58.htm

McLaren, P. (1995). *Critical pedagogy and predatory culture: Oppositional politics in a postmodern era.* New York: Routledge.

McLaren, P. (2005). *Capitalists and conquerors: A critical pedagogy against empire.* New York: Rowman and Littlefield Publishers.

McTell. B. W. (1991). *Statesboro blues.* On *a decade of hits 1969–1979* [CD]. New York: PolyGram Music.

Menzies, P. (producer) & McTierman, J. (director). (1995). *Die hard. With a vengeance* [motion picture]. United States: Cinergi Pictures Entertainment Inc.

BIBLIOGRAPHY

Miles, J. (2004). Religion and American foreign policy. *Survival, 46*(1), 23–37.

Mill, J. S. (1989). The subjection of women. In *On liberty and other writings*. Cambridge University Press.

Millich, K. (2006). Fundamentalism hot and cold. *Cultural Critique, 62*, 92–125.

Moen, M. C. (1996). The evolving politics of the Christian right. *P.S.: Political Science and Politics, 29*(3), 461–464.

Mooney, C. (2005). *The republican war on science*. New York: Basic Books.

Mooney, C. (2006). *The republican war on science* (New Ed ed.). New York: Basic Basic Books.

Morrelli, E. M. (1999). Ressentiment and rationality. *Philosophical Anthropology*. Retrieved December 10, 2007, from www.bu.edu/wcp/Papers/Anth/AnthMore.htm

Morill, C., Snow, D. A., & White, C. H. (2005). *Together alone: Personal relationships in public spaces*. Berkeley, CA: University of California Press.

Morris, M. (2001). *Curriculum and the holocaust: Competing sites of memory and representation*. Mahwah, NJ: Lawrence Erlbaum Associates.

Moser, M. (1999). Have you been saved? Models of identity for maladies of the soul: Evangelicalism and feminist performance art. *Journal of American Culture, 22*(4), 57–66.

Moyers, B. (2004, December). *Speech*. Presented at the Center for Health and Global Environment at the Harvard Medical School, Boston, MA.

Moyers, B. (2005, January 30) There is no tomorrow. *The Star Tribune*, p. 1.

National Center for Science Education (2005). *"Divine design" legislation threatened in Utah*. Retrieved July 22, 2008, from http://ncseweb.org/news/2005/06/divine-design-legislation-threatened-utah-00758

Ness, I. (2004). *Encyclopedia of American social movements*. Armonk, NY: Sharpe.

Ngai, P. (2005). *Made in China: Women factory workers in a global marketplace*. Durham, NC: Duke University Press.

Nietzsche, F. (1989). *On the genealogy of morals* (W. Kaufman & R. J. Hollingdale, Trans.). New York: Vintage Books.

Norris, P. (2005). *Radical right: Voters and parties in the electoral market*. New York: Cambridge University Press.

Nosey Online (2004, July). *Rupert Murdoch*. Retrieved Decemeber 20, 2007, from http://www.noseyonline.com/2004/07/

Nurazzaman, M. (2006). Beyond realist theories: 'Neo-conservative realism' and the American invasion of Iraq. *International Studies Perspectives, 7*, 239–253.

Olasky, M. (2003). Christophobia and the American future. In C. W. Dunn (Ed.), *Faith, freedom and the future: Religion in American political culture* (pp. 41–54). Lanham, MD: Rowman and Littlefield.

Orwell, G. (1984). *1984: Commemorative 1984 edition*. New York: New American Library.

Osten, C., & Sears, A. (2003). *The homosexual agenda: Exposing the principal threat to religious freedom today*. Nashville, TN: B&H Publishing Group.

Ostwalt, C. E. (2003). *Secular steeples: Popular culture and the religious imagination*. Harrisburg, PA: Trinity International Press.

Paige, R. (2002). *Remarks at the White House conference on faith-based and community initiatives*. Retrieved from the United States Department of Education website http://www.ed.gov/news/speeches/2002/10/10102002.html

Passmore, K. (2002). *Fascism*. London: Oxford University Press.

Paxton, R. O. (2004). *The anatomy of fascism*. New York: Vintage Books.

Payne, J. W. (2006, May 16). Forever pregnant. *Washington Post*, (pages/e-).

Pearce, W. B., Littlejohn, S. W., & Alexander, A. (1987). The new Christian right and the humanist response: Reciprocated diatribe. *Communication Quarterly, 35*(2), 171–192.

Perkins, T., & Minnery, T. (2007, December 9). What values voters value most. *The Washington Times*, p. 13.

Pew Forum on Religion and Public Life. (2004, September). The American religious landscape and political attitudes: A baseline for 2004 John C. Green.

BIBLIOGRAPHY

Pierson, A. T. (1900). *Many infallible proofs the evidences of Christianity*. Westwood, NJ: F.H. Revell.

Phillips, K. (2006). *American theocracy: The peril and politics of radical religion, oil borrowed money in the 21st century*. New York: The Penguin Group.

Phillips, P. (2001, January). *American mantra: Freemarket capitalism*. Retrieved December 18, 2007, from http://www.commondreams.org/views01/0103-05.htm

Philips, K. (2004). *American dynasty: Aristocracy, fortune, and the politics of deceit in the house of Bush*. New York: The Penguin group.

Pinar, W. F. (2004). *What is curriculum theory?* Mahwah, NJ: Lawrence Erlbaum Associates.

Pocock, J. G. A. (2003). *Barbarism and religion, Vols. 1–3*. Cambridge University Press.

Potter, K. (2001). *Social gospel theology*. Retrieved from http://spider.georgetowncollege.edu/HTALLANT/COURSES/his338/students/kpotter/theology.htm

Povinelli, E. A. (2005). A flight from freedom. In A. Loomba et al. (Eds.), *Postcolonial studies and .beyond* (pp. 145–165). Chapel Hill, NC: Duke University Press.

Prescott, B. (2002). *Christian reconstructionism*. Retrieved September 22, 2006, from http://www.mainstreambaptists.org/mob4/dominionism.htm

Pressman, E. R., & Stone, O. (producers) & Bigelow, K. (director). (1990). *Blue steel* [Motion picture]. United States: Lightening Pictures.

The president's council on bioethics: Choosing the sex of children. (2004) *Population and Development Review, 29*(4), 751–760.

Prothero, S. (2006). The variety show of religious experience [Review of J. C. Hallman's *The Devil is a Gentleman*]. *The New York Times Book Review*, July 2, p. 15.

Provenzo, E. (1990). *Religious fundamentalism and American education: The battle for the public schools*. New York: SUNY Press.

Puar, J. K. (2007). *Terrorist assemblages: Homonationalism in queer times*. Durham, NC: Duke University Press.

Rankin, D. M. (2005). The midwest: The arching divide. In K. J. McMahon, D. M. Rankin, D. W. Beachler, & J. K. White (Eds.), *Winning the White House 2004: Region by region, vote by vote* (pp. 153–183). New York: Palgrave.

Rau, W., Shelley, N. M., & Beck, F. D. (2001). The dark engine of Illinois education: A sociological critique of a well-crafted (testing) machine. *Educational Policy, 15*(3), 404–431.

Rauschenbusch, W. (1917/1997). *A theology for the social gospel*. Louisville, KY: Westminster John Knox Press.

Rauschenbusch, W. (1912). *Christianizing the social order*. New York: Macmillan.

Rauschenbusch, W. (2007/1907). *Christianity and the social crisis*. Whitefish, MT: Kessinger Publishing.

Reed, A. L. (1999). *Class notes*. Boulder, CO: Westview.

Republican Party Platform. (2004). *Republican party platform 2004: A safer world and a more hopeful America*. Retrieved October 11, 2007, from http://www.gop.com/media/2004platform.pdf

Reynolds, W. M. (2004). The nostalgic turn and the politics of ressentiment. *Georgia Educational Researcher, 2*(1). Retrieved October, 2007, from http://coefaculty.valdosta.edu/lschmert/gera/used_vol2_no1/specFEAT-04.pdf

Reynolds, W. M. (2007). Under siege and out of reach: Steven Seagal and the paradox and politics of new age masculinity. In D. Macedo & S. Sreinberg (Eds.), *Media literacy: A reader* (pp. 340–352). New York: Peter Lang.

Reynolds, W. M., & Webber, J. A. (Eds.). (2004). *Expanding curriculum theory: Dis/positions and lines of flight*. Mahwah, NJ: Lawrence Erlbaum.

Reynolds, W. M., & Gabbard, D. (2004). We were soldiers: The rewriting of memory in the brand name corporate order. In D. Gabbard & K. Saltman (Eds.), *Education as enforcement: The corporatization and militarization of schools* (pp.). New York: Routledge.

Riaz, A. (2008). *Faithful education: Madrassahs in South Asia*. New Brunswick, NJ: Rutgers University Press.

Rich, L., Rachmil, M. I., & Todman, B. (producers) & Malmuth, B. (director). (1990). *Hard to kill* [motion picture]. United States: Warner Brothers.

BIBLIOGRAPHY

Robertson, P. (2004). *Homosexuals: The 700 club*. Retrieved December 13, 2007, from http://www.gainesvillehumanists.org/patr.htm

Robertson, P. (1992). *The new world order*. Nashville, TN: Thomas Nelson.

Robbins, T. (2001). Combating 'Cults' and 'Brainwashing' in the United States and Western Europe: A comment on Richardson and Introvigne's report. *Journal for the Scientific Study of Religion, 40*(2), 169–175.

Rorty, R. (1997). Religious faith, intellectual responsibility, and romance. In R. A. Putnam (Ed.), *The Cambridge companion to William James* (pp. 84–102). New York: Cambridge University Press.

Rosen, J. (2006, June). The day after Roe. *The Atlantic Monthly*, 56–66.

Rozell, M., & Wilcox, C. (1996). Second coming: The strategies of the new Christian right. *Political Science Quarterly, 111*(2), 271–294.

Rubenstein, D. (2008). *This is not a president: Sense, nonsense and the American political imaginary*. New York: NYU Press.

Rubenstein, D. (2003). Did you pack your bags yourself? Governmentality after 9/11. *The New Centennial Review, 3*(2), 303–331.

Rubenstein, D. (1989). The mirror of reproduction: Baudrillard and Reagan's America. *Political Theory, 17*(4), 582–606.

Rubenstein, D. (1992). The anxiety of affluence: Baudrillard and sci-fi movies of the Reagan era. In W. Stearns & W. Chaloupka (Eds.), *Jean Baudrillard: The disappearance of art and politics*. New York: St. Martin's.

Rushdoony, R. R. (1973). *The institutes of biblical law*. New York: P&R Publishing.

Rudin, J. (2006). *The baptizing of America: The religious right's plans for the rest of us*. New York: Thunder's Mouth Press.

Saskia, S. (2002). Counter-geographies of globalization: Feminization of survival. In K. Saunders (Ed.), *Feminist post-development thought: Thinking modernity, post-colonialism and representation*. London: Zed Books.

Sayyid, S. (1997). *A fundamental fear: Eurocentrism and the emergence of Islamism*. London: Zed Books.

Scahill, J. (2007). *Blackwater: The rise of the world's most powerful mercenary army*. New York: Nation Books.

Schaefer, N. A. (2004). Y2K as an endtime sign: Apocalypticism in America and the *fin-de-millennium*. *The Journal of Popular Culture, 38*(1), 82–105.

Schlesinger, P., & Foret, F. (2006). Political roof and sacred canopy. *European Journal of Social Thought, 9*(1), 59–81.

Schmidt, C., Craword, S., Deckman, M., Gray, D., Hofrenning, D., Olson, L., et al. (2003). The political attitudes and activities of mainline protestant clergy in the election of 2000: A study of six denomination. *The Journal for the Scientific Study of Religion, 42*(4), 515–532.

Schrage, L. (2001). From reproductive rights to reproductive Barbie: Post-porn modernism and abortion. *Feminist Studies, 28*(1), 61–93.

Schrage, L. (2003). The electoral politics of abortion. *Dissent, 50*(4), 67–73.

Scherer, G. (2004). The Godly must be crazy: Christian-right views are swaying politicians and threatening the environment. Retrieved December, 12, 2007, from http://www.grist.org/news/maindish2004/10/27/scheerer-christian/

Scott, R., & Polk, M. (producers) & Scott, R. (director). (1991). *Thelma and Louise* [motion picture]. United States: Patche Entertainment Inc.

Schweiker, W. (2003). Theological ethics and the question of humanism. *Journal of Religion, 83*(3), 539–561.

Sears, A., & Osten, C. (2003). *The homosexual agenda: Exposing the principal threat to Religious freedom*. Nashville, TN: Broadman and Holman.

Shaeffer, F. (1981/2005). *A Christian manifesto*. Wheaton, IL: Crossway Books.

Shaeffer, F. (1982). *A Christian manifesto*. Sermon presented at the Coral Ridge Presbyterian Church, Fort Lauderdale, FL.

BIBLIOGRAPHY

Shapiro, M. J. (1997). *Violent cartograhies: Mapping cultures of war*. Minneapolis, MN: University of Minnesota Press.

Shapiro, M. J. (2007). The new violent cartography. *Security Dialogue, 38*(3), 291–313.

Shor, I. (1986). *Culture wars: School and society in the conservative restoration 1969–1984*. Boston: Routledge and Kegan Paul.

Shor, I. (1992). *Culture wars: School and society in the conservative restoration*. Chicago: University of Chicago Press

Sierra Club (2004). *A guide to the Bush adminitrations environmental doublespeak*. Retreived October, 27, from http://www.southshore.com/baedd.htm

Smith, C. (1998). *American evangelicalism*. Chicago: University of Chicago Press.

Smith, O. (2000). *The rise of Baptist Republicanism*. New York: New York University Press.

Sosnik, D. (2006). *Applebee's America: How successful business and religious leaders connect with the new American community*. New York: Simon & Schuster.

Southern Baptist Convention. (2007). Retrieved December 15, 2007, from http://www.sbc.net/

Southern Poverty Law Center. (2006). *Active U.S. hate groups*. Retreived October 2, 2006, from http://www.splcenter.org/intel/map/hate.jsp

Spindel, B. (2003). Conservatism as the 'sensible middle'. *Social Text, 21*(4), 99–125.

Spivak, G. C. (1988). Can the subaltern speak? In C. Nelson & L. Grossberg (Eds.), *Marxism and the interpreation of culture*. Urbana, IL: Univeristy of Illinois Press.

Spring, J. (2002). Political agendas for education: From the Christian coalition to the green party (2nd ed.). New York: Lawrence Erlbaum.

Stahl, L. (2007, December 16). *Military soft on don't ask don't tell? CBS News*.Retrieved December 21, 2007, from http://www.cbsnews.com/stories/2007/12/13/60minutes/main3615278.shtml?source=RSSattr=OME_3615278

Stanley, R. C. (2000). Comparison of changes of population, Southen Baptist churches, and resident members by region and state, 1990–2000. A Publication of Research, North American Mission Board, SBC.

Starr, B. (2003, March 11). *US tests massive bomb, CNN*. Retrieved April 3, 2007, from http://www.cnn.com/2003/US/03/11/sprj.irq.moab/

Sunstein, C. R. (1997). Homosexuality and the Constitution. In D. Eastland & M. Nussbaum (Eds.), *Sex, preference, and family*. Oxford University Press.

Tasker, Y. (Ed.). (2004). *Action and adventure cinema*. New York: Routledge.

Tasker, Y. (1993). *Spectacular bodies: Gender, genre and the action cinema*. New York: Routledge.

Taylor, C. (2006). Religious mobilizations. *Public Culture, 18*(2), 281–300.

Taylor, C. (2002). Modern social imaginaries. *Public Culture, 14*(1), 91–124.

Theweleit, K. (1989). *Male fantasies*. (Vols. 1–2, E. Carter & C. Turner Trans.). Minneapolis, MN: University of Minnesota Press.

Thompson, F. (2007). *Traditional American values*. Retrieved December 13, 2007, from http://www.fred08.com/Virtual/AmericanValues.aspx

Unitarian Universalists Association of Congregations. *Giving public voice to our values and principles*. Retrieved December 18, 2007, from http://www.uua.org/aboutus/18387.shtml

Urbina, I. (2006, August 13). Panel suggests using inmates in drug trials. *New York Times*, pp. A-1, A-18.

Urquhart, B. (2005). Extreme makeover [Review of the book *America right or wrong: An anatomy of American nationalism*]. *The New York Review of Books, 52*, p. 3.

Vann Woodward, C. (1993). *The burden of southern history*. Baton Rouge, LA: Louisiana State University Press.

Vindice, D., & Hill, M. (1994). *League of the south core beliefs statement*. Retrieved October 9, 2007, from http://dixienet.org/New%20Site/corebeliefs.shtml

Virno, P. (2004). *A grammar of the multitude*. New York: Semiotexte.

Wald, K. D., & Calhoun-Brown, A. (2006). *Religion and politics in the United States* (5th ed.). Lanham, MD: Rowman and Littlefield Publishers.

Warner, M. (2000). *The trouble with normal: Sex, politics and the ethics of queer life*. Cambridge, MA: Harvard University Press.

BIBLIOGRAPHY

Warner, M. (2005). *Publics and counterpublics*. New York: Zone Books.

Waters, B. (2006). *From human to posthuman: Christian theology and technology in a postmodern world*. London: Ashgate.

Webber, J. A. (2003). *Failure to hold: The politics of school violence*. Lanham, MD: Rowman and Littlefield.

Weinstein, M. W. (1991). The dark night of the liberal spirit and the dawn of the savage. In A. & M. Kroker (Eds.), *Ideology and power: In the age of Lenin in ruins* (pp. 210–224). New York: St. Martin's Press.

White, C. (2003). *The middle mind: Why Americans don't think for themselves*. San Francisco: Harper.

Why-War (2004). *Deleuze, fascism and the informatic*. Retrieved December 17, 2007, from http://www.why-war.com/news/2004/01/12/bombsand.html

Wilcox, C., & Larson, C. (2006). *Onward Christian soldiers: The religious right in American politics*. Boulder, CO: Westview Press.

Wilcox, C. (1992). *God's warriors: The Christian right in twentieth century America*. Baltimore: John's Hopkins University Press.

Williams, M. C. (2005). What is the national interest? The neoconservative challenge in IR theory. *European Journal of International Relations, 11*(3), 307–337.

Williamson, J. (1984). *The crucible of race: Black-White relations in the American south since emancipation*. New York: Oxford University Press.

Willis, G. (2006). A country ruled by faith. *The New York Review of Books, 53*(18), 1–11.

Willis, G. (2007). *Head and heart: American Christianities*. New York: Penguin Press.

Winnicott, D. W. (1986). *Home is where we start from*. New York: W.W. Norton.

Wolin, S. (1981). The idea of the state in America. In J. P. Diggins & M. E. Kann (Eds.), *The problem of authority in America* (pp. 41–58). Philadelphia: Temple University Press.

Woodruff, J. (2001, September 17). America's new war: President Bush talks with reporters at Pentagon [television broadcast]. Washington, DC: CNN.4.

Wuthnow, R. (1988). *The restructuring of American religion*. Princeton, NJ: Princeton University Press.

Wyatt-Brown, B. (1991). Introduction: The mind of W. J. Cash. In W. J. Cash (Ed.), *The mind of the south* (pp. vii–xxxiii). New York: Vintage Books.

Yoran, H. (2002). The humanist critique of metaphysics and the foundation of political order. *Utopian Studies, 13*(2), 1–20.

Young, I. M. (2003). The logic of masculinist protection: Reflections on the current security state. *Signs: Journal of Women, Culture and Society, 29*(1), 1–25.

Young-Rahn, U. (2003). South-Korea: Human embryo research. *Cambridge Quartley of Healthcare Ethics, 12*(3), 268–278.